T0148786

JACK LONDON'S
STRONG TRUTHS

JACK LONDON'S
STRONG TRUTHS

by
James I. McClintock

Michigan State University Press
East Lansing
1997

Copyright © 1975 and 1997 by James I. McClintock
All rights reserved

Originally published in 1975 as *White Logic: Jack London's Short Stories* by
Wolf House Books, Grand Rapids, Michigan

All Michigan State University Press books are produced on paper that meets
the requirements of American National Standard of Information Sciences—
Permanence of paper for printed materials ANSI Z39.48—1984.

Library of Congress Cataloguing-in-Publication Data

McClintock, James I., 1939-
    [White Logic]
    Jack London's strong truths / by James I. McClintock.
     p.   cm. -- (A Red Cedar classic)
    Originally published: White logic. Grand Rapids, Mich. : Wolf House
    Books, 1975, in series: Wolf House Books monograph.
    Includes bibliographical references (p.   ).
    ISBN 0-87013-471-X (alk. paper)
    1. London, Jack, 1876-1916--Criticism and interpretation.
2. Short story. I. Title. II. Series.
PS3523.046Z765 1997
813'.52--dc21   79-16852
                CIP

Printed in the United States of America

For Will, Amy, Matt, Sally, Jim, Sara
and
Richard Weiderman

PREFACE

Jack London's Strong Truths was originally published in 1975 as *White Logic: Jack London's Short Stories* (Grand Rapids, Michigan: Wolf House Books, 1975) and has remained the standard critical study of London's short fiction. Focused on Jack London's nineteen volumes of short stories, it was one of the first studies to challenge easy, often condescending, generalizations about London's fiction and to offer a balanced, tightly-reasoned analysis of his impassioned, albeit often "exasperatingly uneven artistry." It remains the most frequently cited work on London's short fiction. Long out of print but still in demand, parts have been reprinted not only for their importance in understanding Jack London's life and writing but for understanding short story criticism in general. Now, happily, the entire work will once again be widely available for scholars and students of American literature and culture.

Originally reviewed by Charles Walcutt as "a valuable, in many ways definitive, study," this critical work has aided a generation of London scholars who, as Joan Hendrick says in her own *Solitary Companion* (Chapel Hill: North Carolina University Press, 1982), have built on McClintock's example. Recently, for instance, London scholar Dale Walker described McClintock's study as "rare and invaluable" (*Firsts*, December, 1993). That it is indeed rare and invaluable singles out the two major reasons for its re-issue.

The objectives of *Jack London's Strong Truths* do not admit to simple generalizations. In a study that attempts to describe and evaluate Jack London's nearly two hundred short stories of so protean a nature, no controlling thesis is adequate. Rather, it is best to break down the easy generalizations that have been made about London's fiction and to suggest a more complex understanding of London's art.

The first third of McClintock's study focuses on the initial three years of London's literary life, from 1898-1902, when he learned the craft of short fiction and crystallized his literary theory. It is one of the strikingly original aspects of the book. He details London's self-conducted apprenticeship in his craft when the writer was determined to master "the proper trend of literary art." London studied magazine fiction and short story handbooks to learn form and technique at a time when critics were asking for more dramatic fiction and praising Rudyard Kipling. The first three volumes of London's short stories reveal his gradually developing expertise as well as his debt to Kipling's example. Literary critics were, at the same time, reacting against both Zolaesque "realism" and sentimental romance. They approved of fiction which combined harsh honesty with idealism. Responding to these critical views, London committed himself to stories which combined "strong truths" of "actuality" with "ideals," finding Herbert Spencer's *Philosophy of Style* a "scientific" literary method for undertaking this didactic mission. From this time forward, London was committed to dramatizing and advancing those "strong truths," willing anytime, he said, to sacrifice art for the integrity and impact of ideas.

The second third of this study examines London's Northland fiction, written from 1898-1908, in which London pitted "spirit-groping," idealized protagonists against the "actuality" of the Arctic wasteland. The strong truths derive from the world newly understood through perspective of Darwinian ideas. The explicit theme of the Malamute Kid series is that a code-practicing, rational man can achieve mastery over, or accommodation with, a hostile environment. The implicit theme, however, is that when adventurers challenge the "unknown," rationality fails to sustain humanly satisfying values. The stories which follow these explore more ironic and tragic themes; and, literarily, London's exploration of the non-rational by invoking the violent, the death-dealing and the grotesque, demands limited protagonists and a mythopoeic prose.

The last third of this work falls into two sections. The first, emphasizing stories written in the years from 1906 to 1912, discusses the artistic decline of his short fiction. This view of London's decline has excited more critical controversy than any other aspect of McClintock's analysis, dividing scholars into those who agree in substance, if not always in detail, with McClintock's analysis and those who argue that London's vitality and skill did not diminish, that London merely turned his attention to the novel and other book length projects. The debate is current and, as yet, unresolved. McClintock argues, in any case, that during this period London continued to employ themes growing from his fascination with Darwinian ideas as well ones he had been developing from Marxist political and economic theories. Using them London sometimes produced an excellent story but more often wrote pot-boilers until he gave up the short story genre entirely. Before stopping, he drifted into writing

South Seas stories that portray mechanical misery in a diseased environment meant to return to the Northland theme of mastery but which instead portrayed the collective racial mastery of Anglo-Saxons. At the same time, he wrote a number of socialist or social comment stories meant to affirm strong truths and positive values, a few of which are admirable but most of which are seriously flawed. Gradually incapacitated by his philosophical pessimism and other personal problems, London turned to pot-boilers characterized by inconsequential themes, slapstick humor, sentimentality and bitterness. From 1912 through 1915, London wrote just one story (the unremarkable "Whose Business Is To Live") although a number were published.

The second part of this last section contains another of McClintock's signal contributions to London scholarship and, more generally, American letters. By analyzing a group of Hawaiian stories that London wrote in 1916, McClintock shows that London's rekindled interest in the genre came from finding more strong truths, this time in Jungian and Freudian psychology. The stories are based upon themes and symbols London uncovered in his reading of Carl Jung's *Psychology of the Unconscious*. These last stories repeat a recurring pattern that emerges from all London's fiction: he experienced an initial enthusiasm at having discovered a scientifically justifiable rationale for believing in humanly sustaining values; then a sober realization of human limitations coming from an awareness that death can be understood but not conquered; and, finally, a bitter sense of futility. These late Jungian stories can remind us that London's stories, from the early Alaskan tales to stories set in urban America, were distinctive for the motifs he eagerly garnered from then revolutionary insights into the natural, social and subjective worlds. Often denigrated for his not-even-nice "primordial" vision, London, as McClintock convincingly demonstrates, was the first American writer to undertake a wide-ranging aesthetic response to those "truths." He incorporated a range of radical ideas into the major themes of stories that had to be popular if he were to maintain himself as a writer. It was a remarkable goal, and a remarkable achievement, to be at once popular and searching, so remarkable, in fact, that it has awaited generations of literary critics to be sufficiently appreciated.

Stanford University Press' recent publication of the three-volume *The Complete Short Stories of Jack London*, intelligently and helpfully edited by Earle Labor, Robert C. Leitz, III, and I. Milo Shepard (1993) is an indication of the continuing importance of Jack London's short stories for a new generation of readers as well as for literary and cultural critics and historians. Anyone in possession of this collection and *Jack London's Strong Truths* has a well-equipped library for finding his or her voice in the continuing conversation assessing Jack London's achievements as a writer of short fiction read the world over.

Sam S. Baskett
London, 1997

TEXTUAL ABBREVIATIONS FOR COLLECTIONS OF JACK LONDON'S SHORT STORIES

CF	Children of the Frost
DC	Dutch Courage and Other Stories
FM	The Faith of Men and Other Stories
GF	The God of His Fathers and Other Stories
HP	The House of Pride and Other Tales of Hawaii
LF	Lost Face
LL	Love of Life and Other Stories
MF	Moon-Face and Other Stories
NB	The Night-Born
M	On the Makaloa Mat
R	The Red One
SB	Smoke Bellew Tales
S	A Son of the Sun
SW	The Son of the Wolf, Tales of the Far North
SST	South Sea Tales
SS	The Strength of the Strong
TF	Tales of the Fish Patrol
TT	The Turtles of Tasman
WGL	When God Laughs

CONTENTS

Chapter   Page

I.   Finding the Proper Trend of Literary
      Art: 1898–1902   1

II.   Actuality and Ideals: 1898–1902   35

III. The Malemute Kid   57

IV.   Alaskan Nightmare and Artistic Success:
      1898–1908   79

V.   The Decline: 1906–1911   121

VI.   Rebirth: 1916   151

Footnotes   175

Selected Bibliography   193

Chapter I

FINDING THE PROPER TREND
OF LITERARY ART: 1898–1902

In the summer of 1898, Jack London, just returned from a sixteen month trip to the Klondike and beset by family and financial responsibilities, committed himself to an energetic apprenticeship in the art of the short story. The apprenticeship appeared to be short and successful: a little more than six months later in January, 1899, he published his first Northland story, "To the Man on Trail."[1] Actually, however, this six month period was just a furiously eclectic initial stage in his apprenticeship, and he continued his study of the short story form and technique for several years. This continuing and more directed and controlled quest for an adequate form is evidenced in the changes seen in his first three collections of Alaskan stories: *The Son of the Wolf* (1901), *The God of His Fathers* (1901) and *Children of the Frost* (1902).[2]

Between the apprenticeship years 1898 and 1902, London accomplished several things: he studied the magazines to learn what subject matter was finding a market and what techniques and forms would be suitable for his purposes. Kipling was at that time the most widely heralded short fiction writer, and London studied that writer's methods and appropriated them as his own. The direction in Kipling's fiction, and that of the magazine stories in general, was towards dramatic short stories, a direction found in London's own stories during the first four years of his career. In addition, through Kipling's example and

1

Herbert Spencer's theory in *Philosophy of Style* (Boston, 1892), he fashioned a literary style congenial to his forms and themes. Satisfied with what he learned, he never significantly altered his form, techniques, or style.

Late in his life, London wrote to an aspiring writer advising that "success as a writer" depends upon "a study and knowledge of literature as it is commercially produced today."[3] Probably because it had been his own method for crashing the gates of fame, he was fond of advising young hopefuls to study magazine fiction before submitting manuscripts. His daughter, Joan, writes that during his apprenticeship in the fall of 1898 he "pored over the magazines whose acceptances he coveted."[4] London has left no record of the specific publications he studied, but it seems fair to assume there were many and that they were diverse in what they published. Certainly he studied, if we accept the accuracy of Joan London's observation, the stories in at least thirteen periodicals in which he found berths for his own stories during 1899 and 1900.[5] In addition he submitted articles to magazines that would have brought him in contact with discussions of literary technique and theory: for example, *The Bookman, The Review of Reviews, The Editor* and *The Writer*. Nor were these the only magazines that he scrutinized during his first two years of successful publication. He placed articles in other periodicals: *Cosmopolitan Magazine, Home Magazine, The Wave* and *Junior Munsey*, among others. It does not seem improbable, then, that Jack London took his own advice for attaining successful authorship and acquired a "knowledge of literature as it is commercially produced today."

During the *fin de siecle* decade, a young literary hopeful did not have to come from a home that had a private library or from a college education to feel the literary energy that was being generated. During the nineties, weekly and monthly magazines achieved record circulations and flooded America with serialized novels and short fiction of all literary persuasions. Even the newspapers and their Sunday supplements brought fiction and literary commentary into the lives of the most casual readers. The short story had become big business:

By the later 'nineties the short story had become so established an article of merchandise that the production of it became a recognized industry with numberless workers. The coming of the fifteen-cent magazine and the Sunday supplement stimulated greatly the quantity of the output. By 1900 the short-story stream had become a flood and syndicates had been established to handle it.[6]

In the proliferation of magazine prose the short story found its most viable medium; short stories and magazines joined in a mutual dependency that became profitable for writer and publisher alike. No wonder that the young Jack London believed that "the short story is growing in importance in modern literature ... It almost seems that the novel is destined to become extinct" and decided to link his fortune to the popularity of the short story genre.[7]

"Success as a writer" not only depended upon an awareness of the trends in commercial fiction, London maintained, but also "a knowledge of life."[8] Fortunately for him, the materials of his life coincided with the magazine taste for adventurous experiences. Before trekking to the Klondike, he had adventured with the Oyster Pirates on San Francisco Bay, ridden the rails, hiked with Coxey's Army and sailed aboard the sealer *Sophia Sutherland* as an able-bodied seaman. This last experience sponsored his first literary success, "Typhoon off the Coast of Japan," which won first prize in a *San Francisco Call* contest in 1893 when Jack was only seventeen. Like the content of much of his following fiction, the story is autobiographical and capitalizes upon special information embodied in a use of technical jargon which classifies the author as "authentic," entitling him to comment upon an unusual experience. As he often would later, London chose to identify himself with a masculine group existing outside polite society. The substance of the piece is a dramatic incident in a natural, crisis situation which appeals to a love of action and adventure.[9]

Five years after the publication of "Typhoon," when he began his intensive study of magazine fiction, what he found must have struck a responsive chord in his mind and heart.

Anyone who turns to the magazines to acquire "a knowledge of literature as it [was] produced" in 1898 and 1899 cannot avoid having adventure stories forced upon his attention. A glance at the magazine contents at this time attests to the overwhelming trend in public taste and literary expression for aggressive, adventurous materials; they dominate page after page of the leading big circulation magazines: *Harper's Monthly, Scribner's, Atlantic Monthly, Century, Cosmopolitan, McClure's* and *Youth's Companion*. Frank Luther Mott notes in *A History of American Magazines* that

> With the coming of the Spanish-American War, trumpets blared and swords flashed in the pages of the magazines. This effect came not from war material alone, but from the swashbuckling stories which were the fashion of the moment.[10]

Even a conservative magazine like *Harper's Monthly* felt reader pressure for tales of violence, action, and insurgent masculinity during London's apprenticeship. Characteristic of *Harper's* fiction at this time, for example, were westerns by Garland, Wister and Remington, including Remington's "Sun-Down" series, surrounded by articles about Cuba, Mexico and the Arctic.[11] *Scribner's*, too, indicated its participation in the vogue by publishing Crane's "The Open Boat" which is almost inconspicuous among the other tales in the issue because of the surface qualities of crisis and outdoor adventure it shares with them.[12] The *Atlantic*, dropping in circulation, attempted to regain its readers with stories like "Where Angels Fear to Tred," a dialect tale of shipboard cruelty and mutiny, and "The Commodore" whose title character "rode the waves like a cork and climbed the rigging like a cat," displaying superhuman strength.[13] *Century* joined the other major magazines with its "Heroes of the Deep" stories about Gloucester fishermen which were part of a larger series entitled *Heroes of Peace*.[14] *Cosmopolitan* printed "The Confessions of a Seafaring Blackmailer" and war stories such as Crane's "The Woof of the Thin Red Threads" (later retitled "The Price of the Harness" in *Wounds in the Rain*) set in Cuba and Charles B. Lewis's similar but weaker "The Story of His First Battle."[15] *The Overland Monthly*, London's first consistent market, specialized in stories and articles featuring outdoor life in the West, and more than any other magazine printed articles capitalizing upon the Klondike gold mania.[16] All major publications participated in the worship of active strength and virile adventure. The materials of London's life automatically blended with the materials he studied in the magazines, and eventually he would find markets for his stories in all these magazines.

But it was *McClure's Magazine* which would publish some of London's best stories like "Grit of Women," "The Law of Life," and "The God of His Fathers" and offer him an editorial position, that most consistently printed the kinds of materials which would make London famous. To demonstrate how thoroughly the magazines were saturated with danger, violence and individualistic action set in frontier and exotic locales, one need only examine the *McClure's* pages in the winter of 1898–1899 when London began to publish his Alaskan tales.

Interest centered around the Spanish-American War, an interest allied with larger issues of jingoistic imperialism and masculine adventure in the out-of-doors, both preoccupations of London. Racism is blatantly but unselfconsciously apparent in "500 Years of the Anglo Saxon," an article "documented" with charts showing the "inevitable" domination by the white man.[17] Adjacent to this article is a companion short story, "The Forerunners of Empire," set in the South Pacific, which could have been written by London had he been ready to treat race conflict in the South Seas.[18] In the February issue appeared the most notorious statement of white imperialism and racism—Kipling's "The White Man's Burden" (March, 1899; 190–93). The jingoistic spirit was fed by war articles in these issues, typified by Crane's "Marines Under Fire at Guantanamo" (332–36) and Stephen Bonsal's "The Day of Battle: Stories Gathered in the Field" (223–31). Simultaneously, Alfred Mahan's *The War on the Seas and Its Lessons* appeared monthly.[19] Outdoor life and rugged masculinity provide subjects for the bulk of the remaining pages, focusing upon articles like Garland's "Hitting the Trail" which extols the virtues of a return to nature to replenish a spirit dissipated by civilization (298–304) and his Indian adventure story "Rising Wolf–Ghost Dancer" (Jan., 1899; 241–48). Garland, moreover, shows interest in the new frontier, the Klondike, in his Northland poem celebrating manhood, "The Trail to the Golden North" (April, 505–07).

This list of articles and stories from *McClure's* (similar to lists which could be compiled from most of the major periodicals) glorifying individualism, strength and race identity is extensive. Often these stories are weighted more heavily with the ridiculous than the sublime especially since adult taste had become indistinguishable from the adolescent. The adult audiences of magazines like *McClure's*, for example, could not seem to satiate their hunger for stories like Ray Stannard Baker's "A Story of the Fire Patrol" (Nov., 19–22) and Jasper Ewing, Jr.'s serial *Adventures of a Train Dispatcher* (Nov., 44–48), more suitable for children. And "a boy's story," Frank Norris noted, "must now be all about the doings of men, fighters preferably, man-slayers, terrible fellows full of blood and fury . . ."[20] London would respond to this merger of adult and adolescent imagination, but often rise above the decline in public taste: for example, "To Build a Fire," his most widely known story, was originally published in *Youth's Companion* in 1902 but later issued with some modifications as an adult story in 1910.[21]

If these adventurous materials dominated the magazines, one figure best represented to the reading public what this type of fiction could offer—Rudyard Kipling. Following the 1887 publication of *Plain Tales from the Hills*, Kipling's fame in America had been immediate, and during the nineties, his work was appearing in every major American magazine.[22] Robert Louis Stevenson, until his death in 1894, had been the darling of the magazine story readers, and although his stories and imitations of them continued to be popular for more than two decades, the public gave its first loyalty to Kipling. They were obsessed by Kipling. F. L. Mott writes that "at the turn of the century Kipling was a Colossus bestriding this narrow world of letters."[23]

Fred Lewis Pattee had noted earlier that after Mark Twain and his followers had treated "the sweep and vastness of the American Frontier, and its coarseness and its democratic abandon" came "the Kipling school, raucous, masculine, far-flung in its materials."[24] Kipling's success was meteoric but solidly established, and Kipling imitators fill the magazines with materials that London, too, would use—race, exotic locales, and masculine characters who were do-ers rather than dreamers, who knew "the ropes" of their trades.[25]

The *McClure's* issues, that London probably studied, are again representative of this Kipling mania. During the mid and late nineties, *McClure's* printed Kipling's "Quigierern" (an Eskimo story), "The Ship that Found Herself," "In the Rukh" (a reprint of the first Mowgli story), "Slaves of the Lamp," and two serials: *Captain's Courageous* and *Stalky and Co.*[26] This last serial began in the November 1898 issue, and in the same issue and the December one following it appeared W. A. Fraser's "Raja Singh and Other Elephants" and "A Tiger in the Tea Gardens" which are typical Kipling imitations.[27]

London, who would be called the "American Kipling" by early reviewers, returned from the Klondike, where he had read Kipling's *Seven Seas*, already an ardent admirer of the Englishman.[28] In the following years he would defend Kipling against his attackers and promote an interest in Kipling whenever he could. Perhaps on his arrival in San Francisco, penniless from his adventure in Alaska and the Yukon, he saw the Kipling window display at Doxy's bookstore which a *Bookman* contributor noticed was the center of literary conversation in June, 1898.[29] If London did, it must have confirmed his resolve to seek the same fame. At any rate, Kipling had done what London hoped to emulate—achieved an immediate and unrivaled recognition by writing stories based upon his special knowledge of the remote areas of the world and the lives of men who fought for survival against other men and their environment in order to perpetuate their race.

Jack London did not immediately realize, however, that the Alaskan adventure short story would be his way to fame. During the fall and winter of 1898, he desperately tried to get into print. He ignored Northland short fiction, and sounded the market for popular materials and genres of lighter weight. At this time, the initial stage of his apprenticeship, he dashed off and submitted an assortment of manuscripts including jokes, triolets and essays as well as stories. A few of them found their way into print: "Eggs Without Salt," a joke; "He Chortled with Glee," and "If I Were God for One Hour," poems; and several essays capitalizing upon the information he acquired in the Klondike—"From Dawson to the Sea," "Through the Rapids on the Way to the Klondike," and others.[30] He submitted a 21,000 word serial to *Youth's Companion* but it was rejected, and he began to rely on short stories as his most likely vehicle to success.[31]

When he began to concentrate on stories in the fall of 1898, committing himself to making a living through fiction, he recognized that even though he had materials he was lacking in the literary skills that could shape them into dramatic fiction. In November, he wrote to the "Lily Maid," Mable Applegarth, revealing his intention to acquire technical skills:

> I shall not be ready for any flights till my flying machine is perfected, and to that perfection I am now applying myself. Until then, to the deuce with themes. I shall subordinate thought to technique till the latter is mastered; then I shall do vice versa.[32]

Ideas and his preoccupation with Alaskan adventure would have to wait until he had found the "tricks" that made a story marketable.

"Typhoon off the Coast of Japan," published five years before he chose fiction as his vocation, is a useful example of London's rough writing skill which needed to be harnessed by technique. In "Typhoon" he may have instinctively turned to adventure, but the account is an overly verbal report of an unusual incident. At times he shows power, as in the following passage which is often quoted to document London's early capacity for using colorful detail to achieve evocative effects:

A soft light emanated from the movement of the ocean. Each mighty sea, all phosphorescent and glowing with the tiny lights of myriads of animalculae, threatened to overwhelm us with a deluge of fire.[33]

This leaves a false impression, however, since his early delight in words overwhelms the brief, ten page, story and is more characteristically trite than fresh and specific:

> The waves were holding high carnival, performing the strangest antics, as with wild glee they danced along in fierce pursuit—now up, now down, here, there, everywhere, until some great sea of liquid green with its milk-white crest of foam rose from the ocean's throbbing bosom and drove the others from view. (*DC* 24-25)

And these descriptions of the ocean are the piece's *raison d'etre*—the youthful London had reason to criticize himself for want of technical skill.

Determined to perfect his "machine," Jack began

> like a first year medical student ... to dissect the stories in the current magazines, taking them apart, tracing their nerves and sinews, and striving to reproduce the articulation of their joints.[34]

What he produced as the result of this study are short story equivalents to the light weight jokes and poems which were his introduction into print.[35] Like his autobiographical hero, Martin Eden, he learned the "formula" for successful stories:

> The formula consists of three parts: (1) a pair of lovers are jarred apart; (2) by some deed or event they are reunited; (3) marriage bells. The third part was an unvarying quantity, but the first and second parts could be varied an infinite number of times.[36]

He did place one of these formula stories, "In the Time of Prince Charley," in *Conkey's Home Journal*.[37] In it, the first person protagonist, "Griffin Risingham, captain to our good king, George II," and guardian to the captive Prince Charley, falls in love with a noble Highland beauty. A dashing "black-

bearded Highlander" interrupts the lovers one night, embraces
the lady Aline, releases Prince Charley, and departs with the
willing Aline to France (1). Not until a year later, while "in
France on a secret mission," does Griffin accidentally and jeal-
ously encounter the bearded antagonist who, with the proper
suspense, reveals that he is Aline's brother (2). "What a fool I
had been!" exclaims Griffin, "would she, could she ever forgive
me?" She does, of course (3). The story has villains, heroes,
duels, high passion and noble sentiment—all highly marketable.
London, like Martin Eden, had learned that these stories:

> should never be tragic, should never end unhappily, and should never
> contain beauty of language, subtlety of thought, nor real delicacy of
> sentiment. Sentiment it must contain, plenty of it, pure and noble,
> of the sort that in my early youth had brought applause [from the
> gallery].[38]

This story demonstrates that London was sensitive to the
stock forms that were appearing in the magazines. But it also
reveals that he was not yet aware of new narrative methods and
short story principles. For instance, "In the Time of Prince
Charley" is not really a short story at all but, instead, a condensed historical romance novel with a large list of characters,
multiple and complex incidents, lengthy explanations of the
passage of time and changes of place, and a first person narrator
who sometimes assumes omniscient duties.

Another early story, "A Thousand Deaths" which appeared in
Black Cat Magazine, confirms London's sensitivity to the literary
fads at the turn of the century.[39] *Black Cat Magazine* held prize
competitions in story writing and became famous for a stock
"Black Cat story" which emphasized the bizarre, the weird, and
the grotesque. In January, 1899, London won a place for his
story. Like "In the Time of Prince Charley" it testifies to the
sincerity of London's remark that he would "subordinate
thought to technique." The story is a first person account of a
young seaman from "good, English stock" who had left an
unloving father after committing "the wildest and most auda-

cious folly" and years later is rescued from drowning in San Francisco Bay by his father who no longer recognizes him (33). The father, a mad scientist, takes his son to a South Sea island and uses him as a subject for experiments in the suspension of life (hence, the title "A Thousand Deaths"). Eventually, the young seaman escapes his mad father by developing a scientific technique of his own which disintegrates living tissue, leaving just a whiff of ozone. With it, he murders his father.

"A Thousand Deaths" capitalizes upon pages of pseudo-scientific information, unrelieved sentiment for the unloved and handsome hero, and a taste for horror.[40] Although pompous in its language, a propensity noted in the early "Typhoon" and prominent in much of London's later, more serious fiction, the story is fairly controlled. It is limited to depicting two economically drawn characters (if stereotypes) and a few related incidents. Nevertheless, it is obviously hack work.

During this initial stage of his apprenticeship, then, London produced some poems, jokes, articles and stories that can only be described as hack work, corresponding in form, matter and manner to the popular, light items appearing in the magazines he had been studying. He learned that he could find editors willing to publish these pot-boilers. He had discovered the "trick" of successful authorship that would, at worst, tempt him to prostitute his art when he was capable of composing quality stories.[41]

There was, however, a change in his attitude, and he rebelled against the writing of low quality stories. After he had proved to himself and his friends that he could make money at his typewriter, he tired of these confections. London has Martin Eden write horror stories similar to "A Thousand Deaths," and the narrator describes Martin's disillusionment with them:

> ...his horror stories ... he did not consider high work. To him they were frankly imaginative and fantastic, though invested with all the glamour of the real, wherein lay their power. This investiture of the grotesque and impossible with reality, he looked upon as a trick—a skilful trick at the best. Great literature could not reside in such a field.

Then Eden writes "Adventure," "Joy," and "The Wine of Life," his best work.[42] And London, too, goes from horror to adventure.

Dissatisfied with reproducing stock forms, Jack London decided to attempt "great literature" that would compare favorably with the best stories appearing in the current periodicals. He had been praised by his friends as a professional, not an artist, and had written as such. He had acquired the stock techniques of others but had none of his own. He could imitate but not create. Therefore he began anew:

> The farther I wandered from the beaten track, (I mean the proper trend of modern style and literary art), the more encomiums were heaped upon me—by my friends. And believe me, the darkness I strayed into was heartbreaking. Surely, I have since thought, they must have seen where I was blind. So I grew to distrust them, and one day, between four and five months ago, awoke to the fact that I was all wrong. Everything crumbled away, completely lost—had no conception even of the relative values of the comma, colon, and semicolon. Since then have been digging.[43]

"Between four and five months ago" refers to the time when London had begun to write his Northland tales which appeared in the magazines throughout 1899 and would be collected into his first volume, *The Son of the Wolf*, in April, 1900. This letter to Cloudesly Johns announces the beginning of the second stage of his apprenticeship, his quest for a "modern style and literary art" and his utilization of masculine adventure materials. The pattern of his development can be seen in the stories collected in *The Son of the Wolf, The God of His Fathers* and *Children of the Frost*.

Fortunately, London began to "dissect the stories in the current magazines," to "dig" for a "modern style and literary art," at a time when a new consciousness of the short story as a genre was being expressed. Articles discussing the nature of the short story and sometimes giving practical advice appeared side by side with the growing number of stories in the periodicals.

The specific articles London encountered are unknown, but N. L. Goodrich's extensive bibliography of turn-of-the-century articles discussing fictional theory and technique demonstrates that there were so many that London, studying the magazines, could not have been unaware of them.[44] Moreover, London, himself, contributed to magazines like *The Editor, The Writer* and *Review of Reviews* which emphasized discussion of fictional theory and techniques.[45]

The short story theoreticians were uniformly inveighing against the conception of the short story as merely a condensed novel, and London would respond to them, never again composing stories like "In the Time of Prince Charley." Brander Matthew's essay *The Philosophy of the Short-Story* was the most influential of the many that would appear and found its inspiration in Poe's famous dictum from his review of Hawthorne's *Twice Told Tales* to seek "unity of effect or impression."[46] Others before Matthews had made the same plea; for example, an anonymous critic wrote in 1869 that short story "construction is an art, far more so than is generally believed" because a story:

> has laws, and bears very nearly the same relationship to the novel that the song does to poetry, which always properly possesses one definite idea thrown into a compact, symmetrical form. Writers of short stories cannot hope to attain success unless they make this form of composition a profound study.[47]

But it was Matthews who was most responsible for reaching a wide audience in his advocacy of a short story which differed from a novel "chiefly in its essential unity of impression" acquired by dealing with "a single character, a single event, a single situation."[48] Inspired by Matthews, writers of short story handbooks and manuals joined him in attempting to uncover the "laws" of the short story and combined scholarly competence in describing current fiction with quantities of prescriptive "do it yourself" advice for aspiring authors. For example, the first of these handbooks, Charles R. Barrett's *Short Story Writing. A Practical Treatise on the Art of the Short Story*, appeared in

1898 just as London began his serious study.[49] It, like the deluge of handbooks which followed, begins with Matthews' assumptions, describes the kinds of stories appearing on the market, and goes on to argue that compression, unity, momentum and originality are the unique qualities found in the short story.[50]

This "single effect" advice, to distinguish short stories from novels, was not lost on London, although he naively tended to see the observation of the time and place unities as a sufficient guard against diffusion. London picked up Matthews' conception that "the Short-story fulfills the three false unities of the French classic drama [by showing] one action, in one place, on one day"[51] and applied it to an analysis of the short stories which were collected in his own first two volumes:

> Remember this—confine a short story within the shortest possible time-limit—a day, an hour, if possible—or, if, as sometimes with the best of short stories, a long period of time must be covered,— months—merely hint or sketch (incidently) the passage of time, and tell the story only in its crucial moments.
>
> Really, you know, development does not belong in the short story, but in the novel.
>
> The short story is a rounded fragment from life, a single mood, situation, or action.
>
> ... Take down and open *Son of the Wolf*. Though several of them cover fairly long periods of time—the time is sketched and made subordinate to the final situation. You see, the situation is considered primarily—"The Son of the Wolf" in beginning is hungry for woman, he goes to get one; the situation is how he got one.
>
> "The Priestly Prerogative" is the scene in the cabin—the rest is introductory, preliminary.[52]
>
> "The Wife of a King"—not a good short story in any sense.[53]
>
> "The Odyssey of the North"—covering a long period of time (the whole life of Naass) is exploited in an hour and a half in Malemute Kid's cabin.
>
> Take down and open *God of His Fathers*. First story, single situation.[54]
>
> "Great Interrogation"—single situation in cabin where the whole past history of man and woman is exploited. And so on, to the last

story, "Scorn of Woman"—see how time is always sketched and situation is exploited—yet it is not a short story.[55]

But if London sought a unity of impression through an observation of the unities and by telling a story "only in its crucial moments" to avoid writing condensed novels, he did not immediately grasp the critics' entire message. In general, the short story theorists, and practitioners, too, like Howells, Aldrich and James, were reacting against digressive, expository stories that had their roots in Washington Irving's famous conception of the short story: "For my part I consider a story merely as a frame on which to stretch my materials."[56] The handbook theorists rebelled against the looseness of structure inherent in Irving's idea and found in the practice of countless writers who followed him. It was common practice, before this renewed interest in the "well-made" story, for writers to have pages of digressions both as introductory material and as authorial observations interspersed throughout the story. And London's early stories, despite his attempt to observe the unities, had more in common with the discursive story writers than with the new interest in economy.

When London began dissecting the magazine fiction in order to find "the proper trend of style and literary art" which led to the publication of the Northland stories, one of the first techniques he discovered was the use of the reliable, omniscient narrative point of view. He dropped the loose first person point of view that allowed his stories like "Typhoon," "In the Time of Prince Charley," "A Thousand Deaths" and "The Rejuvenation of Major Rathborn" to ramble in chronicle fashion and began to utilize more narrative control in the Alaskan tales. Switching to the third person narrator brought him into line with the most commonly used narrative method employed by his contemporaries.[57] But with it, he inherited its legacy of authorial intrusion, even though writers were learning to restrict narrative privilege. Many of his stories, particularly in his first two volumes, *The Son of the Wolf* and *The God of His Fathers*, employ an essay-exemplum type of construction reminiscent of earlier writers who prefixed rambling sermons to their stories.[58] In the long quotation above in which London discusses the unities, he unwittingly reveals that he considered "introductory, preliminary" materials organic rather than supplementary, unlike later writers who tried to eliminate the impedimenta. He thought of his short stories as having a block form of introduction-story rather than as a single entity.

In these introductory essays, in order to give the text, London would pose as an Alaskan social historian ("The Wife of a King," "The God of His Fathers," and "At the Rainbow's End"); a modern philosopher ("In a Far Country"); or psychologist ("The Son of the Wolf") among other roles. Then the illustrative story would follow. No doubt, this was the simplest method for presenting unequivocally the peculiarities of life in surroundings unfamiliar to the readers. Since London's first loyalty was to ideas and values, this uncomplicated form allowed him to present them so clearly that no reader could misunderstand. He never forgot his audience, and in these essay-exemplum stories, his didacticism led him to present views rather than to merely use them. Often the essays are superfluous, detachable moralizations whose import is implicit in the stories themselves. "The Son of the Wolf," for instance, begins with an essay on sexual instinct, justifying miscegenation in the Klondike:

> Man rarely places a proper valuation upon his womankind, at least not until deprived of them. He has no conception of the subtle atmosphere exhaled by the sex feminine so long as he bathes in it; but let it be withdrawn, and an ever-growing void begins to manifest itself in his existence, and he becomes hungry, in a vague sort of way, for something so indefinite that he cannot characterize it. . . . he will lose interest in the things of his everyday life and wax morbid; and one day, when his emptiness has become unbearable, a revelation will dawn upon him (*SW*, 21).

The story follows as Scruff Mackenzie, compelled by his sexual drive, travels into the hunting land of the treacherous Tanana Stick Indians to claim a bride. Apparently, London was following the journalistic advice he presents to a novice writer in one of his own short stories, "Amateur Night": "Tell it all in the opening paragraph as advertisement of contents, and in the contents tell it all over again."[59]

By discovering the omniscient narrator, London did improve beyond his early first person experiments. Although he sometimes rambled or padded his materials in these introductory essays which characterize many of his early Klondike tales, he generally used only those ideas which were germane to his story. Still, he was violating the primary concern of the short story theorists, the movement towards a more dramatic story. But call as they would for economical story-telling, the critics were not fully understood by London or other practicing magazine writers. Theory remained, to some extent, divorced from practice. The omniscient narrator did not move unobtrusively behind stories; instead, the narrator continued to impose his personality upon the fiction. He was privy to his characters' minds and hearts, had access to all knowledge and cavalierly interrupted at will to pass judgment upon his characters, situations and life in general.

London's first Northland stories demonstrate that he was not an innovator in this regard. Even after the introductory essays, the narrator insistently performs many functions. The characters do not reveal themselves through their actions and speech; instead, the narrator intrudes to comment and evaluate in passages like the following from "The Son of the Wolf":

> As has been noted, Scruff Mackenzie was a practical man. If he wanted a thing he usually got it, but in doing so, went no farther out of his way than was necessary (*SW*, 23).

and

> ...he went among them [the Indians] single-handed, his bearing being a delicious composite of humility, familiarity, *sang-froid* and insolence. It required a deft hand and a deep knowledge of the barbaric mind effectually to handle such diverse weapons; but he was a past master in the art, knowing when to conciliate and when to threaten with a Jove-like wrath (*SW*, 24).

He does the same with situation as with character, using narrative intrusions not only for evaluation, their main function, but to display the "fine writing" which mars many of the early stories:

> For all the world, it was like a scene of olden time,—a lady and her knight. Mackenzie drew her up full height and swept her red lips with his mustache,—the, to her, foreign caress of the wolf. It was a meeting of the stone age with the steel (*SW*, 28).

Often these intrusions are epigrammatic summaries used to resolve one section of the story before going on to the next. Rather than being inconspicuous, they draw attention to themselves and exist for their own sakes as well as for structural purposes—for example, this aside to the reader from "The Priestly Prerogative," one of the most flagrantly non-dramatic stories he ever wrote: "Some people are good, not for inherent love of virtue, but from sheer laziness. Those of us who know weak moments may understand (*SW*, 130)." Besides the precious, epigrammatic language, the intrusions are often particularly noticeable because of their exuberant, emotional or moralizing tone that draws attention to the highly personalized narrator who is indistinguishable from the author. In "The White Silence" the narrator emotes:

> Happy is the man who can weather a day's travel at the price of silence, and that on a beaten track. . . . he who can keep out of the way of the dogs for a whole day may well crawl into his sleeping-bag with a clear conscience and a pride which passeth all understanding; and he who travels twenty sleeps on the Long Trail is a man whom the gods may envy (*SW*, 6).

Of course, the narrator also performs more normal and less obvious functions like providing build-ups for scenes and indicating transitions in time. In general, though, London's use of this type of narrator corresponds directly with the most common practices and abuses of the popular magazine writers as he deliberately draws attention to the narrator by giving him a voice which is conspicuous in tone and allows him to make dramatically unnecessary observations.

When studying the critical commentary appearing in the magazines and handbooks, it becomes clear that a call for dramatic presentation was not a demand for practices we associate with Hemingway's "The Killers" even though at first it may seem to be. Barrett, for instance, in his handbook describes a variety of short stories appearing in the current magazines and reserves the honored place for the "dramatic story" which he defines as:

> ...a story shorn of all needless verbiage, and told as nearly as possible in the words and actions of the characters themselves ... The short story was *Dramatic Form* when the author's necessary comments correspond to the stage directions of the drama.[60]

At first glance this seems to be a recommendation for a "stage-manager" narrator who simply provides stage directions for the characters and then lets them act out their parts. But the phrases "all needless verbiage" and "as nearly as possible" allowed latitude for what was acceptable practice. Barrett, him-self, after presenting this argument for dramatic fiction, uses Kipling's stories as models of this "highest type of the short story."[61] Kipling may have been more dramatic than the youthful London, but he was no Hemingway. Apparently Barrett and the others were merely interested in eliminating the most flagrant abuses of authorial intrusion.

That London became sensitive to these demands is demonstrated by the perceptible movement in his Alaskan stories towards less narrative intrusion, a heavier reliance upon dialogue and action rather than exposition. He was learning "the art of omission" which he found most difficult but realized that its mastery meant the difference between a powerful story and one whose strength was dissipated.[62] As early as February, 1899, he wrote to Cloudesly Johns advising him to:

> Let the reader learn ... through the minds of the men themselves, let the reader look at the question through their eyes. There are a

variety of ways to do this—the most common would be to have them
talk to each other.

Such a method would have more emotional impact than pure
exposition.[63] And dialogue does begin to replace the narrator in
some stories, but often it is a mere transplantation of the
narrator's essay into the mouths of the characters, as, for
example, Karen's discussion of "race affinity" in "The Great
Interrogation" (*GF*, 56–57). But no matter how amateurishly
executed, this is a step towards depersonalizing the narrator.
Furthermore, London began to find techniques which would
eliminate the author, or, at least, camouflage his operations.
Eventually he would develop a theory which corresponds
directly with Barrett's.

It is revealing that Barrett chose Kipling's stories as the
perfect example of dramatic form. All eyes were turned to
Kipling, and London hit upon a form of which Kipling was the
master—the frame story. In these stories the narrator provides
some kind of setting that permits a character to elicit a story
from another, recalls some story told to him, or provides some
motivation for a character to recall a personal experience.[64]
These frame stories represent London's first major movement
towards a more dramatic form of story-telling. They begin early
in his work, while he continued to produce the essay-exemplum
form, and became a significantly large portion of his total
canon.[65] Significantly there are more frame stories in the second
volume of his short stories than in the first, and more in the
third than in the second. They are a modification of the essay-
exemplum type since the frame takes the place of the essay, and
the story-within often illustrates some idea that is discussed in
the frame section.

"An Odyssey of the North" is a well known London story
which exemplifies his experimentation with this more dramatic
type of story. An omniscient narrator begins by introducing the
characters, familiar from earlier stories, and establishing the
setting. The Malemute Kid and Prince take over the narrative
functions through their dialogue and provide the frame. They

discuss the various Northland types of men who are in their cabin, especially the mysterious visitor who is later revealed as Naass, the central figure who narrates the odyssey in the title. The initial part of the frame ends here. Finally, the tale within the story is told by Naass in the long first person narrative passage which is the central interest of this story. After Naass' tale, the "Odyssey of the North" concludes with the final part of the frame as the Kid and Prince ponder what they have heard.

Narrative functions which were left to the omniscient narrator in previous stories are now fulfilled by the central character. Naass establishes his own reliability through his confession of the murder of Unga, who was promised to him in their early tribal days, and Axel Gunderson, the "blond beast" who married her. The quality of Naass' love, the hardship he endured to find Unga, his respect for the man he murdered, and his honesty in returning a loan to the Malemute Kid testify to his integrity and worth, eliminating the necessity for authorial intrusions. Moreover, Naass' description of his world-wide quest for Unga and the heroic actions of Unga and Axel after Naass has found them are so vivid and complete within themselves that they serve as implicit comments upon the quality of Northland life and the capacity of human beings for love and suffering. There is still too much narration in the introduction, but London was learning to find powerful expression by eliminating more of himself, or his representative, from the story.

In his movement from the essay-exemplum form to the frame story, London was not only responding to a general dramatic trend reflected in the construction of magazine stories, but revealing his indebtedness to Kipling's example. Rothberg and other critics have documented the themes and materials shared by Kipling and London, and Joan London mentioned that Jack attempted to imitate Kipling's style.[66] But no one has noticed the remarkable similarity of their short story structures. Moreover, Jack London's testimony that he studied the magazines when Kipling was in the first rank in order to find the proper short story form and techniques, his open and frequently mentioned admiration of Kipling, and the striking correspondences between the two authors' short story patterns, even plots, are strong evidence that London used Kipling's stories as models for his own.

An 1895 review of some of Kipling's stories mentions that Kipling has a ". . . preaching strain in the background of his soul."[67] And, like London, the moralizing intent of his early short stories, especially those in *Plain Tales from the Hills*, is blatantly apparent in the introductory comments or essays prefixed to the stories which illustrate a point in morals or some phase of human character.[68] In "Three—and an Extra," for example, the introductory comment is "After marriage arrives a reaction, sometimes big, sometimes a little one; but it comes sooner or later, and must be tided over by both parties if they desire the rest of their lives to go with the current.[69] Following this statement is the story of a man who leaves his wife and gives his attentions to the fascinating Mrs. Hauksbee before his wife recaptivates him by displaying her beauty and charm at a dinner dance. London's "Wife of a King" parallels the plot of this story, replacing the wife with an Indian girl and Mrs. Hauksbee with Freda Moloof, a bewitching Greek dancer. He might also have used the same introductory statement, but chose, in the same manner at least, a more lengthy dissertation on man taking native wives and then facing the inevitable attraction of racial "kind" which creates domestic crises (*SW*, 160–161). And this London essay, itself, is parallel to one with which Kipling opened "Beyond the Pale":

> A man should, whatever happens, keep to his own caste, race and breed. Let the White go to the White and Black to the Black. Then whatever trouble falls in the ordinary course of things—is neither sudden, alien nor unexpected.[70]

But the point here is not even the similarity of London's ideas, characters and plot incidents so much as his imitation of form.

Walter Morris Hart, the first critic to undertake a full study of Kipling's short story artistry, notes that most of Kipling's early stories, the Indian tales, follow this pattern and also "definitely betray, in some way, the presence of a narrator behind the narrative."[71] Kipling, like London, does not remain impersonally behind the scenes, but summarizes, takes sides, explains and demonstrates a continual awareness of his audience to whom he does not wish to entrust the obligations of interpretation.

But Kipling, too, de-emphasized this non-dramatic form and turned to the frame story as the other major form for his early work. Some stories in *Plain Tales* and many from *Soldiers Three* use the frame pattern, and Kipling maintained it throughout his long career. How similar in basic form, as well as in content, the two men's stories often are is illustrated by a comparison between Kipling's "The Three Musketeers" and London's "The Death of Ligoun."[72] In both stories the frame consists of a story collector providing drinks to loosen the tongues of men who have special information to impart. Kipling's narrator sits with privates Mulvaney, Ortheris and Learoyd, recurrent Kipling favorites, and says, "They told me this story, in the Umballa Refreshment Room while we were waiting for an up-train. I supplied the beer. The tale was cheap at a gallon and a half."[73] London's narrator, in the Klondike rather than India, remarks to the reader:

> I held the bottle between our eyes and the fire, indicated with my thumb the depth of the draught, and shoved it over to him; for was he not Palitlum, the Drinker? Many tales had he told me, and long had I waited for this scriptless scribe to speak of the things concerning Ligoun; for he of all men living, knew these things best (*CF*, 113).

Not only are the frames sometimes parallel, but also the stories themselves. Kipling's "Dray Wara Yow Dee," for instance, is a story told by a native to a white audience, a tale of his quest over the whole of India to find and kill his wife's lover.[74] The parallel with "An Odyssey of the North" is obvious. London emulated his admired Kipling, so like him in his moralizing impulse, by using the forms that Kipling had proven artistically and commercially sound for presenting the kinds of ideas London wished to communicate.

The price of imitation is often that the disciple rarely duplicates the successes of the master. London was usually more
verbose than Kipling in the essays prefixed to exempla and never
reached the artistic complexity in his frame stories that Kipling
exhibits in a few stories like "The Incarnation of Krishna
Mulvaney" in which the relationship between frame and story-
within is so economical and organic that no less than four points
of view are utilized.[75] But if London was not consistently
artistic in using these forms, neither was his mentor and both
succumbed to the looseness inherent in them. It may be said of
London's work what Hart has said of Kipling's:

> One does not get the impression that he planned his stories carefully
> from beginning to end, as Poe and Stevenson did. He worked ...
> with a strong feeling about the story in hand rather than a definite
> plan as to its form.[76]

There is form, a plan, but the power of the stories often strains
against the mechanical structure.

London did, however, learn to use the frame story ade-
quately, and it allowed him to explore his ideas more thoroughly than the essay-exemplum type. In the essay-exemplum stories
the narrator was constrained to speak in what can only be the
author's authoritative voice rather than through a *persona*. Most
of the explicit comments made by the narrator are awkwardly
overbearing and dogmatic in their attempts to force ideas upon
the reader and commit the story-teller to arriving at definite
conclusions. But London's frame stories, using a teller who is
clearly distinguishable from London himself, allowed him to
present more complicated social and moral situations. For
example, in "An Odyssey of the North" Naass, an admirable and
complex character-narrator, comes into conflict with two other
idealized characters. The situation is morally complex since
Naass's suffering and loyalty are emotionally equivalent to
Unga's and Axel's love for each other, and equally justified. Yet
the two sets of emotions are incompatible, and the story rightly
remains unresolved. Because the point of view is not that
absolutely omniscient and reliable author's, the dilemma can be

left without final auctorial redress and pontifical judgment, making artistic uses of ambiguity and irony. And in the North-land tales as a group we find that the frame tale becomes a frequently employed form for presenting stories which deal with the conflict between civilization and primitive culture, the white man and the Indian, topics complex in their moral overtones.

In general, London, probably influenced by Kipling, came upon the frame story as an answer to the twin demands for a more dramatic presentation and a framework for presenting characters and themes of a greater complexity than he had first attempted. The frame story was an improvement over the essay-exemplum form, although London does not always achieve a tightly organic relationship between frame and story within. The twenty stories in his first two volumes, composed in 1899 and 1900, are a record of his gradual acquisition of dramatic methods, and even though the stories in order of appearance do not follow an orderly progression from exemplum type to frame, the drift is undeniably in that direction.

Sometime in late spring, 1900, only a year and a half after beginning his serious apprenticeship and after composing most of the stories eventually collected in *Son of the Wolf* and *God of His Fathers* and beginning to work on the *Children of the Frost* stories, Jack London began to recognize the need for a more satisfactory dramatic form that would encompass an entire story, rather than being limited to the story within another story. In the course of the next few months he developed his most sophisticated theory and practice of dramatic fiction which brought him close to Barrett's definition of "the highest type of the short story" and allowed him to depersonalize the intruding narrator and to achieve the "single effect" intensity so highly prized by short story theorists.

On June 16, 1900, London wrote an excited letter to Johns that proves his awareness of the critical exhortations for more dramatic fiction. Vehemently he criticized Cloudesly for inter-jecting authorial responses into his stories:

> Don't you tell the reader the philosophy of the road (except when you are actually there as participant in the first person). Don't you

tell the reader. Don't. Don't. Don't. But HAVE YOUR CHARACTERS TELL IT BY THEIR DEEDS, ACTIONS, TALK, ETC. Then, and not until then, are you writing fiction and not a sociological paper upon a certain sub-stratum of society ... The reader doesn't want your dissertations on the subject, your observations, your knowledge as your knowledge, your thoughts about it, your ideas—BUT PUT ALL THOSE THINGS WHICH ARE YOURS INTO THE STORIES, INTO THE TALES, ELIMINATING YOURSELF.[77]

This is more than talk. By this time London had begun to write stories that exhibit these principles more definitely than any stories he had composed in the preceding years. And in the following letter to his friend, London reveals that the source of his enthusiasm in the June letter was the composition of "The Law of Life," one of a series later collected in *Children of the Frost*. This letter analyzing "The Law of Life" is the most thorough critique of his own form that he ever wrote and demonstrates his conscious struggle to acquire more dramatic techniques:

Yesterday I corrected proof sheets of a story for *McClure's*. It was written some eight months ago. It will be published in the February number.[78] Do look it up so that you may understand more clearly what I am trying to explain. It is short, applies the particular to the universal, deals with a lonely death, of an old man, in which beasts consummate the tragedy. My man is an old Indian, abandoned in the snow by his tribe because he cannot keep up. He has a little fire, a few sticks of wood. The frost and silence about him. He is blind. How do I approach the event? What point of view do I take? Why, the old Indian's, of course. It opens up with him sitting by his little fire, listening to his tribesmen breaking camp, harnessing dogs, and departing. The reader listens to every familiar sound; hears the last draw away; feels the silence settle down. The old man wanders back into his past; the reader wanders with him—thus is the whole theme exploited through the soul of the Indian. Down to the consummation, when the wolves draw in upon him in a circle. Don't you see, nothing, even the moralizing and generalizing, is done, save through him, in expressions of his experience.[79]

Indeed, in this story London discovered that he could use a limited, rather than fully omniscient, third person point of view for a dramatic effect powerful in its simplicity. There is no essay in the beginning, and the setting is established in terms of the old man's awareness so that there is no awkward shift from narrative landscaping to action; therefore, the reader is not conscious of a direct bid for his attention. "Even the moralizing and generalizing" could be done dramatically by presenting them as the tenor of the old man's thoughts rather than as the author's own. For example, in this philosophical generalization from the story, the narrator lies just behind Koskoosh's thoughts and gives the illusion that they are the old man's by using short, simple sentences that London associated with Indian speech, sentences unlike the involved, clever ones he had used to display the worldly and urbane generalizations of his previously invoked omniscient narrator:

> It was the way of life, and it was just . . . Nature was not kindly to the flesh. She had no concern for that concrete thing called the individual. Her interest lay in the species, the race (*CF*, 31).

The comments made by the narrator are tailored to the demands of character rather than inappropriately out of the range of the character's perceptions and are so appropriate in tone and style that no unusual emphasis draws attention away from the character's point of view.

Although none of the stories following "The Law of Life" in *The Children of the Frost* (1902) are as rigorous in point of view nor in artistic simplicity, stories like "Nam-Bok the Unveracious," "The Sunlanders," and "Keesh, the Son of Keesh," (told "from the Indian's point of view, through the Indian's eyes as it were")[30] do demonstrate that London was avoiding direct philosophical, social or psychological evaluations of character or setting in the voice of the narrator appealing directly to his audience.

London, then, was learning techniques which allowed him to be more economical and dramatic. The logical extension of this movement toward depersonalizing the narrator voice is a scenic method which uses a stage-manager narrator who merely records what can be seen and heard but who does not enter the characters' minds, analyze their motives, nor explain the source and implications of the scenes. The product of such a method would be similar to a painting, a pictorial representation of a situation.

In theory, at least, London did develop such a dramatic theory and presented it as the theme of "The Sun-Dog Trail."[51] The story (itself, however, in the frame story format) consists of a discussion between a painter and Sitka Charlie, London's most idealized male Indian, about the meaning of several paintings hanging on the cabin wall and a story told by Charlie that illustrates his conclusions. The painter is eager to interrogate Charlie because he is "a sheer master of reality," presumably because he is an Indian who lives in a world of action and whose artistic assumptions have not been corrupted by education: "He had lived life, and seen things" and "had never learned to read or write" (*LL*, 208,203). At first the paintings have no meaning for Charlie because they have "no beginning" and "no end" (*LL*, 205). But through further discussion, Charlie arrives at the conclusion that a painting is like life, a scenic presentation of "something that happened" from which only the picture seared into the brain remains (*LL*, 240). The motives and actions of the figures in the painting remain undefined and uncompleted. Charlie then relates an experience of his own which illustrates this conclusion. He tells of being hired by a woman to take her to Dawson where she meets a man; the three of them travel across the Yukon wastes until they meet another man. The man and woman shoot him. The climaxing murder is committed in an intensely visualized setting: " 'And all about is the snow and the silence. And in the sky are three suns, and all the air is flashing with the dust of diamonds' " (*LL*, 238). He concludes, " 'It was a piece of life' " (*LL*, 241). The point of the story is that Charlie was never aware of the true identities of the woman and two men nor their motives. He remembers the "something that happened" because of the intensity of the image, not because he fully understands why the incident happened.

"The Sun-Dog Trail" thematically seems to demonstrate that London subscribed to the theory of dramatic fiction which describes rather than prescribes, shows rather than tells, presents ideas implicitly rather than explicitly by using scenes rather than exposition. He seconds Barrett's admiration of stories which present a "bit of life" in Dramatic Form."[82]

Ironically, "The Sun-Dog Trail" itself is discursive, a denial of its expository statements. It was written after London had established his basic narrative patterns as represented by "The Son of the Wolf" (essay-exemplum), "An Odyssey of the North" (frame), and "The Law of Life" (limited third person narrator); and he never actually practiced purely stage-manager narration. The theory presented in "The Sun-Dog Trail" written in 1904 yielded to the practices he had acquired from 1899 to 1902.

But there is an extremely important basic correlation between London's theory and his actual practice. From the beginning of his Klondike stories, he had relied upon dramatic scenes as the core around which the rest of the story coalesced. Although the story might contain narrative essays and other authorial interference, an evocative scene lay at the center of dramatic interest in the best of these stories. Even an early critic recognized the visual quality achieved in the *Children of the Frost* as a mark of distinguished writing and wrote that in "The Master of Mystery," "the subject is so interesting and the treatment so powerfully simple and sincere that the picture stands out clear and flawless."[83] The poorer stories, the ones that London himself disliked, such as "The Wife of a King" and "A Priestly Prerogative," fail to focus upon a single dramatic scene or central image. London did realize though that such scenes replace the author, or, more accurately, become the author in the sense that his emotional and intellectual experience can be embodied more compactly and forcefully through scene than through exposition. One of the more frequently mentioned "tips" he gave to aspiring story writers was to "Paint—paint pictures of characters and emotions—but paint, paint, draw, draw" so that the author's voice would be eliminated from the work.[84]

It was intense, direct and powerful experience that Jack London wanted to evoke. And while he was finding the forms that would assist him, he was cultivating a style that would control and unleash that power. "Strength of utterance" fascinated him; he suspected that technical finesse masked dishonest or conventional thinking.[85]

Among the several books that he took to the Klondike, one was destined to crystallize his ideas about forceful, evocative style and how to achieve it—Herbert Spencer's *Philosophy of Style*, consisting of two sections discussing "the causes of force in language."[86] According to Charmian London, Jack had said in later years that this essay:

> taught me ... the subtle and manifold operations necessary to transmute thought, beauty, sensation and emotion into black symbols on white paper; which symbols through the reader's eye were taken into his brain, and by his brain transmuted into thought, beauty, sensation and emotion that fairly corresponded with mine. Among other things, this taught me to *know* the brain of my reader, in order to realize my thought, or vision or emotion. Also, I learned that the right symbols were the ones that would require the expenditure of the minimum of my reader's brain energy, leaving the maximum of his brain energy to realize and enjoy the content of my mind, as conveyed to his mind.[87]

Spencer believed that the reader had only so much mental "energy" at his disposal and that the writer must tap this energy without allowing it to be squandered on peripheral matters. Simple words and sentence structure would conserve the energy and direct it towards the idea or emotion communicated by the writer. London's statement demonstrates that he comprehended Spencer's thesis. But more importantly, his enthusiasm for Spencer's doctrine reveals what London prized in writing. First, he felt that nothing should stand between the reader and the direct apprehension of the writer's ideas. The writer should never confuse the reader by using intricate plots, complex characters, subtleties of emotion or a Latinate vocabulary. All these "waste" the reader's "energy" as a magazine critic influenced by *Philosophy of Style* stated.[88] London accépted Spencer's theory that simple, evocative language was the best way to convey "each thought into the mind, step by step with little liability to error."[89] Secondly, London learned from Spencer that forceful expression could be achieved by selecting "from the sentiment, scene, or event described those typical elements which carry many other along with them"; or, in other words, the most direct method and style is the most suggestive one.[90] So London tried to acquire a simple but evocative structure and style, and, in fact, the height of his stylistic achievement was just this evocative and poetic effect.

Although no other work of literary theory compelled his imagination as much as Spencer's, it is clear that he did not move directly from assimilating this "scientific" theory of style to the practice of his own. London may have found that Spencer's advocacy of simplicity in form and style in order to achieve a forceful communication was a remarkably coherent statement of what he wished to do, and the essay may have provided him with some specific techniques. Still, from theory to practice was too great a leap. Instead, he acted upon another passage from the first page of Spencer's observations:

> ... there can be little question that good composition is far less dependent upon acquaintance with its laws than upon practice and natural aptitude. A clear head, a quick imagination, and a sensitive ear, will go far towards making all rhetorical precepts needless. He who daily hears and reads well-framed sentences, will naturally more or less tend to use similar ones.

Accordingly, in search of a forceful style, London did as he had done when learning appropriate short story forms: he took down his Kipling and "laboriously, in longhand, and for days on end, copied page after page and story after story of Kipling" until he was able to approximate his style.[91]

Often, London's prose is similar to Kipling's in its measured cadence and rhythmical, incantatory movement. Particularly in the Northland Indian stories, London achieved a "haunted sense of unshaped mystery and sound" growing into "melody, a hint of some primeval cradle-song, brooding and weird, merging into words and rhythm" that an early reviewer found characteristic of one of Kipling's stories.[92] London, like Kipling, sought a prose that was simple and direct, yet evoking strong, intense emotion from its short sentences. Both writers, particularly through the speech patterns of their native characters, invested their prose with Biblical overtones by employing allegorical rhetoric.[93] They combined a grandiloquent tone with the matter-of-fact, the exotic with the ordinary, an epic swing with the rapid movement of clipped, journalistic reportage.[94]

Throughout the rest of his career, London continued to rely on the three major short story forms and the evocative style that he learned during these early, apprenticeship years. His social criticism stories and South Seas stories, the good ones as well as the pot-boilers, are cast in these familiar molds. At their best, the stories wed form, content and style while transcending formal and technical deficiencies by emphasizing central, powerful scenes. The essay-exemplum form remained a staple for presenting ideas dogmatically, particularly when introducing new ideas about strange lands or situations whether in the Northland, the South Seas, or among the "submerged tenth" in America. The frame stories allowed him to develop more complex ideas. The more dramatic forms and techniques were used for statements about basic human experiences which needed no explicit introduction, but demanded emotional impact, especially if the perspective were ironic.

Just why London curtailed experimentation in form and technique near the end of 1902 is a moot question. Certainly the oft-repeated slogan that the quest for dollars and the daily routine of 1000 words would not permit development has a measure of truth in it. That is not the entire answer, however. He needed money and wrote a thousand words daily at the beginning of his career when he wrote jokes, poems, and among others, horror stories; and still, obviously, he went on to experiment successfully with forms, techniques and style. Several other factors must have been equally as important in arresting his development.

The reason he had stopped writing hack work and began experimenting with new forms was that his goal had changed. Not satisfied to stay in the ranks of nameless professional hack writers, he had dedicated himself to a higher goal: to finding the proper trend of literary art. From 1899 to the end of 1902, he changed his literary method and accomplished that goal. Afterwards, his conception of art and sense of mission as a writer did not change radically, and neither did his short story forms. Secondly, especially after the publication of *Call of the Wild* in 1903, he became more interested in the novel and less in short stories.[95] But most importantly, once he was convinced that he had adequate vehicles for his ideas and that they were communicating, he had no interest in craftsmanship for its own sake. Early in his career he had remarked that he would "subordinate thought to technique till the latter is mastered; then I shall do vice versa." He saw himself primarily as a purveyor of new ideas and experiences and gave priority to them. Charmian London records that Jack often claimed that:

> I will sacrifice form *every time*, when it boils down to a final choice between form and matter. The thought is the thing.

By the end of 1902, Jack London had come a long way from "Typhoon" and "In the Time of Prince Charley" in understanding the nature of short story craftsmanship. With the aid of stories and discussions of fiction in the magazines, Kipling's example and Herbert Spencer's stylistic theory, as well as his own colossal energy, he was able to define himself as artist and had gotten in touch with the most important literary currents of his age.

Chapter II

ACTUALITY AND IDEALS:
1898–1902

During his apprenticeship, Jack London was not only seeking an adequate form and style for his short stories, but also defining his literary attitudes in relation to the continuing debate between realism and romance. Although he thought of himself as a realist, he was actually struggling to uncover a literary theory that would transcend deficiencies he perceived in both the realist and romantic traditions by uniting the best qualities of each. Since, for him, "the thought is the thing," he needed a literary perspective consistent with his "working philosophy of life," his third prerequisite for "success as a writer" in addition to a knowledge of life and of commercial literature.[96] Somehow that perspective would have to account for the dark truths about nature and man's position in it thrust upon him by his fascination with evolutionary thought. And, simultaneously, that perspective would have to be consistent with a deeply felt intuition that man is noble and that humanly sustaining ideals can be validated.

As we have seen, Jack London began writing when the most influential short story theorists and commentators had fallen under the spell of realistic technique; Brander Matthews, for example, was a disciple and ardent defender of William Dean Howells. London learned from the realists "how to forbear the excesses of analysis, to withhold weakly recurring descriptive and caressing epithets, to let the characters suffice for themselves," to be "dramatic" rather than "tediously analytical."[97] He called Sitka Charlie in "The Sun-Dog Trail" a "sheer master of reality" because he saw "things that happened," reminiscent of the realists' "slice of life."[98] These emphases upon depersonalized narration and scenic method would seem to place London with the realists. Moreover, London used most of the realists' catchwords like "facts," "truth," "reality," and "honesty" to characterize his own intention and practice and to praise the works of other writers whom he admired most. He noted with pride, for instance, that his materials came from experience, making them "real" ("like 90% of my stories, 'The Benefit of the Doubt' is based upon actual experience").[99] In one of the most thorough accounts of what realism meant to London, Robert Holland suggests that the autobiographical emphasis does lead one to identify London with realism:

> ... many of London's characters are real men. Much of his setting is realistic. In fact, the characters and settings, though often unique, are not impossible.[100]

But London's "near-at-hand" truth and his autobiographical materials came from the Klondike, the high seas, and the tropics—familiar places to him but not to his readers. The places and characters are "not impossible" and no doubt were "real" to London, but not real in the Howellsian sense of the "average" or the "commonplace" which were hateful words to London.[101] The experiences London used as the stuff for his fiction had sprung from his lower class existence and included the crude, the violent and the sordid, all "average" to him, but not to Howells who assumed the middle class American as the norm for perception. Literature written from a Howellsian perspective bored London; it was bloodless. He wanted his stories to "live and spout blood and spirit and beauty and fire and glamor."[102] These attitudes and characteristics, the appeal to intensity, seem to make a romantic out of London. Indeed, his fiction has sometimes been called "romantic realism," which, unfortunately, is not a revealing phrase.

Comparing London's critical views with those of Howells, Hamlin Garland and Frank Norris has obvious merit; but London thought within another context. To understand just what London meant when he defined himself as a realist and why romantic elements are found in his stories, it is helpful to examine the magazine criticism appearing in periodicals to which he hoped to contribute. He caught its drift. His literary theory parallels an eclectic compromise between realism and romance implicit in the reviews written by the more fashionable popular magazine critics; and it is strikingly similar to the concepts of literary naturalism formulated by recent academic critics like Charles Walcutt and Donald Pizer.

Virtually every American magazine that printed reviews or literary gossip at the turn of the century had staff members and outside contributors who took part in the battle between romance and realism. Today, of course, university originated critical studies dominate critical exchange, but in 1900 the general magazine was the medium for almost all critical commentary. For over a decade, Howells had been defending realism and attacking romance in *Harper's* on a relatively high level of controversy. Other magazines, like *Lippincott's, The Forum, The Critic* and *The Bookman* had contributed their voices. *The Bookman* and *The Forum* were particularly notable for the consistently good coverage they gave to both sides of the issue.[103]

By the turn of the century, the skirmishing was nearly completed; the major areas of contention defined and almost settled. Intellectually, the battle had gone to Howells and the realists, but the popular victory had gone to the critics who favored stories which in some way managed to combine elements of realism and romance. From this compromise London took his cue, demonstrating his sensitivity to the popular arguments.

The popular critics, like James MacArthur, staff reviewer for *The Bookman* and exponent of sentimental romance, recognized two kinds of literary production: one was "very probable, very life-like, and very disagreeable" and the other "quite improbable, in externals strange, yet true to the motives and passions that

sway men and women."[104] The "very disagreeable" referred to
stories using a wider range of materials than had been used
before, and such expressions usually referred to Zola's novels
which were at the center of critical attacks upon "immoral"
materials. To the popular critic, the use of such materials con-
stituted "realism." Many critics were predicting doom for Zola
and his imitators, as did Edward Fuller: "The pseudo-realism
preached by Zola and echoed by his imitators has ended, or is
ending, in dismal failure . . . the best and most vital literature
cannot be produced in a period of decadence."[105] But James
MacArthur, who called this fiction "disagreeable," reluctantly
admitted, while reviewing *Chimmie Fadden* and *Slum Stories of
London*, that "the enduring novel of New York or London of
the future" would undoubtedly be shaped by such pernicious
materials; thereby indicating that some popular romantic critics
were begrudgingly admitting the inevitability of sordid detail as
fictional material.[106] They stood shoulder to shoulder, however,
with the more intransigeant against any work which seemed to
use naturalistic detail for its own sake and to equate the human
with the bestial.

On the other hand, the "quite improbable" romantic fiction
that MacArthur obviously prefers was also coming under attack.
This literature, represented by Andrew Lang's fiction, itself
imitative of Stevenson's, existed solely for entertainment and
whisked the reader to the pleasant land of noble sentiments and
happy endings that were the substance of the *Trilby* and *The
Prisoner of Zenda* crazes. Even though romance was popular
with the readers, two major and related critical objections, with
which London would have agreed, were being levelled against
this type of story.[107] First, it failed to discuss significant experience. Bliss Perry, for instance, castigates Stevenson and his
followers because, "few or none of these men have revealed
themselves as great personalities seriously engaged in interpreting
the more vital aspects of human experience."[108] Secondly,
romantic fiction was being criticized for ignoring the impact of
new ideas in biology and psychology that were changing old
conceptions of nature. E. F. Andrews, even though he was an

apostle of "moral" literature and an opponent of Zola's influence, finds that he must criticize romantic fiction "if the romantic element prevails to such an extent as to contradict nature . . ."[109] Briefly then, both the purely naturalistic use of sordid detail and the purely sentimental kind of romance were rejected by the popular critics as being ill-conceived extremes.[110]

The view that triumphed, if the repeated testimony in its behalf is the measure of its acceptance, was a combination of what was felt to be the essence of the two positions. The popular critics of both persuasions would accept as artistic any work which combined materials from the world, even though unsavory in isolation, if they were shot through with some kind of idealism. Typical of the critical commentary arising from such a position is this passage from a review of Frank Harris's *Elder Conklin and Other Stories*. The reviewer praises Harris's characters who are like

> The Bret Harte type—only much less sentimental—or hard-fibered, unpolished dwellers in tamer places. It is a grim, unlovely life, and the author paints it very relentlessly, yet letting in now and again a ray of pure idealism . . . We see no searching after the ugly, but a philosophical acceptance of the sordid as forming no inconsiderable part of the life he designs to paint.[111]

The point of MacArthur's and Andrew's articles was to promote this fusion of new materials with idealism, and a legion of critics made the same point: "Without true realism and genuine romanticism—actuality and ideals—good work was never done," one critic put it, and another, "no worthy work of fiction may be properly labelled romantic, realistic or symbolic, since every great work of art contains all these in some proportion."[112] This fusion became the trademark of many stories appearing in print and the mark of success as far as the rank and file critic was concerned.

Even Howells could accept this compromise with some reservations. He did object to those writers who were "content to use the materials of realism and produce the effect of romanticism" since, regardless of the realistic materials, romantic conventions were still operative, producing "effectism" and denying the proper seriousness inherent in good fiction.[113] Nevertheless, Howells did tolerate, as legitimate literature, fiction that avoided the clichés of realism and romance and combined the serious spirit of both modes, that give precedence to principle rather than to mere evocation of passion or to "entertainment."[114] It must be remembered that Howells recognized in Norris and Zola a new kind of romancer whom he could admire and that he praised Kipling by finding his fiction "heroic" rather than "romantic."[115] By making this distinction between heroic and romantic, Howells was actually hitting at the core of the new compromise and accepting it himself: in essence, he was attempting to isolate the "false" romance, one that exists in order to entertain by flattering the reader's sense of his own nobility, from a higher romance which presents spiritual man existing even in an ugly setting. Like the other critics, Howells rejected popular romance but could accept new materials if they were charged by an idealism that was true to nature.

This magazine compromise is the fundamental critical conception behind Jack London's short stories. And an attempt to combine idealism with the rough external world he observed, to balance a vital emotional life with the truths of scientific observation, is a recurrent theme in both London's life and his work. In the summer of 1899 he wrote:

> I early learned that there were two natures in me. This caused me a great deal of trouble, till I worked out a philosophy of life and struck a compromise between the flesh and the spirit. Too great an ascendancy of either was to be abnormal, and since normality is almost a fetish of mine, I finally succeeded in balancing both natures. ... I have small regard for an utter brute or for an utter saint.[116]

This statement, and similar ones, allows one to presume that Martin Eden's literary theory is a statement of London's own. Early in his career Martin learns to avoid both romantic and realistic clichés in his works but to combine the best elements of both realism and romance:

He had discovered, in the course of his reading, two schools of fiction. One treated of man as a god, ignoring his earthly origin; the other treated of man as a clod, ignoring his heaven-sent dreams and divine possibilities. Both the god and the clod schools erred, in Martin's estimation, and erred through too great singleness of sight and purpose. There was a compromise that approximated the truth, though it flattered not the school of god, while it challenged the brute-savageness of the school of clod (*ME*, p. 212).

Like the popular magazine critics, London objected to the "too great singleness of sight and purpose" shown by both sides. On the "clod" side, he objected to the Zolaesque "brute-savageness" if it existed for its own sake. On the "god" side, he objected to a sentimental view of human nature.

At first glance, though, London's fiction would seem to make him an apostle of the sensationally shocking. Joan London noted that "he soon became a pioneer of American 'realism.' He broke every writing tradition long revered in America, seemed . . . ultramodern and shocking" because, like Martin Eden, he used "scenes that were rough and raw, gross and bestial (*ME*, p. 76)."[117] He had contempt for the avoidance of violence and the artistic capitulation to feminine sensitivities. He agreed with Crane's sentiment, "Tradition, thou art for suckling children,/ Thou art the enlivening milk for babes;/ But no meat for men is in thee . . ."[118] Nevertheless, London agreed with the realist and romantic critics who deplored the cataloguing of sordid experience, or, indeed, any kind of detail which did not have a clear relevancy to the fates of the characters. In his review of *The Octopus*, for example, London criticized Norris for his indiscriminate use of detail when describing Hooven's safe, and in another place argues that the writer must employ only those details which have emotional significance, that elicit a response from the depths of the human heart.[119] Like Howells, London believed that facts must have human significance:

When realism becomes false to itself, when it heaps up facts merely, and maps life instead of picturing it, realism will perish too. Every true realist instinctively knows this, and it is perhaps the reason why he is careful of every fact, and feels himself bound to express or to indicate its meaning at the risk of over-moralizing. In life he finds nothing insignificant; all tells for destiny and character . . .[120]

Romantic critics, too, often mentioned this principle of selection as the difference between art and non-art:

There must be no misconception about great fiction being a transcript of life. Mere transcription is not the work of an artist . . . the human significance of facts is all that concerns one. The inwardness of facts makes fiction the history of life, its emotions, its passions, its sins, reflections, values. These you cannot photograph nor transcribe. Selection and rejection are two profound essentials of every art.[121]

London felt privileged to use the "rough and raw, gross and bestial" materials characteristic of the "clod" school but exercised a principle of selection. He wanted only those materials which bore human significance, facts which documented the subjective.

Just as he could accept man's unpleasant surroundings and actions but could not accept the bestial as the total explanation for human nature, London both accepted and rejected elements of the "god" school doctrine. Like the popular critics, he rejected "light and airy romances, pretty and sweet and beguiling."[122] But he wanted to portray a human nature which transcended the animal, that described "spirit-groping and soul-searching" and the "fancies and beauties of imagination" (ME, p. 212). With harsh fact he strove to combine "the stinging things of the spirit."[123] "Actuality" and "ideals" were to be the staples of his fiction. He believed that man's environment and mental-emotional life should not be divorced from one another and hoped they could be integrated.

London's compromise between the "god" and "clod" schools approximates the compromise made by magazine critics. He rejected the commonplace of both groups and attempted to salvage what was serious in both. Neither "airy romances" nor "brute-savageness" should be the exclusive preoccupation of fiction, he believed; instead, he accepted the impulse to root his fiction in an expanding reality of harsh facts and, yet, to depict ideals. Neither the saint nor the brute, or by implication, the pleasant nor the sordid, optimism nor pessimism would dominate his stories.

But where would the emphasis lie in that broad territory between the utter brute and the utter saint? In fixing the proportions of the saintly and the brutish, he favored the positive: "Surely I have learned how vile [man] can be," he remarked, "But this only strengthens my regard, because it enhances the mighty heights he can bring himself to tread."[124]

That optimistic, affirmative impulse, surprisingly, was in part a product of his exploration of scientific thought which was helping him formulate the philosophy of life that demanded a new literary theory and attracted him to that critical compromise theorists were groping for. Had he been alive at the time, he would have been amazed by Vernon Parrington's academically popular formulation that an interest in evolutionary science led literary naturalists to an amoral and pessimistic attitude and a preoccupation with brutal or neurotic characters.[125] London was captivated by the evolutionary optimism of two social Darwinists, one English and the other German. In the exchanges between London and his literary confidant Cloudesly Johns throughout 1899 and 1900, the grand philosophical speculations of Herbert Spencer and Ernst Haeckel are often at center stage.

Spencer's works, especially *First Principles*, drew a grand design which organized all knowledge in terms of the "persistence of force" which must have come to Jack London as a revelation like the one he gave later to Martin Eden:

> And here was the man Spencer, organizing all knowledge for him, reducing everything to unit, elaborating ultimate realities and presenting to his startled gaze a universe so concrete of realization that it was like the model of a ship such as sailors make and put into glass bottles. There was no caprice, no chance. All was law (*ME*, p. 99).

Proud of having fashioned a personal philosophy of life derived from Spencerian thought, he even exhorted Johns to develop a "working philosophy" that goes to "first principles," nagging him to study Spencer so that he too would discover the "dynamic principle" expressing relations between matter, force and motion—this key would explain how all things work.[126]

Spencer's terms, though, are very general. It is London's response to Haeckel's ideas, which are compatible with Spencer's and which London encountered in the popular *The Riddle of the Universe*, that reveals most clearly how he could hold a grandiose conception of man and find it consistent with a biological view of the human condition.[127] As late as 1914, he wrote:

> I have always inclined toward Haeckel's position. In fact, "incline" is to weak a word ... I join with Haeckel in being what ... I am compelled to call "a positive scientific thinker."[128]

Simply put, Haeckel's monist position was that all events are the working out of the law of "conservation of energy" which is synonymous with Spencer's "law of the persistence of force."[129] A materialist, he nonetheless rejected a "theoretical materialism that denies the existence of spirit, and dissolves the world into a heap of dead atoms," a "theoretical materialism" London would associate with the extreme position of the clod school, the realists. Inversely, Haeckel attacked a "spiritualism ... which rejects the notion of matter, and considers the world to be a specially arranged group of 'energies' or immaterial natural forces," a spiritualism London would associate with the god school romanticists. The German biologist and philosopher held that "matter cannot exist and be operative without spirit, nor spirit without matter."[130] Jack London realized that this monist philosophy, which he believed was covertly supported by Spencerian scientism, can provide a scientific rationale for subscribing to a high order of "thought, mind, soul."[131] As of March, 1900, London could say, "Haeckel's position is as yet unassailable."[132] His attachment to Haeckel's ideas accounts for the seemingly bizarre situation of a literary naturalist saying that

"I am an agnostic, with one exception: I do believe in the soul."[133]

London's definition of soul is different from orthodox religion's; still it is the basis for considerable optimism and a clue to the optimistic thread he found running through Darwinian and Marxist thinking in addition to Spencer's and Haeckel's. For him it is "the sum of activities of the organism plus personal habits, memories, experiences, of the organism."[134] Jack London was more Lamarkian than he knew, not surprisingly perhaps, since so were Darwin, Spencer, Haeckel and Marx. All subscribed to the notion of "acquired characters," believing that beneficial characteristics acquired during the struggle for existence would be transmitted genetically to the following generations.[135]

London, then, had what he would consider a scientifically responsible justification for imbuing sordid materials with idealism. He had an intellectual framework and a literary theory he synthesized from magazine criticism, both of which encouraged him to dramatize "spirit groping" and "soul searching" characters pursuing "heaven-sent dreams and divine possibilities" while being true to biology that was altering old conceptions of nature and man's place in it and insisting that struggle was at the core of experience. "Thought, mind, soul" have a place in the natural order; men are not necessarily unthinking, vicious animals driven by amoral instincts.

He had reason to attempt to infuse sordid materials with idealism, ugly truths with self-sustaining values, when he began to compose the Alaskan stories. By 1899, when he broke into *The Overland Monthly* with "To the Man on Trail," the "clods" (Zola's disciples) had rejected a belief in the possibility of achieving personal fulfillment in a universe scientifically described. In February of that year, *McTeague* appeared in which Norris symbolized the death of humanistic values and announced a crisis in the American identity by leaving McTeague stranded in the wasteland, confused and pursued, holding his gilded birdcage in one hand and chained to a dead man by the other. Joan London, in her biography of her father, has catalogued the economic, political, social and spiritual upheaval of the decade during which London became aware of the American ways of life and which provided the background for his awareness that all was not well with the American Dream. Fundamental American values had been dislocated, or as Malcolm Cowley has it, "The American faith that was preached in the pulpits and daily reasserted on editorial pages had lost its connection with American life."[136]

It was characteristic of London, however, that this dislocation of values should be felt personally, temperamentally, rather than as just cultural and scientific abstractions. In *John Barleycorn*, there is an episode from his youth that is emblematic of both the awareness of despair and the formula for modifying it that informs his Alaskan short stories. He recoiled from toiling "twelve hours a day at a machine for ten cents an hour" not because of the subsistence level pay, but because there were "no purple passages in machine toil."[137] Being a mechanical extension of a machine, a "work beast" (a typically naturalistic reductive statement) was repugnant because it eliminated a romantic sense of intense excitement, a sense of "something more." Thereafter, he joined the oyster pirates on San Francisco Bay to recover excitement and vitality. But while London was among the pirates, the pattern repeated itself. The life was sordid, and disillusionment was only temporarily held in abeyance by the boozy illusion of comradely adventure. Once again he confronted futility, this time precipitating an attempted suicide in the bay. What prevented him from drowning, according to his account, was the recurrent promise that wonder, excitement and awe could be felt, suggesting to him that triumph over material circumstances is possible:

> For always, drunk or sober, at the back of my consciousness something whispered that this carousing and bay-adventuring was not all of life. This whisper was my good fortune. I happened to be so made that I could hear it calling, always calling, out and away over the world. It was not canniness on my part. It was curiosity, desire to know, an unrest and a seeking for things wonderful that I seemed somehow to have glimpsed or guessed. No there was something more, away and beyond (*JB*, pp. 112–113).

This romantic "whisper" from beyond the world of sordid appearances enticed him from his life on the Oakland waterfront to the sea and Klondike. The Northland, presumably, is the place where an integrated spirit is possible and annihilation circumvented. The call of romantic adventure to participate in the "stinging things of the spirit" would, he intuited, triumph over "actuality." He thought of himself as a realist, but a romantic intention lies behind his fiction.

The flight from society in order to find completion in a new land indicates that London, unlike Frank Norris, was not ready to admit that the frontier spirit had lost its vitality. The frontier was still the place to "begin anew" (in romantic fashion) if one hoped to shed the decadent values of civilization and to join the "gods": "When a man journeys into a far country, he must be prepared to forget many of the things he has learned, and to acquire such customs as are inherent with existence in the new land."[138] And properly addressed, the "new land" might answer the requirements of the romantic whisper. It could be the land of romantic completion where a man could find the self-identifying and self-sustaining values that assured him of his nobility.

But London was not content to write stories that would escape the import of *McTeague*. The Northland would not be the place of easy romantic identification. Despite the pattern of flight from futility recorded in the "whisper" passage, London presents the Klondike as the land of the "actual," the arena for a confrontation with death. Actuality, the disturbing truths of nature, had to be fused with the romantic. In another place in *Barleycorn*, he wrote a significant description of scientific, deterministic truth, which he calls "primary truth," that the "White Logic" or alcoholically induced imagination will not allow him to escape:

> John Barleycorn sends his White Logic, the argent messenger of truth beyond truth, the antithesis of life, cruel and bleak as interstellar space, pulseless and frozen as absolute zero, dazzling with the frost of irrefragable logic and unforgetable fact . . .

that "destroys birth and death," rendering insignificant the land-marks of life (*JB*, p. 308).[139] What is revealing in this description of an order of truth that strips man of hope and is "the antithesis of life" is that London uses the imagery of the Northland to evoke it. It is cosmic, cold, and "pulseless." The burden of cosmic truth is death, and it saturates the Arctic landscape. Compare the introduction of *White Fang*, for instance, with the description of primary truth:

> A vast silence reigned over the land. The land itself was a desolation, lifeless, without movement, so lone and cold that the spirit of it was not even that of sadness.
>
> . . . .
>
> It is not the way of the Wild to like Movement. Life is an offense to it, for life is movement; and the Wild aims always to destroy movement.[140]

The new land that calls men to be yea-sayers is infused with a law of necessity, with cold, stillness and death that spell an ever-lasting No.

That the Northland is a symbol of death needs no complete examination here since recent critics, particularly Maxwell Geismar, have recognized that the Northern wilderness is a "wasteland" and "London's typical figure a voiceless traveler journeying across the ghostly leagues of a dead world."[141] This idea is examined more fully by Earle Labor, and he concludes that a Just God rules over the Northland nature but is indif-ferent to man's aspirations.[142] Both men cite this passage from "The White Silence" as the source of their commentaries (the source of Geismar's vocabulary as well):

> Nature has many tricks wherewith she convinces man of his finity,—the ceaseless flow of the tides, the fury of the storm, the shock of the earthquake, the long roll of heaven's artillery,—but the most tremendous, the most stupefying of all, is the passive phase of the White Silence. All movement ceases, the sky clears, the heavens are as brass; the slightest whisper seems sacrilege, and man becomes timid, affrighted at the sound of his own voice. Sole speck of life

journeying across the ghostly wastes of a dead world, he trembles at his audacity, realizes that his is a maggot's life, nothing more. Strange thoughts arise unsummoned, and the mystery of all things strives for utterance. And the fear of death, of God, of the universe comes over him,—the hope of immortality, the vain striving of the imprisoned essence,—it is then, if ever, man walks with God (*SW*, 7).

When London makes this aside in "The White Silence," the characters are on the trail, and the pattern for many London stories is a ritual trip to confront death and Self. Earle Labor notes that the Northland tales have a "pervasive oneric quality" as figures on the trail pass archetypally into the "other world."[143] In many stories the trail movement that "lays a man naked to the very roots of his soul" is at the center of the narrative, working subtly upon the characters' awareness.[144] Sam Baskett compares "In a Far Country" with Joseph Conrad's "An Outpost of Progress" and notes that when London presents his statement of "the horror" that lies within man and nature, he, unlike Conrad, makes no attempt to "use the traditional imagery and symbolism of the voyage to Hades which Conrad, like Virgil and Dante employed 'to create that otherwise formless region into which not only the artist but every man must descend if he wishes to understand himself.' "[145] But in other stories London does. In "An Odyssey of the North" Axel, Unga and Naass, on the trail, follow a map in their quest for gold and finally move into the unchartered land. In this passage the archetypal, romantic descent to the nadir of experience where life and death confront each other is presented entirely. Naass narrates:

> One looked for a valley beyond, but there was no valley; the snow spread away, level as the great harvest plains, and here and there about us mighty mountains shoved their white heads among the stars. And midway on that strange plain which should have been a valley, the earth and the snow fell away, straight down toward the heart of the world. . . 'It is the mouth of hell,' he [Axel] said; 'let us go down.' And we went down.
>
> And on the bottom there was a cabin, built by some man, of logs which he had cast down from above. It was a very old cabin; for men had died there alone at different times, and on pieces of birch bark

which were there we read their last words and their curses. . . . And the worthless gold they had gathered yellowed the floor of the cabin like in a dream (*SW*, 240–241).

The most famous trip of this kind occurs in *The Call of the Wild*, presented in almost identical language, causing Geismar to remark: "Could anything be better than the long trip into the wilds in search for hidden treasure, from which no man had ever returned: this 'great journey into the East,' past the tall peaks which marked the backbone of a continent, into the land of gold and death?"[146]

The Northland, then, is the unchartered land of the spirit where man seeks his identity by facing death, by participating in life's essential contest for preservation of meaningful selfhood. It is not merely the place to escape from civilization; instead, it is the place where men could confront the disturbing natural facts of life (actuality) and undertake a romantic quest for identity (ideals). The Alaskan landscape, the cosmic landscape, is identified with a naturalistic logic that denies human significance. This is startling because London sees the frontier unlike any writer who preceded him. Hamlin Garland in his short stories, for instance, had his characters withdraw from civilization to find new identities only to be disappointed by the dreary facts of the middle-border; but no one, until London, had put this confrontation in such darkly dramatic and universal terms.

The Northland nature itself is clearly not a source of positive values. Isolated, the "White Silence" passage makes a convincing argument that man is just a finite "speck" traveling in a "dead world," and man's impulse to define himself heroically and transcend his mortality is "mere striving." If London had made the rest of the story consistent with the import of this poetic essay, he would have made his characters into mindless, brutal McTeagues. But it must be remembered that London hoped to combine with the "world of actuality" the record of man's "spirit-groping" and "soul-reaching." "Actuality," which he associated with the unpleasant, he found by leaving civilization where death is "a prearranged pageant, moving along a well-oiled groove to the family vault, where the hinges are kept from rusting and the dust from the air is swept continually away" to the Arctic where death stalks "about gruesome and accidental."[147]

Values, "spirit-groping," the god-like in man, must be shown as the product of man, himself, responding actively to the whisper calling to completion. The early Northland stories do combine the "actual" and the "ideal," the realistic and the romantic, since romantic heroes quest in an environment suggesting terror and futility. The external would be the actual and the internal the ideal.

London may have thought of himself as a realist because he believed that he was engaged in recording truth honestly and would have agreed with Howells that the goal of the writer is to describe reality and that "all tells for destiny and character." But London's conceptions of truth, reality and character were remarkably different from the realist's. Holland was correct in assuming that "the deeper philosophical points of departure always color the work and interweave themselves into the story and set the pace and determine the impact of the fiction."[148] Something happens to London's fiction when he promotes ideas. Jack London was seriously recording truth, but not mere truth. He desired to present "strong truth," and to make absolutely clear to his reader his own conception of that truth.[149] To him, a neglect of either the external or of man's subjective experience would be an abandonment of that truth-seeking: the realist's "fact" had to be converted into a romantic "truth." It is this impulse to didacticism, his compelling desire to communicate "strong truth" forcefully, that leads to the romantic intensity of his fiction.

Howells conceived of reality as changing but still rather static in its undramatic process from event to event. London, on the other hand, thought of the cosmic process as more vital, operating according to a dynamic principle. He never explicitly defined this principle, but it is implicit in his use of Herbert Spencer's "force." Like Martin Eden, "he had accepted the world as the world, but was not comprehending the organization of it, the interplay of force and matter (*ME*, p. 88)." Force is the most significant and underlying fact in the universe. Arthur

McDowell, as early as 1918, realized that this belief is fundamentally hostile to realism:

> ... just as there is a form of art which regards life as the embodi-
> ment of some one guiding thought or feeling, so it has been a
> common trait of philosophers to choose one element of the universe
> and look in it for the meaning of the whole. So Spinoza chose
> substance, Schopenhauer chose will, while modern theorists who start
> from physical science interpret everything in terms of activity or
> force. This point of view realism also repudiates as deceptive in its
> assumptions and its simplicity.[150]

London's reading of Darwin, Spencer, Haeckel and Marx, to
name a few, hastily but energetically undertaken when he began
to incorporate serious ideas into his stories, demanded that he
"interpret everything in terms of activity or force."[151]

London applied the notion of force to his conception of
character psychology as well as to his philosophy of external
environment. Character and destiny were bound together with
powerful emotion, "the splendid stinging things of the spirit,"
"wild insurgencies," "stress and strain," "terror and tragedy."
(*ME*, p. 108). London believed that primitive emotions lay at
the center of the struggle for existence. Fear, in particular, was
the basic emotion which nature evoked in man and which men
either learned to live with or perished.[152] But an intense love of
life complemented that fear and compensated for it. Portrayal of
intense emotions became not only his fictional goal but also the
yardstick by which he measured the success of other writers and
the rationale behind his praise for Kipling, Gorky and Upton
Sinclair.[153] For Howells, with his mild moral ethic, this reliance
upon powerful emotions must have seemed an "itch of
awakening at all cost in the reader vivid and violent emotions"
that he deplored in romance.[154]

To fictionalize this interplay of forces and dramatize intensity
demanded of London something more than a mere objective
documentation of external nature, "the world as world" as
London called it, in order to avoid the "endless book-keeping of
existence" as Philip Rahv describes the naturalistic tendency.[155]

As we have seen, he assimilated Herbert Spencer's theory about "the causes of force in language," as the best way to communicate his intellectual and emotional intensity and adopted Kipling's practice as a guideline. Style, he felt, is the medium which unites "strong truth" and forceful emotion. Consequently, he poeticized his descriptions in order to charge them with life, energy and force. Indeed, so strong is the poetic and evocative element in London short stories that Fred Lewis Pattee declared it the feature which distinguishes London from his predecessors in the craft.[156]

In a June, 1899, letter, London made a passing comment about Walt Whitman's style which is not without significance, for in many ways his apprenticeship demonstrates that he was Whitman's literary child.[157] London's "god" and "clod" eclectic literary theory demonstrates that like Whitman he wished to embody in his fiction both matter and spirit, both the body and the soul, and to forge a new relationship between them. With Whitman, and other serious romantics, London shared a sense of active participation in a dynamic cosmos that was lacking in Howellsian realism. This vitality had died in popular romance, too, which retained the vestiges of idealism in the form of a sentimental moralism allied to an aristocratic conception of society and disembodied from new philosophical and psychological information. London hoped to shock his readers into a sense of active, masculine forces shaping their characters and destinies and to drag them bodily into an awareness of new values. Like Whitman, he felt the prophetic impulse and lurked egotistically in and behind his stories, exuding a self-conscious intensity and recommending a new approach to life. And if Whitman used prose-poetry to evoke a sense of cosmic power, London employed a poetic prose style to infuse his grand landscape with mythic significance. In many ways London was seeking to do for prose what Whitman had done at mid-century for poetry.

The comparison with Whitman is a little too flattering. London's dogmatically expressed theories and good intentions are not always consistent with his practice. He might deride the conventionalities of sentimental romance or commonplace realism, but both find places in the nineteen volumes of collected short stories. Even in work which cannot be described a hack, he would glaze his strenuous idealism with sentimental platitudes or lace his evocative prose with insignificant detail.

But by no means was the young Jack London without insight, profundity and real understanding. His visions of nightmare and glory as they erupt from his Alaskan stories prove that his fiction is more than popular art. Although he did learn from the magazines and handbooks that there would be a market for fiction that presented bold materials—the adventurous, violent, even sordid—if they were shot through with idealism and that critical acclaim went to those stories which were presented dramatically and created a single impression, his short fiction is more than a prefabricated construction built from the commentaries of magazine critics. The union of his personal experiences, his individual understanding of Spencer's and Haeckel's ideas as they bore upon a redefinition of man's potential in a scientifically describable nature, and his willingness to dramatize those strong truths by concentrating upon mythic settings and characters struggling to affirm meaningful values, differentiates his work from both his predecessors and from countless practitioners whose stories appeared in the magazines London studied.

Early in his career, then, Jack London had formed a literary theory, the heart of which was a dynamic tension between actuality and ideals, between the disturbing natural truths thrust upon the imagination by evolutionary thought and a sense that a humanistic conception of man is not inconsistent with a scientific perspective. Those students of American literary history who think that literary naturalists, especially Jack London, wanted to dramatize man's insignificance in a Darwinian world are necessarily going to be baffled by London's propensity for making value judgments, espousing causes and creating heroic characters and to take them as signs that he could not control his "romantic temperament." At worst, they will continue charging him with unknowingly celebrating sentimental, optimistic versions of the American Dream of Success. But revisionist critics like Charles Walcutt and Donald Pizer have built a new context for examining naturalistic fiction that leads to a more thoughtful and sympathetic assessment of London's fiction. Their views about naturalism are almost synonymous with London's own sense of his literary directions and mission. Naturalism, according to Walcutt, encompasses two streams of thought:

> One, the approach to Spirit through intuition, nourishes idealism, progressivism, and social radicalism. The other, the approach to Nature through science, plunges into the dark canyon of mechanistic determinism. The one is rebellious, the other pessimistic; the one ardent, the other fatal; the one acknowledges will, the other denies it. This "naturalism," flowing in both streams, is partly defying Nature and partly submitting to it.[158]

He concludes that "all 'naturalistic' novels exist in a tension between determinism and its antithesis."[159] Donald Pizer's characterization of naturalism comes even closer to London's understanding of his intention. In naturalistic fiction, he suggests, there is a tension "between the naturalist's desire to represent in fiction the new, discomforting truths which he has found in the ideas and life of his late nineteenth-century world, and also his desire to find some meaning in experience which reasserts the validity of the human enterprise."[160]

Jack London would not have denied that statement; he would have taken it for granted.

Chapter III

THE MALEMUTE KID

Jack London's quest for a form, technique and philosophy of composition was characterized by his desire to present truth in the most forceful manner. In his moments of self-characterization, he thought of himself foremost as a truth-seeker and a public educator and, secondarily, as an artist. He mastered the rudiments of short story form and technique and assimilated Spencer's philosophy of composition, which had as a premise that the forceful communication of ideas and emotions was the primary function of fiction.

The forceful truth London wanted to demonstrate to the world was that life-giving values could be operative in a death-dealing environment, that ideals could triumph over actuality. Consequently, upon the cosmically cold, pulseless and deterministic "primary truth" embodied in the Northland landscape, he superimposed a more optimistic, idealistic order of truth—"secondary truth," he would later call it. In *Barleycorn* he writes of secondary truth:

> This is the order of truth that obtains, not for the universe, but for the live things in it if they for a little space will endure ere they pass. This order of truth . . . is the sane and normal order of truth, the rational order of truth that life must believe in order to live . . .
>
> What is good is true. And this is the order of truth . . . that man must know and guide his actions by, with unswerving certitude that in the universe no other order can obtain (p. 308).

The "whisper" in *Barleycorn* hints the truths from the

secondary order, ideals like love, courage and individual completion that are missing in civilization, can be restored by responding to the call to adventure. Ideals may be revitalized even in the face of a naturalistic actuality.

The Malemute Kid series of stories in *The Son of the Wolf*, which drew initial critical attention to the young writer during 1899 and 1900, are the results of London's attempt to combine realism and romance, "actuality and ideals," or "primary" and "secondary" truths.[161] "I am an emotional materialist," London explained, and associated the external world with realistic materialism and subjective man with romantic idealism.[162] These stories which have the Malemute Kid as a central character or as a by-stander supplying the moral norm for the stories, are fictional attempts to validate the efficacy of the intuited whisper that somehow the individual man, a "spirit-groper" in love with the "stinging things of the spirit," can outwit a stultifying environment and find "things wonderful." In his youthful idealism, while writing the Malemute Kid series, he tried to stack the deck in this contest between actuality and ideals to prove that the ideal was possible even in a naturalistic universe. The ideal, the Kid, was to conquer actuality. His explicit theme for these stories is an optimistic affirmation of man's power to defy determinism and reassert life-giving ideals.

The implicit theme of these stories, however, contradicts his optimism. Throughout these stories, London demonstrates an ambivalence rooted deeply in his temperament; the actual and the ideal are never bonded and remain an emulsion. The Kid stories that argue that man is powerful and can control his fate through the exercise of thought wedded to action are, in the final analysis, morally confused and artistically feeble. It must be remembered that if the whisper telling of the rewards of adventure is an illusion, despair and death are the inevitable alternatives (the suicide would have been consummated if the whisper had not intervened). Since what the whisper promises is an empirically unproven intuition, it could well be merely the vain promptings of the human heart that lead to a further and final disillusionment. And in fact, the drift of the Malemute Kid series is towards a dominance of primary, naturalistic truth. The explicit theme of mastery metamorphosizes into a more compelling implicit theme of failure.

Jack London identified himself strongly with the Malemute Kid and saw him, probably, as an idealized extension of himself. He wrote to Cloudesley Johns about this character:

> You surprise me with the aptness of your warning, telling me I may learn to love him too well myself. I am afraid that I am rather stuck on him—not the one in print, but the one in my brain. I doubt that I ever shall get him in print.[163]

Even the "Malemute" half of the character's name has a personal connection with the writer because London, it is well known, used the nick-name "Wolf" with intimates and idealized dogs in several fictional works.[164] The "Kid" part of the name, too, identifies London with the character since London in his autobiographical comments took obvious pride in the "Sailor Kid" "monicker" bestowed upon him by the brotherhood of waifs on the road. London had a great personal stake in this character who embodied what man could hope to achieve by responding to the whisper that called him to adventure. Through him can be found the pattern of London's quest for life-sustaining values and the failure of that quest.

Franklin Walker writes that the stories in *The Son of the Wolf* "are held together by their northern settings and by the appearance and reappearance of a group of characters of whom Malemute Kid is the most noteworthy," and that early reviewers immediately recognized the Kid's literary forefathers:

> Reviewers at once labelled Malemute Kid an Argonaut Mulvaney, recognizing the Kipling influence as truly in the central character as in London's use of the paragraph of aphorisms, 'the vague and choppy abstract,' as one critic put it, with which he opened many of his tales. They also recognized that the Kid was a descendant of some of Bret Harte's characters. Malemute Kid is a sourdough with a heart of gold. Though he has 'lived on rabbit-tracks and salmon-belly' and can both think straight and act quickly and, if necessary, roughly, he is sensitive to all finer emotions.[165]

The Kid rules over *The Son of the Wolf* collection, and as Earle Labor succinctly puts it, is its "central intelligence."[166] The Kid has literary antecedents, personal relevance and a structural and thematic function.

In the romantic tradition, the Malemute Kid comes from an unknown origin and is not tied to civilized institutions such as marriage or business. He is the spirit of the Northland human experience and is free to fulfill his promise by pitting his virtues against the cosmic odds. As a citizen of the Arctic wastes, he is not insulated by society from life's central problem of death and has faced it many times. When a tree crushes Mason in "The White Silence" while Mason, the Kid and Ruth, Mason's Indian wife, are on the "Long Trail," the narrator interjects: "The sudden danger, the quick death,—how often had the Kid faced it! (10)." The narrative focus at this crucial moment in the story is shared equally by the natural event described as "the tragedy of life" and the Kid's reactions to it. Mason, dying, is of secondary importance. The real interest for London is in portraying an idealized man, the Kid, reacting to the facts of violence and death—ideality confronting actuality.

Through the Kid's reactions to this tragedy, London presents the masculine code that preserves human dignity and worth and dramatizes the imposition of secondary truths upon primary. For London, like Joseph Conrad, the code is "that belief in a few simple notions you must cling to if you want to live decently and would like to die easy".[167] Experienced in the ways of life and death, the Kid leaps into action because "those of the Northland are early taught the futility of words and the inestimable value of deeds (11)." At the moment of imminent death, London's characters act from habit, or instinct, and abstractions are suspect because action, after all, is man's sign of living in an Arctic environment that equates stillness with death. Strength is the dynamic of action, and the Kid is "capable of felling an ox at a single blow (5)." Such strength is, as Malcolm Cowley has pointed out, not only a physical but a moral attribute to naturalists.[168] The Kid then builds a heat reflector from some canvas, "a trick which men know who study physics

at the fount of experience (10)." Often the instinctual or
habitual action taken in the face of death is a ritualistic one or
in some way demonstrates expertise that symbolically represents
human control over natural forces. Ritual, whether it is in the
more symbolic realm of journeying on the "Long Trail" or in
the more denotative fashion of using Northland lore, is always
allied in London's fiction with self-definition or self-preservation.
The building of the reflector shows not only that the Kid is
experienced in Northland ways, but demonstrates that he knows
the tricks that bring the light and warmth associated with life.[169]
To understand process and to perform perfectly are implicit
goals for London's characters in their quest for identity. Wholeness of personality is not a given in his fiction and must be
accomplished through the ability to act with style.

Experience, action, strength and expertise, although the
basic virtues of the code, are not enough, however. Tenderness and love must temper courageous action. The ideal man
should be not only "practical insofar as the mechanics of
life were concerned" and "brave and game" but "delicate
and tender . . . an all around man."[170] The motive for action
is to preserve life and to exhibit the love that makes life
worth living. The Kid, already shown as strong and practical,
is tender and "could not bear to beat the poor animals. . . .
almost wept with them in their misery (5)." Such sympathy
is mawkishly sentimentalized particularly since the Kid's
emotions are described in similar terms when he faces and
carries out the mercy killing of Mason that closes the story.
Nevertheless, love for all living creatures is a hall-mark of
London's idealized characters.[171] Mason is only an inch less a
man, and he dies. He is, of course, killed by the "great
tree, burdened with its weight of years and snow," which
"played its part in the tragedy of life (10)." But preparation
is made for his death by contrasting the Kid's tenderness for
the dog Carmen with Mason's impatient cruelty with the
lash. In typical London fashion, the author is ambivalent
about whether the responsibility for Mason's death is naturalistic or human because he violates the code which stipulates

that when on the trail, close to death, true manhood is defined not only through strength but through generosity, control and compassion.

Many critics have seen that struggle, action and strength, arising from a Darwinistic conception of the human situation, color the Northland characterizations. But no one, with the exception of Earle Labor, has given attention to the key quality possessed by the "spirit-groping," idealized characters— "imagination." In the ideal comrade passage from Joan London's biography mentioned above, London also demanded that his soul mate be "fanciful, imaginative, sentimental where the thrill of life was concerned."[172] An active imagination is synonymous with the capacity for adventure. London's unimaginative men, like Edwin Bentham in "The Priestly Prerogative," do not have this capacity and are content merely to make money in the Klondike rather than to find riches of the spirit through adventure.[173] Only complete men have the imaginative capacity that speaks to them in a "whisper." Most important, through the exercise of the imagination London's characters avoid the "clod" label because they have active consiousnesses. They face the naturalistic environment not only with their brute strength held in common with nature, but with a zestful mental and emotional awareness.

The imagination concept is more complicated than the capacity for responding to the whisper. Earle Labor writes that in London's fiction,

> ...the man who is to endure the long arctic winter must be exceptionally gifted in that highest of human faculties—imagination: he must understand the ways of the northland so sympathetically that he can anticipate its emergencies before they occur, always adapting himself to nature's laws, never attempting foolishly to impose the frail, devious customs of society and civilization upon the inviolable wilderness.[174]

Possibly "To Build a Fire" was in Labor's mind when he wrote this description of imagination because it is there that London makes his most explicit statements about this faculty. The man in "To Build a Fire" dies because he does not understand the Northland laws of nature and, consequently, can not intuit the danger that waits for him:

> The trouble with him was that he was without imagination. He was quick and alert in the things of life, but only in the things, and not in the significances. Fifty degrees below zero meant eighty-odd degrees of frost. Such fact impressed him as being cold and uncomfortable, and that was all. It did not lead him to meditate upon his frailty in general, able only to live within certain narrow limits of heat and cold; and from there on it did not lead him to the conjectural field of immortality and man's place in the universe.[175]

The two ingredients of, or qualities prerequisite to, the possession of imagination in this story are instinct, found in the dog in the story, and experience, represented by an old sourdough's admonitions. These qualities permit one to understand the human significance of the facts of nature.

The Kid in "The White Silence" possesses the imagination that the unnamed man in "To Build a Fire" lacks. Keeping the Kid from becoming a sentimentalized romantic idealization, London gives him the power of imagination which tells him that the significance of the Arctic cold is death unless he acts unhesitatingly. And because of his experience he is able to act swiftly, instinctively, and, finally, decisively by shooting Mason in order to allow Ruth and himself to live. Because he perceives the human significance of natural facts, he is not ruled by the sentimental code of civilization that would deplore the mercy-killing and urge him to stay with his friend Mason even though it would mean the death of all three characters.

An understanding of the operation of the imaginative faculty in London's short stories is essential if one expects to appreciate fully the import of the Malemute Kid series. London's concept of this faculty is both more simple and more complex than either Labor's estimate or as a sign of the capacity for adventure because it operates in different ways in different stories. Let it suffice for the present, however, that the imaginative faculty permits the Kid to be aware of the threat of the Northland environment and to challenge it by calling the code into play to avoid disaster.

If the theme of "The White Silence" is two-fold, that nature is indifferent to man but that man, equipped with imagination, can find meaning by practicing the code of manhood, "To the Man on Trail" is a further development of the second. In this and the three Kid stories which followed it, London tried to make the ideal dominate actuality. This is the story that first drew attention to London, and in it he presents the most positive view of manhood he could muster.

The story takes place on Christmas day as the Kid, "a born raconteur," surrounded by a democratic fellowship of Northland friends, encourages the host to make the drinks stronger and begins the heroic tale, which had passed into Arctic folklore, of acquiring a bride for Mason. The tale told, the Kid proposes a toast: " 'A health to the man on trail this night; may his grub hold out; may his dogs keep their legs; may his matches never miss fire' " which is a prayer for human life to prevail over death (105). This serves as an incantation. As the toast concludes, noises are heard outside the cabin, and, shortly, Jack Westondale enters:

> He was a striking personage, and a most picturesque one, in his Arctic dress of wool and fur. Standing six foot two or three, with proportionate breadth of shoulders and depth of chest, his smooth-shaven face nipped by the cold to a gleaming pink, his long lashes and eyebrows white with ice ... he seemed, of a verity, the Frost King (106).

From the description it is apparent that this is another of London's idealized, virile characters, experienced in the ways of the trail and strong. He grips hands with the Kid and "though they had never met, each had heard of the other, and the recognition was mutual (108)." A corollary to the code of manhood is that its practitioners instinctively know each other. It is a recognition of wholeness of character. The Kid's close friendships have as their bond this mutual recognition of completed identity or, at least, the potential for it. Prince, a young

mining engineer, is the Kid's protege who is learning the Northland ways in order to complete his potential for manhood.[176] It
is this bond, too, that is the basis of mutual respect between
Sitka Charlie and the Kid. In "The Wisdom of the Trail" Charlie
proves that he can undertake "an unknown journey through the
dismal vastnesses of the Northland, and he knew it to be of the
kind that try the souls of men (149)" and still live by the code,
"the honor and the law," which means death if it is broken
(148, 154). The last of the integrated spirits is Father Roubeau
who "but one in all the Northland knew [as] the man Paul
Roubeau, and that man was Malemute Kid . . . Before him alone
did the priest cast off the sacerdotal garb and stand naked"
because they had shared "the last and inmost thought, on the
barren stretches of Bering Sea, in the heartbreaking mazes of the
Great Delta, on the terrible winter journey from Point Barrow
to the Porcupine."[177]

In "The Wife of a King" the Kid hears the Priest's confession,
and this is significant because as the ideal man of imagination,
experience, action and compassion, the Kid is the true priest of
the Northland morality. He is the high priest in the new land.
He becomes the moral norm for the stories in which he appears
and the "law-giver" that London admired so greatly.[178]
Returning to "To the Man on Trail," after the story has
presented the Kid as the ideal and Westondale as a kindred
spirit, the Kid, knowing that Westondale is a fugitive from the
Mounted Police, deliberately helps him to escape. When the
other men in the cabin, who represent the Northland
democracy, discover that the visitor had stolen $40,000 from
McFarland's gambling casino, they are angry with the Kid for
misleading them. The resolution of the story is the Kid's rationale for helping the thief escape, the basis of his Northland
morality: " 'It's a cold night, boys.' " Westondale has " 'traveled
trail' " and you " 'know what that stands for,' " he tells them
(117). He had been " 'taking care of his partner with the
scurvy' " when another partner lost $40,000 of Westondale's
money gambling and dashed the hopes he had of returning to
the " 'wife and boy he's never seen' (118)." Consequently, he

stole " 'exactly what his partner lost—forty thousand' (118)."

Legally, also logically, of course, Westondale is guilty, and London even idealizes the Mounty representing civilized law. But the Kid is spokesman for the law of the Northland code that transcends a civilized morality. Westondale is acquitted because he is a completed spirit who has faced the essential facts of life (the trail, the cold and misfortune) and mastered them. Moreover, he had practiced the masculine code by obeying the law of comradely self-sacrifice and remaining loyal to his tender love for his wife and child. Finally, he maintained his integrity by taking only what had been his, money lost not through natural misfortune but through a corrupt social institution—the gaming table.[179] Westondale is justified because he is wronged in a way that society is incapable or unwilling to rectify. He, therefore, is judged by the Northland code that admires masculinity kept in spite of hardship and is found justified in his actions. The ethic that lies behind this story and the code, as Earle Labor has noticed, "is not an eat-or-be-eaten Darwinian ethic but a situational ethic predicated upon joyous, selfless love of man for his fellow man."[180] London, incidentally, was not satisfied with this ending, perhaps because of the doubtful morality that Charmian London noticed; nevertheless, it is consistent with his portraiture of idealized men and valuable as an example of the Kid acting as law-giver.[181]

If "The White Silence" demonstrates the qualities inherent in the Kid that make him the ideal man and person most likely to explain to others how a meaningful life can be lived while facing death and violence and "To the Man on Trail" shows him actively, although arbitrarily, imposing his code in order to resolve a moral dilemma, "The Men of Forty-Mile" and "The Wife of a King" extend the thesis that the Kid, educated in the truths of Northland life, is a law-giver, truth-bearer and righter of wrongs. Both of the two later stories, however, are artistically and intellectually weak, testifying to London's difficulty in sustaining an ideal hero and, consequently, a belief in the ideal.

In "The Men of Forty-Mile" Lon McFane and Bettles, two of

London's regulars in the early Northland tales, both frustrated
by the Arctic winter, squabble over an insignificant matter, and
despite their friendship, decide to settle the issue by dueling
with rifles. The two men leave the cabin to prepare for the
encounter, and the narrator comments, "There was no law in
the land . . . The Mounted Police was also a thing of the future"
as he prepares for the entrance of the law-bringer Kid (57).
After a few more comments on the customs of settling differences on the lawless frontier, there is "a scurry of moccasins and
loud cries, rounded off with a pistol-shot. . . . Then the storm-
doors opened and Malemute Kid entered, a smoking Colt's in his
hand and a merry light in his eye (58)." Once again, as in "To
the Man on Trail," there is the melodramatic entrance of the
ideal man of action. The problem is presented to the Kid, he
takes "charge of the affair" and makes this pronouncement
about human nature: "Life's a game, and men the gamblers.
They'll stake their whole pile on the one chance in a thousand.
Take away that one chance, and—they won't play (60)." The
chance that each of the contestants believes in is that the other
will die and he will live. Both have "an unswerving faith in the
God of Chance (66)." What the lawbringer proves to the men is
that ultimately there is no chance and that all men must die. He
declares that he will hang the winner of the duel. McFane and
Bettles see the wisdom of this and call off the contest just as a
rabid dog tears into the camp and leaps to attack Bettles.
McFane intercepts the dog; and, finally, Bettles shoots the
animal. In a frame-work of farce, London has presented the
dominant theme of the Malemute Kid series: among good men,
the knowledge of the inevitability of death calls them to self-
sacrifice and comradeship. The Kid teaches the law of necessity,
and the men have never known him to lie. His spirit presides
over the men's instinctual decision to practice the code that
cheats death and units them in brotherhood.

But despite the serious theme of "The Men of Forty-Mile,"
the story does not evoke the mythic-poetic spirit of the Northland that serves as a backdrop for a heroic journey into a
dangerous knowledge of the outer world and of Self. Instead,

the focus of this story is upon the comical, impetuous and quarrelsome men of little learning and polish who, conventionally, have hearts of gold beneath crude exteriors. Irish and working class dialects give humor to the serio-comic banter. The narrator interrupts the dialogue to mention the Arctic customs and psychology and to sustain the action. The result is a local color story with the heroic Kid superimposed upon it. The Kid, himself, is reduced to little more than a master of the revels who is necessary to the story only because he holds the device, the trick, which restores order after the foolery has spent itself.

It is the Kid as "trickster" that is the most symptomatic change in "The Men of Forty-Mile." The change is fundamentally an over-simplification of the concept of "imagination" that turns the story into a tale of conventional heroics more closely associated with London's juveniles than with the complex stories like "The White Silence." *Tales of the Fish Patrol*, for example, which is a collection of adventure stories about the oyster pirates and lawmen of San Francisco bay written originally for *The Youth's Companion*, contains "moral purposes insidiously inserted."[182] One of the morals he advocated was the necessity of using a less complicated kind of imagination than the Kid uses in "The White Silence" and the kind that he does employ in "The Men of Forty-Mile." In "A Raid on the Oyster Pirates" the boy-hero's life is saved because his adult comrade, Charley, has the foresight to envision the course of the action and to alert the law to stand guard on the beach.[183] The story ends with this moral tag: " 'That comes of imagination . . . When you see a thing, you've got to see it all around, or what's the use of seeing it at all?' (102)." And the burden of the moralizations in the *Fish Patrol* series in general is that success in outwitting the forces of lawlessness and death depends upon possessing an imagination which allows one to see the pattern of human affairs and upon using "ingenuity," a clever plan of action, to avoid disaster. An imaginative grasp of the whole combined with a plan of action permit the good to live.

The Kid's imagination in "The Men of Forty-Mile" is like Charley's. It is merely the exercise of intelligence and reason acting upon a knowledge of human nature that allows him to "see it whole" and devise a trick to solve the problem; not the instinctive and emotional, as well as intelligent, apprehension of nature's laws that elicits the implementation of the code in "The White Silence." Instead of pitting a spirit-groping man against cosmic odds, London presents a lesser confrontation between an intelligent man and comical caricatures. Because of the inequality of the contestants, trickery can replace the code in exercising death. Apparently, London was having difficulty in creating artistically, intellectually and emotionally provocative stories that had at their center the consciousness of an ideal man.

From toast-master who invokes the law of the Northland in "To the Man on Trail," to master of the revels in "The Men of Forty-Mile," the Kid degenerates into the head of a finishing school in "The Wife of a King." This story, mentioned earlier as one purloined from Kipling, uses the *Pygmalion* device that so delighted the Victorian mind when it took its fantasy holidays from rigid social and class distinctions and pretended that training was more important than birth. Its importance in the Malemute Kid sequence is that it shows the idealized man as a righter of social injustice and a restorer of "real" values. Cal Galbraith, the Klondike "King," leaves his Indian wife, Madeline, lured to the glittering tent cities which were socially dominated by white women. These pretentious white women had "come last" to the Northland, "knew least, but . . . ruled the land (164)." One of the first rules they legislated was that Indian women are inferior to white. The narrator announces sententiously, "There were false ideals in the land. The social strictures of Dawson were not synonymous with those of the previous era, and the swift maturity of the Northland involved much wrong." The "Malemute Kid was aware of this" and "he was minded to teach a great lesson (168)." The Kid, with the aid of Jack Harrington, Bettles and Prince, teaches Madeline the social graces—proper carriage, the art of dancing and even techniques of bullying, wheedling and patronizing—in the manner of the sophisticated white women. At the masked ball that concludes the story, Madeline uses these bewitching accomplishments to rescue Cal's interest in her. In short, the Kid turns her into a white woman and, ironically, London has shown the Kid not correcting "false values" but reinforcing them. This unintended ambiguity ruins the story.

A brief interlude in the story is more characteristically London than the finishing school antics, indicating that the Kid is still to be taken as the spirit of the Northland experience as it is presented in more successful stories. Sandwiched between the education of Madeline and the climaxing masked ball is a page on which the Kid confronts Cal with his neglect of Madeline. In this place only are the "real values" presented and a "great lesson" taught. Just as the Klondike King begins to rationalize, the Kid stills him with a gesture as they step out of the cabin into the Northland night reigned over by the "miracles of color" of the aurora. The mythic atmosphere is evoked. A dog begins to howl, and the Kid again restrains Cal from speaking. The passage which follows contains the logic of the Northland for which the Kid stands, the source of values that are most important for joining man and woman:

> Dog and dog took up the strain till the full-throated chorus swayed the night. To him who hears for the first time this weird song, is told the first and greatest secret of the Northland; to him who has heard it often, it is the solemn knell of lost endeavor. It is the plaint of tortured souls, for in it is invested the heritage of the North, the suffering of countless generations—the warning and the requiem to the world's estrays.
>
> Cal Galbraith shivered slightly as it died away in half-caught sobs. The Kid read his thoughts openly, and wandered back with him through the weary days of famine and disease; and with him also was the patient Madeline, sharing his pains and perils, never doubting, never complaining (179).

The "White Logic" speaks to Cal of the vanity of human desires and mocks man with his futility. The only important values are found when two people share a love that withstands suffering, despair and death. The Kid stands in the night with Cal and is

the Northland priest who mediates between imperfect man and a
higher truth. Cal is reminded that love and loyalty, aspects of
secondary truth, must be given the highest value if finite man is
to endure in the face of a crushingly impersonal primary order
of truth infused in nature and threatening tragedy.

The tone and import of the above passage is in keeping with
the spirit of seriousness that is in London's best stories but fails
to raise the Kid above the characterization in the rest of the
story—as an organizer and participant in a social comedy, a
gallant who can too easily correct injustice because "in him was
centered the wisdom of ages, that between his vision and the
future there could be no intervening veil (168)." Again, he
exercises the imagination of mere intelligence and ingenuity.

The Kid is a liability to the story as a comparison with "The
Great Interrogation" demonstrates.[184] In that story, David Payne
faces the similar problem of choosing between an Indian wife
and a wealthy woman who appeals to his "race affinity." The
white woman is presented forcefully and is not the narrative
abstraction found in "The Wife of a King." Therefore, the
temptation is presented more strongly, Payne's indecision is
greater and more dramatically presented. He decides to remain
with his Indian wife for the reasons which appear in "The Wife
of a King" Northland "dog chorus" but not because she
becomes "whiter." "The Great Interrogation," as a result, is a
stronger indictment of culturally sanctioned racial bigotry and a
more convincing resolution of it. No outside agent, like the Kid,
is needed to trick the character into solving his dilemma.

Two final stories result in the Kid's fictional demise. "The
Priestly Prerogative" and "An Odyssey of the North" are
extremely diverse artistically and thematically, but they share
the device of using the Malemute Kid as a passive observer to a
moral dilemma, as the moral norm. In the first, possibly the
weakest of London's Alaskan tales, the Kid is little more than
an echo to social convention. Grace Bentham, one of London's
idealized white women who practice the code of masculinity
despite their sex, wants to leave her husband, Edward Bentham,
whom London surrounds with a barrage of pejorative attributes:

he tears wings from butterflies, is a "selfish cry-baby" with "a skin-deep veneer of culture and conventionality" and, most contemptible, permits his wife to break trail for him (121). He is one of London's "incapables" who lack self-knowledge, self-respect and an imaginative response to adventure. Grace falls in love with Clyde Wharton, who has a capacity for manhood and love, and decides to live adulterously with him. In the Kid's cabin, Father Roubeau convinces her that adultery is wrong because it will do emotional damage to the bastard children and disgrace her family. Taken by this logic, Grace is reduced to groveling on the cabin floor and returns to her hellish marriage (139). The priest, while on the trail with the Malemute Kid, reveals that he is distressed by the consequences entailed in making her go back to Edward; nevertheless, the burden of the story supports the moral code of Mrs. Grundy's civilization, and the Kid gives his tacit approval to the resolution. This is the lowest point in London's extended characterization of the Malemute Kid, who, as the spirit of the Northland, the new land beyond the pale of bankrupt social institutions with their hollow or moribund morality, has stood for new values that bring dignity to essential human relationships. All the Kid's experience and imagination, implicit in the story because of his presence, result in a degrading reinforcement of society's conception of a proper marriage, one that may be spiritually bankrupt as long as appearances are maintained.

The last portrayal of the Kid occurs in the powerful story "An Odyssey of the North." Once again he passively oversees a moral dilemma, but this time admits that he can not resolve it. The confusion is integral to the theme and characterization rather than a flaw in the narrative. There is no need for the Kid to point out the lesson of the Northland's cosmic logic nor to recommend the code as a solution to it because the central characters (Axel, Unga and Naass) travel into the wasteland, practice the code and, yet, do not preserve life or love. Naass kills Axel and Unga. The Kid admits that there is no moral basis for judging Naass: " 'There be things greater than our wisdom, beyond our justice. The right and the wrong of this we cannot

say, and it is not for us to judge' (251)." Neither the simple
imagination that weds common sense to American ingenuity nor
the imagination that through intelligence, instinct and experience
senses disaster and sponsors the active code to mitigate the
threat are adequate concepts for dealing with death and
violence. The Kid is the passive witness to the central problem
London has raised in the Kid series, but no longer can act as an
active agent of good, the righteous lawgiver and Northland
priest. Naass's adventure does not make him a whole man, the
journey and the code do not provide men with self-completion.
There are indeed "things greater than our wisdom" and man can
not "see it all around."

The message is that man is limited. Consequently, London's
perfect man, the Malemute Kid, must cease to exist; he disappears from London's stories. From his serious stories, at any
rate. Years later he was resurrected, rechristened "Smoke
Bellew" and "David Grief," and made the hero of two more
volumes of short stories.[185] Intended to show that he could "still
turn out ... stuff that is clean, alive, optimistic," even though
by that time he no longer believed in optimistic "illusions," they
do not have the vitality of the early Malemute Kid stories
written when London believed that affirmation was within
grasp.[186]

The Malemute Kid series was a noble experiment attempting
to prove the hypothesis that man, who "alone among the
animals, has the awful privilege of reason" that "can penetrate
the intoxicating show of things and look upon a universe brazen
with indifference towards him and his dreams," can act meaning-
fully and morally to preserve the dream of his significance (*JB*,
p. 207). "Only in man is morality, and man created it—a code of
action that makes toward living," London states in *John Barleycorn*, a statement which could have been the theoretical basis
for the Kid's characterization (315). The Kid, through the
exercises of common sense, intelligence, ingenuity, integrity,
loyalty, love and active strength within the context of adventure, challenges the Darwinian nightmare with his code. An
awareness of actuality, of primary truth, challenges man to

reaffirm humanly satisfying values from the order of secondary truth so that he can achieve a sense of worth and dignity.

Austin M. Wright in his *The American Short Story of the Twenties* suggests, indirectly, the importance to literary history of London's undertaking.[187] Wright demonstrates that the awareness of mortality, of death, of the dissolution of the individual identity, is the insight common to writers like Sherwood Anderson, F. Scott Fitzgerald and Ernest Hemingway that prompted them to use disillusioned characters who in fear and resentment at the loss of their capacity for wonder, awe and appreciation of beauty engage in adventure to restore them.[188] In the stories of the twenties, he continues, adventure is associated with youth and undertaken with a sense of urgency since "to lose is to die."[189] The parallel with the motives of London's stories is provocative and establishes London's thematic relationship with the short story writers who followed him. A more apt parallel historically with London's attempt to use youthful adventure as a buffer between man and death, however, is Conrad's fiction, particularly *Youth*. The young Marlow ships aboard the "Judea" whose motto is "Do or Die" in response to an inner, romantic voice calling him to the mysterious East.[190] Marlow's disillusionment is the explicit theme of the narrative.

The same disillusionment is the implicit theme of London's Malemute Kid series. Stories like "To the Man on Trail," "The Men of Forty-Mile," "The Wife of a King" and "The Priestly Prerogative," which show man in control of his fate, are artistically puerile, scarred with moral confusion, and were recognized by London himself as little more than popular successes. Although the explicit themes and characterizations of these stories promote the efficacy of a man-made morality, their intellectual and artistic failure deny it. The "whisper" turns into derisive laughter.

The failure of these stories was implicit in London's conception of the short story which claimed that the world of actuality, the Darwinian cosmos, could be infused with the ideal. He did incorporate the wasteland into his fiction; but, with the exceptions of "The White Silence" and "An Odyssey of the North," it is superficially imposed upon the stories. Beneath the gloss of unpleasant subject matter—theft, brawling and adultery—the illusions that infested the pleasant land of romance control his stories. The operative values, the idealized qualities of the Kid, are straight from the American Dream: a belief in the power of the human will, a trust in the legendary American common sense and ingenuity, a commitment to personal integrity and love, and above all a faith that these potent virtues are capable of securing the dignity of the individual and restoring a humane social order. Rationality provides not only a scientific description of the universe, but mastery over it. London, it seems, had brought with him to the Northland the optimistic baggage of a dead morality that had already been undermined by newer, more pessimistic, conceptions of the universe that he, ironically, simultaneously promoted. He tried to solve a twentieth century problem of alienation, despair, futility, suffering and death with a nineteenth century set of values that presumed a rational, man-centered world order.

It has long been recognized that London's themes are confused and confusing. Partly this is due to the cursory nature of his reading, undertaken with more excitement and energy than method and analysis, when he was discovering the "strong truths" he hoped to communicate.[191] Faced with this confusion, Gordon Mills argues, the most important function a critic can perform is not to find the specific sources of London's themes, but to uncover the principle that organizes his ideas. Mills argues perceptively, for example, that the much debated issue of whether London was an individualist or a socialist has little meaning because London was ruled by two desires rooted more deeply in his personality than in his reading: "the desire for adventure, combat and power" and "the desire for friendship, justice, and a serene intellectuality," regardless of whether the topic was socialism or individualism.[192]

It is Erich Fromm in *Escape From Freedom*, however, who provides the most useful key to London's temperament and, consequently, to an understanding of the ambiguity in his themes. Fromm remarks that in some men's inner lives there is a dialectical exchange between a growing sense of freedom and a developing sense of futility:

> On the one hand it is a process of growing strength and integration, mastery of nature, growing power of human reason, and growing solidarity with other human beings. But on the other hand this growing individuation means growing isolation, insecurity, and thereby growing doubt concerning one's own role in the universe, the meaning of one's life, and with all that a growing feeling of one's own powerlessness and insignificance as an individual.[193]

This same dialectic, an ambiguity in London's thinking, informs the Malemute Kid series of stories. In his excitement with his own intellectual and artistic growth and in his haste to communicate his new found "strong truths," ambivalence necessarily resulted, an ambivalence between ideals and actuality, between secondary and primary truths.

Later in his career London recognized the logical inconsistency, albeit the emotional necessity, of what he had done. In *Barleycorn*, after he had defined the "White Logic" and before concluding his remarks on man-made morality, he states that the code that "makes toward living," "secondary truth," is "of the lesser order of truth (215)." Friendship, strength, the sensation of mastery that comes from a successful adventure, and all the values the Kid represents, are but human constructs desperately formulated to insulate him from the primary truth of their futility. The rest of *Barleycorn* testifies to London's own inability to maintain an emotional commitment to these life-giving truths against the onslaught of primary truth. So, too, does his early fiction prove that London was unable to sustain artistically and intellectually a belief in the secondary truths as a buffer between life and death. A passage in Conrad's *Youth* captures the essence of London's early disillusionment, the dissipation of his early enthusiasm to advance the dogma that responding to the call of adventure will infuse life with the ideal. Marlow, having taken his voyage to the East, the fabled land of romance, reflects upon his own disillusionment:

I remember my youth and the feeling that will never come back any more—the feeling that I could last forever, outlast the sea, the earth, and all men; the deceitful feeling that lures us on to joys, perils, to life, to vain effort—to death; the triumphant conviction of strength, the heat of life in a handful of dust, the glow in the heart that with every year grows dim, grows cold, grows small, and expires—and expires, too soon, too soon—before life itself.[194]

"The White Silence" and "An Odyssey of the North," the only stories in his first volume that conclude tragically, contain the desperate struggle between "primary truth" and "secondary truth" for ascendancy. At the end of the first story, the Kid who has brought all the talents of the imaginative, code-practicing hero to bear upon the fact of death, flees the scene in terror: "The White Silence seemed to sneer, and a great fear came upon him. There was a sharp report; Mason swung into his aerial sepulchre; and the Malemute Kid lashed the dogs into a wild gallop as they fled across the snow (19- 20)." The conclusion is unresolved. There is a delicate balance between the magnificent example of the Kid's courageous and decisive actions and his terrifying glimpse into the futility of his prideful manhood that undercuts his usual composure. The end of "An Odyssey" is also inconclusive, and the "things beyond our wisdom" threaten to turn to mockery any rational basis for finding a unity between man's desires and the cosmic facts of life. In both stories, the central characters practice the code but the mythically invoked Northland atmosphere, that speaks of tragedy, penetrates the action so that the characters become participants in violence and death rather than bringers of law and life.

The whisper that called to completion becomes a call to face human limitations. From this point on, London's better fiction portrays limited or deficient characters who live in a universe that actively seeks their destruction rather than completed heroes who wrest mastery through imagination. London had opened the door leading to fear and irrationality and would have to give some response to Charley's question in "A Raid on the Oyster Pirates," that when one can't "see it all around" then "what's the good of seeing it at all?" What was a rhetorical question in that early story becomes the crucial problem in London's mature fiction.

Chapter IV

ALASKAN NIGHTMARE AND
ARTISTIC SUCCESS: 1898-1908

It has been shown that the fundamental philosophical assumption behind the characterization of the Malemute Kid as he is presented in "The Men of Forty-Mile," "The Priestly Prerogative," and "The Wife of a King," the least artistic of the stories in *The Son of the Wolf*, is that man can master his fate by rationally comprehending the ways of men and the cosmos. He is at home in the "new land," a citizen of the Northland, and can "see it all around." He is a protector of the American Dream.

Most casual critics and some London scholars discuss the entire London canon of fiction as if, at its base, it merely reflects the American Dream that all inevitably leads to individual mastery and social perfection. For them the idealized Malemute Kid must represent the most important aspects of London's thought and fiction. Abraham Rothberg writes in "The House That Jack Built" that:

> Actually, [London] was committed to an earlier heritage of absolutist ethics fundamental to the thinking of the mid-19th century. These ideas were derived chiefly from 18th-century ideas of nature and moral law. Here nature was favorable to man rather than indifferent or hostile; the concept of historical development was both progressive and optimistic rather than retrogressive and pessimistic; rather than a view of life in which man's nature is conceived of as beastly and irrational operating in a completely determined fashion,

ruled over by blind forces or brute forces, man's nature was conceived as reasonable, and his behavior was based on free will
operating in a universe governed by a benevolent providence.[195]

Kenneth Lynn in his *Dream of Success* characterizes London,
and presumably his fiction, as a product of the Horatio Alger
myth.[196] And even so recent a critic as Warner Berthoff, although he admits "darker, more complex intuitions" in
London's fiction, places his emphasis upon the theme of mastery
and domination in London's stories:

> He had a shrewd instinct for the chronic main currents of middle-
> class hallucination, especially a kind of retributive daydreaming about
> acts of pure domination or unconditional conquest. He appealed
> strongly to readers who wanted their daydreams explained a little,
> dignified by an overglaze of objective theory.[197]

The condescension exhibited by such commentators is not
wholly unjustified when discussing London's weaker fiction, but
it has occupied too prominent a place in London criticism. For
the triumphant Malemute Kid disappears early in 1899 from
London's fiction, and birth is given to a new Kid, the one in
"The White Silence" and "An Odyssey of the North," who
receives a terrifying glimpse of human finitude. After this revelation, the hero as completed and masterful man is no longer
possible and the limited, code-practicing protagonist takes
London's stage. Pessimism is the pervasive mood of *The Son of
the Wolf*; pessimism, rather than optimism, sponsored the major
themes of his stories from the beginning of his career. To "The
White Silence" and "An Odyssey of the North" can be added
two more excellent tales from *The Son of the Wolf*—"The
Wisdom of the Trail" and "In a Far Country"—making in a
collection of nine, four superior stories which deny the
American Dream of drifting optimistically towards perfection.
They present the nightmare of "things greater than our wisdom"
which suggest tragedy, horror, irrationality and human impotence.

Rather than portraying characters who master themselves and

their environments, London depicted them either reaching an uneasy accommodation with internal and external forces or being destroyed by them. In the best stories in *The Son of the Wolf* and the following collections, indifferent or even sadistically irrational forces inhibit man's puny efforts to control his fate; they are not man-oriented or man-controlled. Rather than nineteenth century preoccupations, London engaged twentieth century concerns: alienation, disenchantment, ironic ambivalence, and impotence. Early in his career he began to compose excellent stories within this pessimistic context and continued for ten years.

Although he wrote and published short stories from 1898 until his death in 1916, most of what are judged his superior stories were written in a ten year period between the fall of 1898 and the spring of 1909, when he stopped for a variety of personal reasons. During this decade he wrote stories which were eventually collected into the six volumes of Alaskan tales that established his fame then and continue it now: *The Son of the Wolf* (1898–99), *The God of His Fathers* (1900–01), *Children of the Frost* (1900–02), *The Faith of Man* (1901–03, but primarily 1903), *Love of Life* (1904–06) and *Lost Face* (1905–08).[198] The height of London's technical and thematic achievement is recorded in these six volumes of Alaskan stories. The "socialist" stories, the other group of tales upon which London's literary and popular fame rests, were also written during this decade, but they were written primarily during 1906 and 1907. The most important collection of these is *The Strength of the Strong*.[199] In addition to the Northland and socialist stories, this ten year period also saw the composition of two volumes of tales set in a South Seas locale: *South Seas Tales* and *House of Pride* (written by 1908).[200] The order of these three groups of short stories is not merely chronological; it also indicates a pattern of decline— the Northland stories are often excellent, the socialist and South Seas tales rarely as good.[201]

The encounter of limited man with a mysterious cosmos, an encounter which defines the limits of rationality, is the major theme of London's best fiction. London continually readjusts the boundary between the rational and the suprarational: from the intuitive and rational Kid living in an imaginatively and rationally comprehensible universe, London begins to portray protagonists who live by various kinds of laws which they apply to the knowable parts of their existence while being aware of the ultimately unknowable and incomprehensible nature of life. At first these limited characters find some way to maintain identity; but eventually, the characters participate with, or are crushed by, the nonrational. London finally portrays protagonists who become victims of the irrational elements in the unknowable because there is no law which affords protection. This pattern of readjustments by limited characters to the "Unknown" is the dynamic thematic principle which gives life to London's finest short stories.

In the Malemute Kid stories that emphasize rationality, control and mastery, the poetic landscape of the "white silence" plays no integral part in the fates of the characters; in fact, it is almost unmentioned. In the best stories, the reverse is true and the landscape is constantly crushing in upon the characters' consciousness. That the stories which evoke the mythic wasteland are the same in which the protagonists fail to "see it all around" is no accident; for, as has been mentioned, the Alaskan landscape symbolizes the uncharted land of the spirit where man must confront but can not conquer the supra-rational if he is to experience life fully. Perhaps the importance of the mythic landscape as a symbol of the region beyond logical comprehension, indicating London's awareness of the limits of positivism, can be more fully realized if one recalls London's early enthusiasm for Herbert Spencer's *First Principles* and acknowledges the connection between the landscape and Spencer's doctrine of the "Unknowable."[202] Commenting on the nature of the scientist, Spencer summarizes his doctrine of the "Unknowable":

> He learns at once the greatness and the littleness of the human intellect—its power in dealing with all that comes within the range of experience; its impotence in dealing with all that transcends experience. He realizes with a special vividness the utter incomprehensible-

ness of the simplest fact, considered in itself. He more than any other, truly *knows* that in its ultimate essence nothing can be known.[203]

London, as we have seen, was torn between the "greatness and the littleness of the human intellect ... its power [and] its impotence." This is the lesson of the "white silence," and often London's characters learn, as London did from Spencer, "the absurdity of the finite contemplating the infinite." The North-land landscape is the "unknowable" which can not be comprehended through positivistic logic and must be evoked symbolically and poetically. Spencer also writes that

> ... when the size, complexity, or discreteness of the object conceived becomes very great, only a small portion of its attributes can be thought of at once, and the conception formed of it thus becomes so inadequate as to be a mere symbol; that nevertheless such symbolic conceptions ... are indispensible in general thinking.[204]

Again and again, London's best protagonists move into the unchartered, unknown land and experience awe, mystery and terror that arise spontaneously as the landscape speaks to them symbolically. The characters are compelled to confront the mysterious unknown and to learn either how to live amidst it or to perish. Like an aspect of mind, destructive forces cannot be escaped nor conquered: "These protagonists consider that the world is a dark and futile place," Sam Baskett writes, "but even as they investigate this insight they struggle with that darkness and futility."[205] Earle Labor claims that the Northern land of the unknowable "is a region to escape from—not to"; but, be that as it may, London and his characters are compelled to explore its dimensions.[206]

That the Unknowable is not completely accessible to logic is a sub-theme in both "The White Silence" and "An Odyssey of the North." While the Kid analyzes the alternatives he confronts when Mason is injured, he must consider the inevitability of his and Ruth's deaths as well as Mason's. He considers the logic of the crisis: "In the abstract, it was a plain mathematic proposi-

tion,—three possible lives against one doomed one" (the third is
Mason's unborn child).[207] A sense of brotherhood makes him
hesitate, but finally he acts in accord with the "mathematic
proposition," with reason, and shoots Mason. The man of reason
has killed rationally, but rather than mastery and conquest, the
consequence is ambiguous. He has preserved his life, Ruth's and
the unborn child's. But as important, he ironically has discovered the limits of his power, the limits of logic. The symbolic
unknown has been brooding behind the events, and as he acts
rationally, he experiences terror as the White silence "sneers"
(*SW*, 19–20). The non-rational unknown teaches the Kid the
lesson that he is limited. Although he acts logically, he is aware
that his action forces him to cross a boundary between rationality and a threatening non-rationality. Similarly in "An
Odyssey" reason, legality in this case, tells Prince that Naass's
slaying of Unga and Axel convicts Naass of murder. But the Kid
intervenes with his observation that "there be things greater than
our wisdom" that necessitate violence and killing. Why is
beyond explanation. Even Naass, the killer, has discovered that
premeditation has not led to mastery and that the personal
implications of his actions are unclear. He senses that he can
neither submit himself to the law for judgment (only the
possibility that they will hang him and he "will sleep good"
appeals to him) nor return to his native village and live on "the
edge of the world (*SW*, 250)." Neither the civilized nor the
primitive, the rational nor the instinctual or non-rational, provide solace. Both are necessary components of the internal and
external worlds, but even together they yield no completely
satisfactory basis for action nor for understanding the consequences of action. At the end of the story, Naass remains
undecided and confused and can only stammer, " 'Yet—no; I do
not know' (250)."

The impotence of rationality when confronting the unknown
in effect demands that London turn to violence and death. Only
in death is there finality, and only in non-rational action can
one identify himself with his environment. The "unknowable"
symbolized by the Alaskan landscape is organically linked with

violence and death. It is significant that in the stories that portray the Kid as master and conqueror not only is there no artistic evocation of the landscape, but no death either by murder or by accident. But in "The White Silence" and "An Odyssey" death is the basic experience which raises the crucial issue of the limits of man's powers in the unknown. Death is at the center of almost all of London's important stories. Placed in a crisis situation without comforting landmarks, the protagonist defines the border between the rational and the supra-rational, the known and the unknown, by acting violently. His violent actions, even killing, force him to move beyond the rational and to participate with the death-dealing unknown. Violence may not justify his existence, but it defines it.

The predominance of death and violence in London's short stories disturbed some of the early critics who rejected him as a sensationalist, and very few later critics have realized that through violence London was probing experiences neglected by his contemporaries. Moreover, he probed with an integrity, sincerity and insight rarely associated with him. For Earle Labor, at least, "London deserves some attention as one of the first modern writers to realize the significance of death and violence as a central motif in twentieth century fiction."[208] Death and violence serve as an "initiatory rite into manhood."[209] And "manhood" can be more fully understood as a full awareness of the individual's participation with the unknowable universe that has an anti-human malignancy as one of its components. The act of killing is a concession to the unknowable and an admission that man has an internal counterpart to destructive natural forces.

The introduction of violence and death coupled with the unknown into London's fiction has important artistic consequences: it demands limited characters who can not predict all the implications of their actions nor understand all their consequences; the supra-rational is wedded to the rational and mystery to the known; tragedy rather than comedy becomes the mode; irony rather than a confident certainty becomes the mood.

"The Wisdom of the Trail" contains the elements that go into one kind of excellent London story: a limited protagonist ventures into the unknown; he lives by a code that permits, even demands, that he kill; and death tragically and ironically defines the fluid boundary between rationality and the threatening supra-rational.[210]

Sitka Charlie, the Siwash Indian protagonist, who is the "sheer master of reality" in "The Sun-Dog Trail," contracts with Captain and Mrs. Eppingwell to "go beyond the pale of the honor and the law" by undertaking "an unknown journey through the dismal vastness of the Northland, and he knew it to be of the kind that try to the uttermost the souls of men (146, 149)." The story opens on the trail, and Charlie has become the guide because he has the "wisdom of the trail" lacking in two other Indians, Kah-Chucte and Gowhee, "who had bragged that they knew every landmark of the way as a child did the skin-bales of the tepee, [but had to] acknowledge that they knew not where they were (151)." Charlie, uncertain of their exact location (he does not suffer a damning hubris about the unknown), knows that they have passed the "Hills of Silence" and are moving towards the Yukon River. His "wisdom" means more than a knowledge of geography however; it also means that he knows that "honor and law" are what precariously separate men from annihilation. He is a code hero. Tortured by the trail, Kah-Chucte and Gowhee break honor and law by stopping to rest and stealing a little, but life-sustaining, flour from the provisions. Charlie reminds them that they had contracted to live by the law, passes the judgment, and shoots them. Immediately afterwards he hears other shots that indicate that the travelers have reached the safety of the Yukon settlement.

The story invokes the mythic powers of the unknown that threaten tragically to destroy worthy individuals. Like the lesser characters on this ritualistic journey to confront the dangerous but fascinating unknown, Charlie has little notion of where he is and, at the end, is surprised to learn that he has reached safety. Since it is the human condition, Charlie, like both the fit and the unfit, suffers physically and emotionally because he struggles to survive in "such places [where] death was quick and easy (148)." But Charlie survives for two reasons: The first, the will to live, he shares with the others since in all men "the ego seemed almost bursting forth with its old cry, 'I, I want to exist!' the dominant note of the whole living universe (147)." The second, which he shares only with Captain and Mrs. Eppingwell, is that he is a code hero who lives by the "honor and the law" that "forbade a mighty longing to sit by the fire and tend his complaining flesh (148)." This law demands that he be willing to kill coldly, lucidly, in order to maintain his dignity, control and life. What the code does is to give some certainty, some internal logic to human relationships. Without the law, chance rules and the human community dissolves into competing individuals who will not only destroy one another, but themselves as well. The code is an artificial, sometimes inhumane, order imposed upon the rationally unknowable cosmic condition and replaces, in London's fiction, individual, logical comprehension of an orderly universe.

The ending of "The Wisdom of the Trail," like the endings of "The White Silence" and "An Odyssey of the North," is an important turning point in London's fiction because it is ironic. A simple kind of dramatic irony is discernible in a story like "The Men of Forty-Mile" or "The Wife of a King" since the audience is privy to a joke upon one of the principals. Tragic irony is, however, impossible because the central consciousness in such stories has the power to restore order so that all is eventually resolved comically. But in "The Wisdom of the Trail," even the best human is limited, permitting a more mature irony. The rigid, but orderly code, representing the zenith of man's control over himself and his environment, like the men who practice it, is not perfect. On the symbolic level, the code killing at the end and climax of the story brings salvation. The ritualistic murder purges the destructive element in man and "magically" Charlie and the Eppingwells discover that they have endured long enough to escape the white silence and find "the Men of the Yukon." Ironically and tragically, it is killing that brings life. But it is also the sign of tragic limitations in man and code. The code provides man with a way to exist, but not with a way to "see it all around." Charlie, practicing the code, discovers that the execution of the two Indians was unnecessary. Since the code is practiced not for sadistically punitive reasons, but, instead, to preserve life, it is tragically ironic that safety had been reached without the execution. Charlie's limited nature permits this irony and tragedy. But because he is aware of his limitations, represented by his miscalculation, and aware of the ironical and tragic quality of life, Charlie experiences no remorse. He accepts the situation because he has made a partially successful accommodation with the unknown and assumes that violence is unavoidable: He can "smile viciously at the wisdom of the trail" because he recognizes that violence and evil are inherent in nature.

Sitka Charlie can live in an ambivalent situation; the individual and the code may be limited but he has a sense of dignity and inner worth. Killing, although destructive, is partially redemptive. Not only killing by the code, but dying by it as well, provides a measure of salvation. Gowhee and Kah-Chucte give last messages for Charlie to convey to their families and are asked, " 'Are ye content to die by the law?' " They respond stoically, " 'We are' (159)." Their acceptance of the penalty demanded by the law ennobles them and counterbalances the two men's earlier hubris and cowardice. Dignity is available to all men who realize that suffering, violence and death are unavoidable consequences which must be accepted if one has the courage to explore the unknown.

Implicit in this story is an irony that becomes a dominant motif in later stories which focus upon the suffering experienced on the long trail. In "The Grit of Women," which has been called one of London's best because it has an organically related "theme, character, setting, mood," Sitka Charlie is again on the trail that has been the cause of suffering, sorrow and death and considers the irony of human existence:[211]

> "Life is a strange thing. Much have I thought on it, and pondered long, yet daily the strangeness of it grows not less, but more. Why

this longing for life? It is a game which no man wins. To live is to toil hard, and to suffer sore, till Old Age creeps heavily upon us and we throw down our hands on the cold ashes of dead fires. It is hard to live. In pain the babe sucks his first breath, in pain the old man gasps his last, and all his days are full of trouble and sorrow; yet he goes down to the open arms of Death, stumbling, falling, with head turned backward, fighting to the last. And Death is kind. It is only Life, and the things of Life that hurt. Yet we love life, and we hate Death. It is very strange (*GF*, 176–77)."

Trouble, suffering, sorrow and futility are the primary elements of life; but, ironically, life is dear to Charlie, and he practices a code which the limited man must impose upon the unknown as a buffer between his imperfectly ordered existence and certain annihilation demanded by a destructive universe.

"In a Far Country," also in the first volume of collected stories, concentrates on the grotesque misery in life; and in it, London attempts to reinforce his code premise by reversing the coin. London means to portray what happens when two men, Carter Weatherbee and Percy Cuthfert, face the unknown without the code. He intends these two to be deficients since they lack heroic qualities available to them. However, within the story there is an unintentional shift of emphasis that unveils a far deeper pessimism than revealed in any previous story. The malign, irrational powers of the cosmos are so predominant and so destructive that they make codes ludicrous attempts at self-deception. The basic irony of life found in "The Grit of Women" and "The Wisdom of the Trail" is resolved because life is no longer dear. In this story London explores the irrational demands made by the unknown and, implicitly, concludes that the deficient man in the beginning of the story is really the best he can be, a limited man. "Limited" and "deficient" become synonymous terms. The major part of the story becomes a parody of what London has claimed for the ritual journey into the unknown and for the practice of the code which demands love, imagination, and, sometimes, ritual killing in order to give a measure of dignity to limited human beings.

The story begins as if it were to be an exemplum for a text

about Darwinian adaptability separating the fit from the unfit. Jacques Baptiste and Sloper are fit men who live by the code. They contract to guide the "Incapables" or deficients, Weatherbee and Cuthfert, into "the Unknown Lands" and begin the "arduous up-stream toil" of the long trail (*SW*, 74). But the two deficients refuse to meet the hardships of the trail and decide to remain during the heart of winter in a remote cabin. The rest and most important part of the story is an account of Weatherbee's and Cuthfert's physical and mental deterioration which climaxes in their killing one another.

Together, the two Incapables represent a perversion of the ideal man of reason and imagination: Weatherbee has the doggedly pedestrian and literal mind of an ex-clerk, and Cuthfert possesses a sentimental dilettante's imagination "which mistook ... the true spirit of romance and adventure (72)." They follow "civilized" codes of behavior and are unequipped, therefore, to confront the demands of the unknown as would Charlie or the Kid by exercising comradeship and discipline. So in the depths of winter, in *terra incognita*, without the protection of the rational-imaginative man's code as a buffer between life and death, they are vulnerable to the message and power of the "white logic." Defenseless as they are, the central power and interest in the story becomes the unknown and its death-dealing attributes. At first the men deteriorate socially and physically, but the last fifteen pages of the story catalogue the effects of the unknown upon their sanity. They experience "the Fear of the North ... the joint child of the Great Cold and the Great Silence, [which] was born in the darkness of December (86)."

Fear inspired by the unknown causes the unimaginative Weatherbee to hallucinate men rising from two graves beside the cabin who tell him of their suffering. Death and suggestions of death continue to pervade the story. But it is through the imaginative man, Cuthfert, that the nature of the unknown is revealed. Early in the story London had made the point that his "imagination" is deficient because it provided him with illusions about the meaning of adventure. But for the rest of the story his imagination gives him valid insights into cosmic truths.

Without the aid of the code to protect him, the message of the white logic captures his spirit:

> He dwelt upon the unseen and the unknown till the burden of eternity appeared to be crushing him. Everything in the Northland had that crushing effect,—the absence of life and motion; the darkness, the infinite peace of the brooding land; the ghastly silence, which made the echo of each heart-beat a sacrilege; the solemn forest which seemed to guard an awful, inexpressible something, which neither word nor thought could compass (88).

Cuthfert's discovery that life is an illusion is captured in a passage that typifies some of London's most suggestive prose:

> Once, like another Crusoe, by the edge of the river he came upon a track,—the faint tracery of a snow-shoe rabbit on the delicate snow-crust. It was a revelation. There was life in the Northland. He could follow it, look upon it, gloat over it. He forgot his swollen muscles, plunging through the deep snow in an ecstasy of anticipation. The forest swallowed him up, and the brief midday twilight vanished; but he pursued his quest till exhausted nature asserted itself and laid him helpless in the snow. There he groaned and cursed his folly, and knew the track to be the fancy of his brain; and late that night he dragged himself into the cabin on hands and knees, his cheeks frozen and a strange numbness about his feet. A week later mortification set in (90).

This passage is a parody of the archetypal quest motif in London's other stories. Rather than to accommodation or mastery, this quest leads to disillusionment. Archetypally, man wants to explore and discover (like Crusoe) and ecstatically follows a faint trail, despite the agonies of the flesh, so that he can affirm life. He enters the wilderness and passes the brief day of his life. At the end of the brief span, he loses his illusions and learns that life has been a cheat, and he is filled with an agonizing self-mockery. Exhausted, disillusioned, he senses his imminent death.

Cuthfert possesses London's third and final kind of imagination, the "thrice cursed gift of imagination."[212] This kind of imaginative man does not "see it all around" so that he cannot act constructively, nor does he "understand the ways of the northland so sympathetically that he can anticipate its emergencies before they occur, always adapting himself to nature's laws."[213] Instead, this imagination fills him with "soul-sickness, life sickness":

> He sees through all illusions. He transvalues all values. God is bad, truth is a cheat, and life is a joke. From his calm-mad heights, with the certitude of a god, he beholds all life as evil. Wife, children, friends—in the clear, white light of his logic they are exposed as frauds and shams. He sees through them, and all that he sees is their fraility, their meagerness, their sordidness, their pitifulness. No longer do they fool him. They are miserable little egotisms, like all the other humans, fluttering their May-fly life-dance of an hour. So is he (*JB*, pp. 13-14).

This is the imagination that allows London's limited and deficient characters to merge. The code, the law and the honor, are merely life-giving lies, frauds, tricks to avoid recognizing that life is a mockery and death and pain the reality. Cuthfert, despite the contempt with which London surrounds him in the opening of the story, perceives truths that make the basis of that contempt inoperative. Cuthfert is everyman; instead of being deficient, he turns out to be limited, the best that men can be. And the fundamental qualities of his life and eventual death are grotesquery, malevolency, degeneracy and insanity.

The end of the story is an ironic and grotesque parody of London's other stories that use the ritualistic killing to ennoble both killer and victim. Weatherbee, gone mad, approaches Cuthfert with an axe:

> There was neither pity nor passion in his face, but rather the patient stolid look of one who has work to do and goes about it methodically (97).

Cuthfert shoots him in the face, but Weatherbee swings the axe which "bit deeply at the base of the spine, and Percy Cuthfert felt all consciousness of his lower limbs leave him (98)." They fall together in a final clinch, an image that ironically recalls to the reader the embrace of tender fellowship described two pages earlier and, more generally, London's emphasis upon comradeship as part of the code in other stories. This double killing, described in terms of lucid, rational action, does not ennoble. Instead, it is grotesque. By killing, Sitka Charlie and the Malemute Kid had made concessions to the white silence, but simultaneously had salvaged dignity for themselves and their victims. Cuthfert and Weatherbee become one with the malevolent unknown. The disappearance of Baptiste and Sloper in the beginning of the story, despite London's intention, symbolizes the death of the code as anything more than a system of illusions.

In "In a Far Country," then, London explicitly attempts to reaffirm the necessity of the code, but implicitly he denies the efficacy of a code in the face of the message revealed to Cuthfert. London wanted desperately to announce the revitalizing nature of "true adventure" and intended to satirize the enervating effects of civilization upon Weatherbee and Cuthfert who were unequipped to live according to new laws demanded by the new land; but he found this impossible. Eagerness to believe succumbs to the impossibility of belief. Not only has mastery become impossible, but accommodation as well. Sam Baskett, commenting upon this story, captures its fundamental revelation: "London goes beyond a concern with social theory to make a final comment on life . . . Essentially this comment is—the horror.[214] The stories which follow "In a Far Country" eventually make explicit its implicit concerns: *The God of His Fathers, Children of the Frost, The Faith of Men, Love of Life* and *Lost Face* pursue the nature of the code or the "law" as London makes a series of adjustments to the terrifying insights in "In a Far Country." No adjustment, however, could prevent him from coming to the edge of the abyss.

The Son of the Wolf collection of stories written in 1898 and 1899, in summary, has a range of talent and depth of insight unexpected in a first volume of short stories. Against a Northland landscape, poetically invoked because it is a symbol of the unknown which lies beyond factual, logical comprehension and control, characters actively explore the dimensions of their internal and external worlds. London dramatizes a mythic encounter with the tragedy that man's most highly prized attributes are merely self-sustaining illusions which cannot protect him from the terrifying suspicion that life is empty of significance and the irony that the best man's clearest thoughts and most purposeful actions have ambiguous consequences. Forced to live on the edge of annihilation and to participate in violence, code practicing protagonists act violently, even kill, so that they can revitalize the spirit of adventure and experience "the intense personal satisfaction that comes from knowing one is self-sufficient in a dangerous world."[215] But finally, as in "In a Far Country," the code is inoperable and characters kill because they are linked to a destructive cosmic evil which demands death and violence.

The importance of London's achievement in *The Son of the Wolf* and his independence from popular tastes can be appreciated, perhaps, when it is pointed out that W. M. Frohock in *The Novel of Violence in America* concludes that the treatment of violence by writers of the twenties, thirties and forties is the distinguishing mark of twentieth century American fiction.[216] His generalizations about the elements of this fiction reveal London's originality as he labored in the first decade of this century. "At their best," Forhock writes, "these tragic novels ... conceive of violence as the characteristic mark of the human, and acts of violence themselves are performed with great lucidity."[217] Furthermore, he characterizes the literary structure and techniques that necessarily belong with this subject matter, and they are applicable to London's fiction:

> To discuss such [fiction], one is almost forced to adopt terms borrowed from the drama: "situation," "mounting tension," "climax," "resolution of tension." Inversely, certain concepts traditionally useful for the criticism of fiction hardly apply. One does not look in the novel of violence for "rounded" or "three-

dimensional" figures; such notions as "density" or the "rich texture of life" are rarely of value.[218]

London's best stories meet this description and join content and form artistically. Characters, in a crisis situation, kill or act violently but "lucidly" and, thereby, expand their conceptions of self and their connections with the cosmos. The dramatic focus upon situation, tension, and climax that Frohock sees inherent in the "novel of violence" are terms descriptive of short story form and theory as London understood and practiced it.[219] London is a legitimate predecessor of such writers as Ernest Hemingway, John Steinbeck and Norman Mailer.

Although London's second collection of Alaskan stories, *The God of His Fathers* containing stories written during 1900 and 1901, continues the author's concern with violence, horror, the code and the unknown, it is generally inferior to *The Son of the Wolf*. "Grit of Women," for example, has already been mentioned as similar in matter, theme and technique to "The Wisdom of the Trail"; but it, despite its virtues, suffers slightly from a sentimental treatment of women that more seriously mars "Siwash," another Sitka Charlie story, and "The Great Interrogation." This last story, like "Which Makes Men Remember," "Where the Trail Forks," "A Daughter of the Aurora" and "At the Rainbow's End," all in the same volume, is flawed by thematic confusion. For example, in both "The Great Interrogation" and "Where the Trail Forks" the white protagonists' motives for kindness towards Indians are unclear—do they sacrifice themselves because they love and appreciate for themselves the good qualities of these women or do they merely act chivalrously as "white men"? Social comedy, like that found in the clumsy "The Wife of a King," is resurrected in "The Scorn of Women" and given a perverse twist in "A Daughter of the Aurora," a story that appears to be a product of London's efforts to write his first and unfortunate novel, *A Daughter of the Snows* (1902). "Jan the Unrepentant" is another "The Men of Forty-Mile" in its portrayal of comic violence erupting among isolated miners; but like most of these stories which have a parallel in *The Son of the Wolf*, it is more cynical about human nature. In this volume, too, there is less emphasis upon the demands of the mythic unknown and more upon the demands of the "law" of Anglo-Saxon race supremacy. Generally, then, this volume lacks the stature of its predecessor because of its recurrent appeals to sentimentality and adolescent humor, its thematic confusion and its use of race theory as an explanation for motive and action.

The title story of *The God of His Fathers* does, however, represent an important transition linking the best stories in *The Son of the Wolf* with the best stories in *Children of the Frost*, London's third and, perhaps, finest collection. "The God of His Fathers" is an attempt to deny the implications of "In a Far Country" but without returning to the use of the personal code. London attempts a return to the theme of mastery by emphasizing a new law—race supremacy.[220]

The story is set in the Northland's "forest primeval" at "the moment when the stone age was drawing to a close (1–2)." Hay Stockard, his Indian wife and child, and Bill, his companion gold-seeker, are in an Indian camp attempting to get an assurance from Baptiste the Red, an independent, dignified but hostile half-breed chief, that his tribe will not molest them in the quest up the unchartered Koyukuk River. They are joined by another white man, Sturgis Owen, a self-righteous and fanatical priest. Baptiste the Red refuses to let them pass unless they renounce the Christian God whom he hates because priests had refused to legitimatize his birth, to solemnize his marriage to a white woman, and to punish the Factor who raped and killed Baptiste's daughter. Sturgis Owen refuses to blaspheme, and out of race pride the non-religious Stockard refuses to turn over the missionary to torture. A bloody battle results, at the end of which the missionary recants to save his life and Hay Stockard is killed, a martyr to the "God of his fathers,"—his race.

This is the first of London's stories in which race is the dominant theme.[221] Race is the true God:

[Sturgis Owen's] courage, if courage it might be called, was bred of fanaticism. The courage of Stockard and Bill was the adherence to deep-rooted ideals. Not that the love of life was less, but the love of race tradition more, not that they were unafraid to die, but that they were not brave enough to live at the price of shame (25).

This sentimental fillip reinforces a major London theme of individual tragedy accompanying racial triumph. Hay and Bill "fair-faced, blue-eyed, indomitable men, incarnations of the unrest of their race," die; and the narrator generalizes melo-dramatically:

So many an unsung wandered fought his last and died under the cold fire of the aurora, as did his brothers in burning sands and reeking jungles, and as they shall continue to do till in the fulness of time the destiny of their race be achieved (2).

The story is sententiously phrased and loosely structured; nevertheless, it is significant in the development of London's major themes. Earlier, as has been shown, London had written poor stories attempting to show the mastery of the individual in an orderly cosmos; then, because of a deepening pessimism suggesting a more complex view of reality, he had written more probing stories using more artistic control in which limited protagonists like Sitka Charlie reached an accommodation with a hostile, chaotic cosmos by living by an imposed code; finally, he recorded the failure of individual accommodation in "In a Far Country." Having found individual identity impossible to integrate, London turns to race identification, a blood brother-hood, in "The God of His Fathers" and, thereby, returns to the theme of mastery. His pessimism is held in temporary abeyance. The individual human may be weak, but law and order are restored to the cosmos and link man (white men, at least) with nature. After the collapse of the powers of reason and imagina-tion in "In a Far Country," London now romantically asserts a unity beyond the appearance of flux. This time, however, his optimism depends upon mastery achieved by the aggregate rather than the individual. Group identification for sustaining humanly meaningful values supplants the powerful individual wresting mastery on his own terms. That London found this new theme personally sustaining is demonstrated by the exuberant tone of the racial theory passages, like the one above, in "The God of His Fathers."

Literarily, race theory had the advantage of allowing London to continue some of his best practices. He did not have to yield his concept of the limited individual. In fact, in a later story, "The Terrible Solomons," the narrator defines the major limitation of the "inevitable white" who is the hero of London's racial stories which have white men as protagonists:

> . . . the white man who wishes to be inevitable, must not merely despise the lesser breeds and think a lot of himself . . . He must not understand too well the instincts, customs, the mental processes of the blacks, the yellows, and the browns; for it is not in such a fashion that the white race has tramped its royal road around the world.[222]

Characters like Stockard, a blasphemous, adulterous, violent man, could serve the inevitable law which, ironically, demands that he support the fanatical Sturgis Owen and attack the more noble Indian, Baptiste the Red. Moreover, by means of race theory, London's impulse towards power and mastery could be joined with his sense of insignificance and powerlessness since all individuals are impotent participants in the working out of the inexorable natural law. Finally, the mythic could be invoked since, as George Becker suggests, teleological concepts are implicitly epical and mythic, demanding poetic effects rather than the use of mundane details found in realism of the commonplace.[223]

However, the race theory has disadvantages as well. The protagonists, whom London means to be positively received, often degenerate into brutal fascists, especially when London's racism is less consciously used than in "The God of His Fathers." The lines which precede the above passage from "The Terrible Solomons" capture the racism that goes beyond race theory in some stories:

[The protagonist] must have the hall-mark of the inevitable white man stamped upon his soul. He must be inevitable. He must have a certain grand carelessness of odds, a certain colossal self-satisfaction, and a racial egotism that convinces him that one white is better than a thousand niggers every day in the week, and that on Sunday he is able to clean out two thousand niggers. For such are the things that have made the white man inevitable.[224]

The bigotry and savagery necessary in such a character's make-up are not, despite London's intention of course, heroic; they disgust. And if Wayne C. Booth in his *The Rhetoric of Fiction* is correct that in making aesthetic judgments, the beliefs of the reader necessarily and legitimately influence critical evaluations, these stories are aesthetic failures on that basis alone.[225]

Fortunately, the "unimaginative" white protagonist who carries out the dictates of his heredity by inflicting personal and social injustices is not often a positively portrayed hero in London's Northland short stories. There is injustice, but since London's more responsive emotional and philosophical milieu was a tragic and ironic sense of failure, his artistic efforts are more often sympathetic with the, albeit "inevitable," despair of the Indians who suffer at the hands of the white invaders. London might write that a white "unimaginative man" (in the sense that he is indifferent to and unaware of the human values of non-whites) is the ideal and that "we must come to understand that nature has no sentiment, no charity, no mercy; we are blind puppets at the play of great, unreasoning forces; yet we may come to know the laws of some of the forces and see our trend in relation to them"; but his Northland Indian stories in *Children of the Frost* show London, himself, "imaginative," "sentimental," "charitable," and "merciful."[226]

The stories collected in *Children of the Frost* were composed from 1900 to 1902 at the same time London was writing those collected in *The God of His Fathers*; but they are more dramatic, mythic, tragic and ironic, a continuation of the best in *The Son of the Wolf*. Despite Earle Labor's claim that "most of the stories are mediocre in artistry," "The League of Old Men" and "Keesh, the Son of Keesh," although sometimes too discursive, rise above some structural awkwardness by evoking the epic struggle of the individual rebelling against the demands of social and cosmic law and compare favorably with "The White Silence" and "An Odyssey of the North."[227] "The Death of Ligoun," "The Sickness of Lone Chief" and "The Law of Life" are dramatically and economically written and capitalize upon the mellifluous style arising from the dignified language London associated with Indian speech. Technical flaws are not difficult to uncover; however, these stories were written at the height of London's apprenticeship in short story technique and theory. This means, for example, that this volume avoids the essay-exemplum form and concentrates on more dramatic forms.[228] At this time his letters reveal his enthusiasm for the genre, and he published more reviews and articles about the writing craft than at any other time in his career. And in 1903 he also published *The Call of the Wild* which climaxed his early literary control and competence.

Although he would write other excellent stories, no single volume of short stories is as consistent in quality of artistry and control of theme as *Children of the Frost*. Moreover, the collection demonstrates a more explicit treatment of "the horror" than he was capable of handling in *The Son of the Wolf* or *The God of His Fathers*. To George Brett, his publisher, London wrote:

> The idea of *The Children of the Frost*, is the writing of a series of tales in which the reader will always look at things from the Indian's point of view, through the Indian's eyes as it were. Heretofore the viewpoint in my Northland stories has been that of the whiteman's.[229]

Because of the Indian point of view, the special pleading and exhortations found in earlier stories are curtailed and the demand for ideal characters is diminished. He might have added to his note to Brett that the theme linking the stories would be inevitable loss. The Indians in all of these stories had possessed all that London's white conquerors came to the Northland to find: individual dignity, courage, contact with and adjustment to the elemental strength of nature, and a sense of community within the tribe. Such a theme was compatible with London's emotional gestalt and could be handled with a consistency unmatched in even the best stories in the first two volumes which threatened to break apart upon the ambivalent requirements of mastery and failure. The Indians are limited protagonists who are victims of both cosmic and social laws. London returns to his theme that human values are tragically inappropriate, but redeeming, in a hostile cosmos. But eventually, he suggests that they are not even redemptive.

Hay Stockard in "The God of His Fathers" is a martyr for his race: his death, and the deaths of other white men, will be redemptive for the Anglo-Saxon race. "The League of Old Men" in *Children of the Frost* is a companion story since it too employs race martyrdom as the dramatic situation; however, the latter story has the power of tragedy, while the former only pathos. Unlike Stockard who is a contributor to group mastery, Old Imber the Indian protagonist is a social and cosmic rebel and martyr. If London admired the "glad perisher" epitomized by Stockard, his growing pessimism made him more at home with this new glad perisher for "lost causes."[230]

The basic nature of the race theme in "The League of Old Men" is the same as in "The God of His Fathers"; the judge's thoughts at the end of Imber's trial for murdering scores of white adventurers, reveals both the theme and the judge's admiration for the Indian:

> ...all his [the judge's] race rose up before him in the mighty phantasmagoria—his steel-shod, mail-clad race, the law-giver and world-maker among the families of men. He saw it dawn red-flickering across the dark forests and sullen seas; he saw it blaze, bloody and red, to full and triumphant noon; and down the shaded slope he saw the blood-red sands dropping into night. And through it all he observed the law, pitiless and potent, ever unswerving and ever ordaining, greater than the motes of men who fulfilled it or were crushed by it, even as it was greater than he, his heart speaking for softness (160).

Although the judge subscribes to race theory, his heart is moved by a pity not appealed to in "The God of His Fathers" because that story does not focus on the tragedy and irony that is at the center of interest in this.

Old Imber, the last of his kind, a "bronze patriot," remembers his Edenic youth when "the land was warm with sunshine and gladness" and when "men were men (152)." Therefore, he organizes a band of old men to assassinate the white men who had brought whiskey, gambling, smallpox and tuberculosis and had taken away women and young men and turned them against tribal customs and honor (155–56). Because of his pride, Imber refuses to accept white culture and rebels against it, consequently rebelling against the cosmic law. The "old men departed up river and down to the unknown lands," where they murdered. Eventually, only Imber was left, and exhausted, "it being vain fighting the law," he surrenders to the police (159–60). It is both tragic and ironic that men like Imber who are courageous, loyal and intelligent must suffer and die at the hands of contemptible whites acting out nature's "law." Imber's martyrdom is moving and even suggests to the judge something like the "things greater than our wisdom, beyond our justice" at the end of "An Odyssey." Moreover, the tragedy of this story goes beyond the pathetic death of Stockard since Imber's rebellion against and final submission to social and cosmic injustice will not be redemptive; his nobility ends with his death. So, although the situation and underlying beliefs might be the same as in "The God of His Fathers," the emphasis shifts from the Hay Stockards of the North to the Red Baptistes and Imbers, from a somber optimism to inevitable tragedy. London has invested his racial theme with the rhetoric of defeat and submission rather than conquest and triumph.

"Keesh, the Son of Keesh," is similar in theme to "The League of Old Men" since it dramatizes the loss of racial identity as the non-whites fall before their Anglo-Saxon superiors. But, contrary to the critics' usual response to this story, it is more than social criticism that reveals London's ambivalency towards non-whites; for the theme of loss in

Children of the Frost is more than the loss of racial identity. The tragic loss is the death of London's previously held illusions that some code, some system of belief, some systematic description of reality, would redeem men from fear, violence, death and despair, or at least that the archetypal journey would yield a self-sustaining myth as a buffer between man and the terrors of a meaningless universe.

Keesh, a young chief of the Thlunget Indians left his tribe to be educated in the "higher morality" by Mr. Brown, a Christian missionary, and had learned that killing is immoral. Since this emasculates him in the eyes of other Indians and allies him with the white oppressors, he is denied the hand of Su-Su, the daughter of the chief of the Tananaws. She agrees to disobey her father if Keesh will "bring me, not scalps, but heads . . . three at least (108)." At first loyal to his catechism, Keesh finally decides to "go to hell" and returns to Su-Su's camp which is described in terms suggesting the place of archetypal confrontation:

> [It was] in an open space, striving to burrow into the snow as though for shelter from the appalling desolateness . . . Ringed all about, a dozen paces away, was the sombre forest. Overhead there was no keen, blue sky of naked space, but a vague misty curtain, pregnant with snow, which had drawn between. There was no wind, no sound, nothing but the snow and silence (109–110).

There he murders Su-Su's father and three other men who spoke against him, decapitates them and then allows Su-Su to guess what he has wrapped in the moose hide. After she plays her coy and sexually exciting guessing game, he rolls the heads before her:

> There they lay—the soft-featured Nee-Koo; the gnarled old face of Gnob; Makumuk, grinning at her with his lifted upper lip; and lastly, Nossabok, his eyelid, up to its old trick, dropped on his girlish cheek in a suggestive wink. There they lay, the firelight flashing upon and playing over them, and from each of them a widening circle dyed the snow to scarlet (112).

A dog sniifs at the head of Su-Su's father and raises a "long wolf-howl" as the girl bears her throat to Keesh's knife, ending the story.

There is social criticism in this story. In eloquent speeches, the men whom Keesh eventually murders list the injustices: whites had married Indian women, breaking the unity of the tribe; had degraded the men by making them do "squaw work"; and are driving the Indians from their land. Moreover, the whites are hypocritical since, although they speak of killing as both criminal and immoral, they kill at will (104-05). As in "The League of Old Men" it is tragic and ironic to London that the dignified Indian had to give way to cultural pressures.

But the power of the story goes beyond social criticism. It arises from the tension between conflicting codes or value systems, each of which is unable to sustain positive human values. Neither the white man's way of life nor the Indian's code of honor leads to an integration of the spirit; instead, the one is hypocritical and, metaphorically, will not permit Keesh the basic privileges of a wife, children and honor, and the other is inhumanely grotesque. Life has become a mechanical ritual for Keesh: he contracts to undergo an ordeal, a ritualistic task, which leads to nihilism. Although he performs perfectly and exhibits the kind of control that saves the Kid and Sitka Charlie, the contract is demonic and the tortured ritual ultimately meaningless so that he is neither damned nor saved. Rather than a synthesis of the two systems, all that links the white and the Indian codes are ugly emotions and grotesque violence. In this story abstractions are rejected as useless and what remains are the horrible details that describe the severed and bleeding heads and the wail of misery from a half-savage dog. As London begins to doubt "Laws," codes and other abstract systems of belief, he turns to a greater emphasis upon ugly physical details as the most meaningful facts of existence.

"The Death of Ligoun," a tersely written frame story, confines social commentary to the frame. The story-within the frame is told by an old, degraded and drunken Indian and pursues the theme of "Keesh, the Son of Keesh" that abstractions no longer give meaning. His tongue loosened by whiskey, the Indian narrator recollects the days of his youth when he escorted Ligoun to a "potlach" with other chiefs where Ligoun hoped to convince them that peace, rather than warfare, solidarity rather than struggle, should characterize inter-tribal relations. First among violent men in his young manhood, Ligoun is now "loudest, ever, for peace . . . being the greatest of chiefs (115)." At the potlach, however, rivalries are fanned until the chiefs, including Ligoun, revert to practicing the "Thlinket Code—Blood for blood, rank for rank (113)." According to the code, to maintain honor men must avenge killings, but only by killing someone of higher rank. Consequently, Ligoun is killed by Niblack, the next in rank, in a lengthily described and minutely detailed massacre which climaxes the story. To "Kill by the law," does not ennoble men; it degrades and destroys and, in effect, kills peace and solidarity (120). London adds to his list of impossibilities, peace and brotherhood.

"The Sickness of Lone Chief," structurally similar to "The Death of Ligoun" because it dramatically utilizes the frame that reveals social loss, pursues London's motif that life is merely a mechanically ritualistic task and that life-sustaining values are illusions. But in this story, he goes closer to the abyss than in the other stories previously discussed from *Children of the Frost*. As in "Keesh, the Son of Keesh" and "The Death of Ligoun," life in the abstract is so vacuous that the climactic act of a man's life is destructive, violent and grotesque; but in this story, London comes close to dramatizing the "horror" that the malignant, destructive nature of the "white silence" is one with the nature of life, making life indistinguishable from death. In short, he returns to make explicit the implicit theme of "In a Far Country."

Lone Chief, with the aid of Mutsak, another old Indian, and the encouragement of spirits provided by a white man who is collecting tales of Indian life before the coming of the white men, tells the story of how he became chief. The last son of a dying chief, Lone Chief was unable to accept his tribal legacy because his mind had been deranged by a head wound inflicted by a bear. Bitterly disappointed and angry, his father ordered that Lone Chief's funeral be celebrated while he was yet alive. Since hs is considered dead, after the ceremony Lone Chief is sent to perish in battle against a rival tribe. In the bloody battle he is struck upon the head, restoring his mind and his manhood so that he brutally defeats the enemy, kills the false shaman of his own tribe, and becomes both chief and religious leader.

This is a pedestrian plot, perhaps accounting for the story's neglect by the critics, but the mythic element gives it a meaning that transcends the limitation imposed by the stock device of a blow to the head restoring a lost mind. Life for Lone Chief in the beginning of the story is death-lin-life. He says, ". . . to them I was dead, so was I to my own mind dead . . . I did not know when, or how, yet did I know that I had surely died (95)." His shock of self-realization is that he is dead and life has no meaning; in the "unknown land" he has no real and vital identity. Life and death are the same. In the funeral oration and in Lone Chief's speech after killing the shaman at the end of the story, the land of death is described precisely as London had portrayed the Alaskan landscape which in other stories is the place where men journey in order to sustain life. An Indian elder describes the land of death as a place of "darkness and silence [and] great spaces [the] soul must wander through (95)." It is the "Unknown" where tormented souls "howl forever in the dark and endless forest" terrorized by "great beasts" and destructive phantoms (95, 100). This is the land in which the "dead" Lone Chief lives.

No longer is death the release longed for in "The Grit of Women" and stoically accepted in "The Wisdom of the Trail." Death and life have become indistinguishable states of darkness and terror. Ironically, Lone Chief's journey and bloody participation in carnage bring him back to life that is death since the land of death and the Northland are identical. His only reward, that makes him both chief and priest, is that he can perceive the meaninglessness that others have not:

> Alone among men I have passed down through the gateway of Death
> and returned again. Mine eyes have looked upon unseen things. Mine
> ears have heard the unspoken words (101).

He has seen and heard that which the "white logic" had revealed
to his creator.

This revelation it would seem, brings some consolation
because, after all, Lone Chief is both a temporal and spiritual
leader and prophet. But the story ends with an ironic under-
cutting of even this solace. The frame around Lone Chief's
narrative reveals that he has lost his position because of the
white man's liquor and money. The parallels with London's
desire to be a cultural prophet, his disillusionment and
destructive attraction to cash and whiskey may be too prophetic
to be considered frivolous.

The only law of life is the law of death. In the most
economically, and dramatically conceived and written story in
this volume, "The Law of Life," Old Koskoosh perceives this as
he sits by the fire waiting the inevitable conclusion of life and
recalls the basic lessons taught him by experience:

> Nature was not kindly to the flesh. She had no concern for that
> concrete thing called the individual. Her interest lay in the species,
> the race ... Nature did not care. To life she set one task, gave one
> law. To perpetuate was the task of life, its law was death (33).

What dignity the old man retains arises from his ability to
perceive this law and his stoical resignation to it, although terror
threatens to undermine his composure. He has performed well,
having sired a chief and perpetuated the race, but the performance is mere "task." His stoicism, too, is not totally
redemptive because the law is merely descriptive and is not
humanly satisfying or meaningful. The fundamental quality of
life remains its savagery and terror.

In this story, London gives his metaphor of the human
situation which shows how far he has travelled from the
optimism of his earliest stories. It is the poetry of this story that
discloses the horror, the nightmare of existence. Left to die as

the snow begins to fall, armed with a few sticks of wood to feed
the small fire, the blind Koskoosh remembers that in his youth
he had seen an old Moose cut from the herd by wolves, surrounded by them and, finally, felled and torn apart:

> Then on his darkened eyes was projected the vision of the moose—
> the old bull moose—the torn flanks and bloody sides, the riddled
> mane, and the branch-horns, down low and tossing to the last. He
> saw the tongues, the slavered fangs. And he saw the inexorable close
> in till it became a dark point in the midst of the stamped snow
> (37-38).

As in other stories, London uses savage animals as a reminder
of the bestial quality of life that threatens to break loose and
overwhelm man. The dogs in "The White Silence" overcome
Ruth's discipline, significantly just after Mason has been crushed
by the tree; a sick wolf stalks the man in "Love of Life"; and in
"Batard" the half savage dog is always waiting for the
opportunity to kill his master.[231] The moose-wolf analogy to the
old man's situation in "The Law of Life" is as powerful in its
simplicity and implications as it is obvious. And London continues the parallel and ends the story by applying it directly to
Koskoosh's situation:

> ...a ring of crouching, jaw-slobbered grey was stretched round
> about. The old man listened to the drawing in of the circle. He
> waved his brand wildly, and sniffs turned to snarls; but the panting
> brutes refused to scatter. Now one wormed his chest forward,
> dragging his haunches after, now a second, now a third; but never
> one drew back. Why should he cling to life? he asked, and dropped
> the blazing stick into the snow. It sizzled and went out. The circle
> grunted uneasily, but held its own. Again he saw the last stand of the
> old bull moose, and Koskoosh dropped his head wearily upon his
> knees. What did it matter after all? Was it not the law of life? (38).

The pattern of life is suggested by the light-dark image motif in
this passage and in the story as a whole: the story opens with
white snow falling, moves to the ring of grey wolves, and to the

black of oblivion, the "dark point in the midst of the stamped snow." The light has flickered and gone out. Here is London's metaphor of the human condition. A man of limited vision is enclosed by an inexorably constricting trap, surrounded by savagery. At the center of the trap, he awaits by a dying fire, a feeble light amidst the grey-black circle bringing a violent and grotesque end as the light goes out.

Life, in "The Law of Life," is no longer of consequence. Koskoosh refuses to cling to life because it does not "matter after all" and drops the brand. The will to live that dominates all the men in "The Wisdom of the Trail" and is the fundamental irony in "The Grit of Women" is gone. The "white logic" has won despite London's earlier enthusiasm for racial law that promised order beyond the multiplicity of existence. Once man has assimilated the meaning of the "white logic," London later wrote in *John Barleycorn*,

> ...he knows that he may know only the laws of things—the meaning of things never. This is his danger hour. His feet are taking hold of the path that leads down into the grave (12–13).

The law that brings an orderly inevitability denies human significance and transforms life into a mechanical task, an empty ritual, to be undertaken until imminent death teaches its emptiness.

The theme of loss, then, in *Children of the Frost*, is more than an account of Indian cultures falling before the inevitable white supremacists. Romance had gone out of the Northland which had once promised a revitalization by immersion in the "stinging things of the spirit." Nothing stands between man and "the horror." Truth terrifies; illusions are impossible to sustain. Death, rather than the peaceful sleep Naass longed for, has become a nightmare indistinguishable from life.

It would seem that London's pessimism had reached its nadir. However, the demonic asserts itself in the Alaskan stories which follow "The Law of Life"; nature is actively and motivelessly evil. The characters who live in this environment become one with its demonic, motiveless malignancy, as the grotesque pervades the stories in *The Faith of Men, Love of Life* and *Lost Face*.

"Simple horror," writes Austin Wright, "involves the emergence of grotesque evil in a character or world that initially appears to be morally neutral."[232] The grotesque arises when we perceive "horror in the face of facts about life that we know to be universal, normal rather than abnormal."[233] The world presented in "Batard," first published in 1902 as "Diable—a Dog" and later included in *The Faith of Men*, is a place of horrors that is grotesque because the "abnormal" has become the universal norm. Evil has become the active force in man and the cosmos.

The two principals in "Batard" are Black Leclere, who struggles to master the malign forces in the "unknown," and his dog, Batard, who embodies those hostile powers. Eventually, the animal kills the man, and London has presented a perverse modification of his previously held cosmic view.

At first it would seem as if London's description of Leclere makes him as another ideal, imaginative character, perfectly suited to survive in the Northland:

> He was a man who lived much in the open, beyond the sound of human tongue, and he had learned the voices of wind and storm, the sigh of night, the whisper of dawn, the clash of day. In a way he could hear the green things growing, the running of the sap, the bursting of the bud. And he knew the subtle speech of the things that moved, of the rabbit in the snare, the moody raven beating the air with hollow wing, the baldface shuffling under the moon, the wolf like a gray shadow gliding betwixt the twilight and the dark. And to him Batard spoke clear and direct (208).

Apparently, he is at home in nature, and his instinctive understanding of her inner-workings should allow him, like the Malemute Kid and Sitka Charlie, to compete successfully. But Leclere's imaginative power is London's third kind of imagination that allows one to perceive the horror, and he has become a "devil" in order to attempt matching the malign cosmic powers

(201). Throughout the story, he tortures his dog, hoping to break his spirit and to master the unknown.

Batard, known as "Hell's Spawn" to the other men of the Northland, has inherited the savage and malignant spirit of the land. He is "sinister, malignant and diabolical," a bastard product of a savage "great timber wolf" and a treacherous and depraved bitch with a "genius for trickery and evil" passed to her off-spring as a "congenital inequity (203)." His howl is a wail of misery "fit for hell," and he possesses a deliberate, patient, destructive cunning (220, 204). By gazing into the dog's eyes, Leclere, through the exercise of imagination, perceives that by competition with the dog, he has "bucked the very essence of life—the unconquerable essence ... He pitted his puny strength in the face of things, and challenged all that was, and had been, and was yet to be (220–21)." Past, present and future demand doom for man and triumph for the diabolical "unconquerable essence" of savagery and iniquity. With a "fiendish levity" Batard finally knocks a cracker-box from under the defenseless Leclere and hangs him. The "unnatural," an illegitimate product of savagery and evil, has become the indomitable power of the unknown, of nature.

London's world view has altered perversely. Leclere, as do earlier protagonists, recognizes that he cannot escape the challenge of the unknown and refuses, therefore, advice to sell or kill Batard. But heroic confrontation does not save. Nor does comradeship, even when its principle is inverted: Leclere's and the dog's "hate bound them together as love could never bind (207)." Violence in earlier stories had become a necessarily evil that helped man to preserve his life and values; and violence pervades "Batard" as Leclere at first practices "crude brutalities" and, then, "refinements of cruelty (204)." But he is unable to accommodate himself to the environment. Finally, the atavism that gave a measure of salvation to men like Hay Stockard, who responded to the call of blood ties, does not save Leclere. At one point in the story, Leclere and Batard battle one another on terms of equal animality as London resurrects the "circle of savagery" metaphor in "The Law of Life":

> It was a primordial setting and a primordial scene, such as might have been in the savage youth of the world. An open space in a dark forest, a ring of grinning wolf-dogs, and in the centre two beasts, locked in combat, snapping and snarling, raging madly about, panting, sobbing, cursing, straining, wild with passion in a fury of murder, ripping and tearing and clawing in elemental brutishness (212).

Devolution affords no sanctuary. Even the man who deliberately identifies himself with the bestial, cruel and diabolical powers of the unknown must perish, and the demonic triumphs.

Motiveless malignancy characterizes the best stories which follow in *Love of Life* and *Lost Face*, expressing the darkest of London's pessimism, while hack work takes more space in these and subsequent volumes. Unexplained murder is the subject matter of "The Sun-Dog Trail" in *Love of Life*, for example. In "The Wit of Porportuk" in *Lost Face* the ideal woman (El-Soo is an aristocratic Indian girl who is adaptable, spirited, and loving) and the ideal man (Akoon is strong and "had been to all the unknown wastes and places") undertake a journey that would, in earlier fiction, prove the perfection of their love (199–200). But they are pursued and caught by an old, jealous suitor from whom El-Soo had run away. Porportuk, the suitor, agrees that she is more suited to live with Akoon; but, then, he shoots her through the ankles so that she will never walk or run again. This final act is grotesque since as a punishment its brutality exceeds the requirements of the offense against Porportuk. Evil, in this later fiction, exceeds expectation in London's non-rational, dehumanized world. But the most grotesque story is "Lost Face" which demonstrates that the quest into the unknown territory ultimately leads to terror and annihilation. Its situation and technique is similar to "The Law of Life." The limited third person narrator presents Subienkow's thoughts as he waits to be tortured and killed by the Indians who had captured him. "A dreamer, and a poet, and an artist," the imaginative man, he had traveled over the globe, continually eastward, only to find that he is "doomed to live in raw and howling savagery, and to die in this far land of night, in this dark place beyond the last boundaries of the world (5)."

"Always it had been savagery—brutal, bestial savagery" behind every experience, the only universal absolute. While he waits for his execution, he listens to the grotesque screams of another man under torture and, fighting hysteria, successfully plans to avoid torture by tricking his captor into decapitating him. Pain, hysteria and grotesque horror have become the only human experiences, and the only rational act left is the deliberate planning of suicide.

Love of Life and *Lost Face* were the last collections of Northland stories London produced, with the exception of his *Smoke Bellew* volume that London, himself, acknowledged as hack work. Many of the stories in *Love of Life* and *Lost Face* are obviously pot-boilers also or recreate the dehumanized world of "Batard" and "Lost Face" that threatens to become more bizarre than terrifying. "The central mood" in these two volumes, writes Maxwell Geismar, is "inhuman, but almost mechanical misery"; and the extreme of the grotesque brings the fiction close to the merely sensational.[234] However, each volume included a story destined to become ones by which London is remembered: "The Love of Life" in the first and "To Build a Fire" in the second. Published in 1905 and 1908, respectively, each had its genesis earlier when London was writing consistently good stories that had not yet become "mechanical" in their pessimism. "Love of Life" is based upon an article from *McClure's* entitled "Lost in the Land of the Mid-night Sun," written in 1901; and "To Build a Fire" is a revision of an identically titled story London wrote for *Youth's Companion* in 1902. Neither story depicts the motiveless malignancy which brought the black imagery of oblivion to stories like "Batard"; but neither do they evoke the mystical whiteness of "The White Silence." Instead, a cold gray encloses the two protagonists as they move between, but never experience consciously, a redeeming illumination and a damning recognition of the powers of darkness.

"Love of Life" describes the ordeal of a nameless prospector who has been abandoned by his partner and must wander alone through the forbidding Alaskan landscape if he is to survive.

Only his tenacious, instinctive will to live, despite the pain and apparent hopelessness of his situation, permit him to reach the safety of a ship anchored in an Arctic bay. Atavism saves him. This affirmation of the impulse towards life, modifies the theme of a perversity controlling the stories in these later volumes; nevertheless, the details used to dramatize his theme, threaten to contradict its import.

Although the theme of the story is the triumph of the will to endure, the patterns of the story convey disintegration. In the beginning there are two men, the nameless wanderer and Bill, his companion, and then just the one human; then, the man and diseased wolf, man and brute; finally, only the man is left, but now dehumanized, brute-like himself. He is an "it," "something that was alive but which could hardly be called a man . . . It squirmed along the ground like some monstrous worm (40)." At first he is not lost, but then he enters the "Barrens" and is. His awareness of the world and contact with reality also undergo a similar pattern of disintegration. In the beginning he turns and "slowly took in the circle of the world that remained to him" which is outlined by "formless mists and vapors, which gave an impression of mass and density without outline or tangibility (5–6)." As the story continues, the movement is towards the center of this circle. His awareness constricts, and he no longer looks slowly at the horizon but compulsively at his immediate surroundings: he counts his matches over and over (10–11); sees a moose he can not shoot, a ptarmigan he can not catch, and finally he captures some fish the size of minnows as the physical world diminishes in its size and he becomes more impotent (11–18). A fog in the valley restricts his vision and, simultaneously, he begins to hallucinate about that world, so that it is not only constricted but unreal (24); the mist that was on the horizon, and then in the valley, now fogs his mind (25). Increasingly, he becomes aware of his own physical state—his blurred vision, the rhythm of his breathing, the throbbing of his heart. Detailed, basic physical needs are foremost in the description as the man moves between sanity and delusions, between conscious and increasingly more frequent unconscious states. The real in his world has been reduced to his instinctual will to survive and the functioning of his involuntary physical processes within a context of pain and fear.

Before the man becomes totally unconscious, he does awaken to a new awareness of the world about him when he hears a cough. He discovers that he is being followed by a sick wolf that has been patiently stalking him, moving closer, "licking hungrily" the man's "bleeding trail" left by his knees which "had become raw meat like his feet":

> Then began as grim a tragedy of existence as was ever played—a sick man that crawled, a sick wolf that limped, two creatures dragging their dying carcasses across the desolation and hunting each other's lives (36).

The new awareness of the world is that it is diseased, destructive, death-dealing, tragic and grotesque. Finally, the man sinks his teeth into the wolf's throat, killing it, and drinks its blood. This is the grotesque climax of the story:

> . . . the face of the man was pressed close to the throat of the wolf and the mouth of the man was full of hair. At the end of half an hour the man was aware of a warm trickle in his throat. It was not pleasant. It was like molten lead being forced into his stomach, and it was forced by his will alone. Later the man rolled over on his back and slept (39).

Up to this point in the story, London has depicted human physical and emotional disintegration and an environment that alters from a misty circle encompassing desolation to a diseased, brutish and grotesque power. He had done this artistically by exercising care with detail and control over his omniscient narration by limiting it, as in "The Law of Life," to the prospector's awareness. His "love of life" theme, however, demanded that the character not die. Consequently, London added a two page, contrived epilogue from a totally omniscient point of view that describes the rescued man's return to the human community aboard ship. He portrays the man's compulsive eating and hoarding of food. In the last sentence, the narrator assures us that he would recover from the eccentric behavior: "He would recover from it, the scientific men said; and he did, ere the *Bedford*'s anchor rumbled down in San Francisco Bay (42)." The inartistically presented epilogue is unconvincing. Madness, pain, decay and disease are not easily dismissed. In effect, the arctic landscape has triumphed, and London's theme that life can be sustained through atavism unintentionally and ironically undercut. Life has been stripped of its dignity; not only has the code failed, but instinct as well.

"To Build a Fire" is London's most mature expression of his pessimism. The nameless "chechaquo" or tenderfoot who confronts the white silence in this short story possesses neither the imagination that gives man an intuitive grasp of the laws of nature and allows him to exercise his reason to accommodate himself to them, nor the "thrice cursed" imagination that convinces man of the absurdity of confronting the unknown with ridiculously finite human powers:

> The trouble with him was that he was without imagination. He was quick and alert in the things of life, but only in the things, and not in the significances. Fifty degrees below zero meant eight-odd degrees of frost. Such fact impressed him as being cold and uncomfortable, and that was all. It did not lead him to meditate upon his frailty as a creature of temperature, and upon man's frailty in general, able only to live within certain narrow limits of heat and cold; and from there on it did not lead him to the conjectural field of immortality and man's place in the universe (65).

He does not recognize that man is so finite that the bitterly cold Alaskan landscape inevitably destroys the individual. The rest of the story suggests that man is totally unequipped to face the unknown and inherently too limited to explore life's mysteries and live. If the individual is to survive, he must avoid truth-seeking and "spirit-groping."

Only two other living beings are mentioned in "To Build a Fire": the "old timer" and the dog who accompanies the tenderfoot along the "hair-line trail" into the "unbroken white" of the mysterious land (64). The old timer offers one way to survive, and as it turns out, the only way. In the autumn before the young man takes his fatal journey, "the old timer had been very serious in laying down the law that no man must travel alone in the Klondike after fifty below (80)." His experience has given him the imagination to continue living; but, significantly, he adjusts to the unknown by refusing to venture into it. He remains with other men, away from the trail during the heart of winter. The lesson he attempts to teach the young wanderer is that if one hopes to survive, he must retreat from a solitary confrontation with cosmic power, "the full force of the blow" delivered by "the cold of space" at the "unprotected tip of the planet (80)." The kind of accommodation the Kid makes, practicing the code in order to adjust, is impossible. The dog, however, accompanies the reckless young man into the cold and does survive. Instinct protects him. Nevertheless, instinct gives no comfort to man, since it is unavailable to him. The dog has "inherited the knowledge" from his savage ancestors who, like he, had never been separated from the brutal landscape by civilization. In fact, the dog is part of the inhuman Alaskan wilderness and, like it, "was not concerned in the welfare of the man (77)." The old timer's imagination, then, warns that man cannot confront the depths of experience and live; the dog's instinct for survival is unavailable to man. Having been divorced from nature by civilization, no man is fit to undertake the most arduous journey.

In addition to imagination, the quality that permitted the Malemute kid and other protagonists to survive in the Northland had been their knowledge of the concrete and their mastery of facts. Suspicious of abstractions, London had given his characters control over the factual. For example, Sitka Charlie may not understand the reasons for the bizarre occurrences in "The Sun-Dog Trail," but he sees the details in the "picture" and knows how to respond to them effectively. The Kid, too, is able to master situations because he knows Northland lore, knows facts and can order them rationally. But by the time London had written "To Build a Fire" he had lost his faith in the potency of reason.

The chechaquo in this story has a command of facts and is "quick and alert in the things of life (65)." Clell Peterson argues perceptively and convincingly that the young man is not, as many readers assume, merely "a fool who dies for his folly"; he is "not a fool" but the "modern, sensual, rational man."[235] Rather than a deficient character, he is another of London's limited protagonists; and his death denies the efficacy of reason. The plot presents the mythic journey of the limited man into the unknown where his reason, his only support, no longer can sustain him:

> The "dark hairline" of the main trail in the "pure snow" on the broad frozen Yukon suggests the narrow limits of man's rational world compared with the universe beyond his comprehension . . . The events of the story take place in a world devoid of sunlight, of day-light, which is also the light of reason and common sense. Thus the absent sun, "that cheerful orb," represents the dominant qualities of the man which are useless in a sunless world where reason fails and common sense proves unavailing.[236]

The power of reason has collapsed. London has even lost his faith in "facts": symbolically, the man falls through the snow into the water, the accident which begins his desperate struggle to live, because there are "no signs" indicating where the snow is soft (78). The man's tragic flaw has been his masculine pride in his rationality.

Neither the abstract nor the concrete, imagination nor reason, sustain life. The romantic and the realistic impulses both lead nowhere. Without their protection, the unknown becomes a destructive agent whose white logic is the "antithesis of life, cruel and bleak as interstellar space, pulseless and frozen as absolute zero." The landscape in "To Build a Fire" has become killer. What remains for London to do in this story, which everyone agrees he does masterfully, is to record the grotesque details which describe the nightmare of impaired physical activity that is the prelude to the modern man's death. In "To Build a Fire" London has employed a controlled artistry to present the theme that was struggling to life in "In a Far Country."

Now that London's everyman has become merely a helpless victim of the killing landscape, the mystical light goes out of the Alaskan sky. Rather than, as some would have it, portraying man's insignificance but unsystematically depicting affirmations of the American Dream, the reverse had happened: London tried to dramatize a new version of human dignity but unintentionally drifted towards the pessimism which undeniably informs these Northland stories. Throughout the best of his Alaskan stories, London had made a series of adjustments in order to stave off a darkening vision and to preserve some reason for "spirit-groping." Although his temperament and reading called upon him to affirm life, he exhausted the positive as he found himself forced to move from themes of mastery, to themes of accommodation, to themes of failure. His honesty compelled him to deny affirmations. Even the archetypal quest motif and the evocative imagery of the wasteland, artistic elements which distinguish his stories from those of lesser writers, disappear from his fiction as he discovered that it is not undertaking the dangerous and desperate quest that determines the quality of life but, instead, inexorable, external forces of nature and man's irrationality, his link with that nature. The Alaskan nightmare had reached its conclusion, and London retreated from the "Unknown."

Chapter V

THE DECLINE: 1906-1911

Martin Eden, London's autobiographical hero, sailing for the South Seas aboard the *Mariposa*, broods over the failure of his individualistic philosophy to furnish him with values that would be at once optimistic and true and decides to commit suicide. *Martin Eden* was published in 1909, and Eden's suicide almost marks the death of Jack London's best short fiction. During the next two years, 1910 and 1911, London squandered his creative energies in penning *Smoke Bellew* (New York, 1912) and *a Son of the Sun* (New York, 1912), the first, a series of connected stories about the Klondike and the second, a series of related stories about the adventures of David Grief in the South Seas. These, even London admitted, were pot-boilers, and they signaled the end of his story-writing for five years.

Although from 1906 to 1911, London wrote a few Alaskan stories such as "Love of Life," "To Build a Fire," and "Lost Face," new emphases appear in his subject matter, themes and techniques that reveal a growing loss of literary vitality even though a few excellent stories were composed. These new emphases are found in three general categories of stories: socialist stories, which attempt to reaffirm positive values; South Seas tales, which continue the grotesque misery of the later Alaskan stories; and many pot-boilers, including some socialist and South Seas stories, which show London's retreat into the inconsequential.

To understand the emergence of London's socialistic fiction, the pessimism of his South Seas stories and his retreat into pot-boilers, written from 1906 to 1911, it is helpful to return to the events of London's life from 1903 until 1906. 1903 saw the beginning of serious personal problems for London. In that year he was separated from Bess, his first wife, beginning a widely publicized scandal that continued while London covered the Russo-Japanese War for Hearst in 1904 and climaxed with a divorce from Bess and marriage to Charmian Kittridge in 1905. This period from 1903 until 1905 was the time of London's Nietzschean "long-sickness" that he often referred to in *John Barleycorn* and his letters. He writes in *Barleycorn:*

> I had read too much positive science and lived too much positive life. In the eagerness of youth I had made the ancient mistake of pursuing Truth too relentlessly. I had torn her veils from her, and the sight was too terrible for me to stand ... This long sickness of pessimism is too well known to most of us to be detailed here. Let it suffice to state that I had it very bad. I meditated suicide coolly, as a Greek philosopher might (253-54).

In a letter to Carrie Sterling, he recalls the summer of 1903 that began his affair with Charmian and disintegration of his marriage:

> You will remember yourself, the black moods that used to come upon me at that time, and the black philosophy that I worked out at that time and afterwards put into Wolf Larsen's mouth.[237]

The allusion to *The Sea-Wolf*, written from 1903 to 1904, is illuminating. Larsen's philosophy is that which had taken over the Alaskan landscape; he was the master of "positive science" and, symbolically, suffers from a cancerous brain tumor that at first destroys his voice, then blinds, and finally kills him. Larsen had "made the mistake of pursuing Truth too relentlessly" and could not, with intellectual honesty, accept appealing romantic illusions. He was committed to an emotionally dehabilitating materialistic pessimism.

Like Larsen, London was losing his "voice" as pot-boilers increased in number. The pessimism apparent in his later Northland stories was incapacitating him. *The Sea-Wolf*, as critics have often noted, moves unconvincingly toward a romantic affirmation as Maude Brewster and Van Weyden find comradeship, then love, after Larsen dies. London denies the white logic and superimposes life-sustaining illusions.[238] Similarly, in his composition of short stories, London moves literarily from the Northland landscape that has become identified with "positive science" and pessimism to socialist stories in an effort to affirm life. In the "long sickness" passage from *Barleycorn*, quoted above, London writes that after the white logic had exposed success, fame and money as illusions, he was spared from suicide by "the PEOPLE":

> ... the PEOPLE saved me. By the PEOPLE was I handcuffed to life. There was still one fight left in me, and here was the thing for which to fight. I threw all precaution to the winds, threw myself with fiercer zeal into the fight for socialism ... Love, socialism, the PEOPLE ... were the things that cured and saved me (254, 256-57).

Socialism was not an entirely new interest of London's: from the beginning of his career almost until his death, he was involved in the socialistic cause. Philip Foner's *Jack London: American Rebel* is still the most thorough account of London's association with the socialist movement and eliminates the necessity of trying to summarize here this important aspect of London's biography.[239] Such a summary would be superfluous, anyway, since, despite London's continued interest and contrary to popular opinion, his socialism sponsored very few stories of artistic distinction, and these were written from 1906-1909. Instead of writing stories, he aided the cause primarily through articles, essays, reviews and speeches.[240]

In the summer of 1906, he threw himself into the composition of his famous revolutionary novel, *The Iron Heel* (New York, 1908). At the same time, he began to compose socialist stories. Among the few socialist stories he wrote, these, in the order of their publication, are the few which still elicit interest: "The Apostate" and "A Curious Fragment" which are collected in *When God Laughs* (New York, 1911), the volume which followed *Lost Face*; "The Dream of Debs" and "The Strength of the Strong" which are collected in *The Strength of the Strong* (New York, 1914), the most widely known collection of stories with a social emphasis; and "The Mexican," collected in *The Night-Born* (New York, 1913).[241]

The thematic break with the Alaskan stories which was entailed in writing socialist fiction is not as dramatic as one would expect; the new emphasis is a matter of degree. Early, London had emphasized comradeship as a saving element of the Malemute Kid's code, and it is a simple step from this to class solidarity. Similarly, he could turn from race theory involving a melioristic natural law to socialism's telic forces. Injustices perpetrated against Indians by gold hungry whites from civilization are like those inflicted upon "wage slaves" by their capitalist masters. This shift from individual and racial mastery to social mastery, then, is not a total departure from his earlier themes and motifs but, instead, a realignment of his ideas to effect a more optimistic view of life. He moves from the Alaskan nightmare to social ameliorization, a kind of change which Frederick Hoffman, in more general terms, believes characteristic of modern literature:

> When once the shock of violence is unaccounted for, unseen, unreal, and unreasonable, the self is separated from most doctrines of sufficient reason; it has to make its "separate peace." Since the self cannot be sustained without some viable code or some illusion, there are many contrived readjustments.[242]

The most important unifying bonds between the Northland and socialist stories are that London could approach the different subject matter didactically and prophetically, his most comfortable authorial stance, and that both kinds of stories were justified by "scientific" theories. In the beginning of his career he hastened to find techniques to allow the presentation of "strong truths," derived in part from science; and in the socialist stories, the role of the artist as propagandist for a scientific Marxism is a recurring motif that demonstrates his messianic impulse, the sincerity of his conviction, and his continuing trust in scientific theories.

London's interest in the artist's social role as prophet and propagandist accounts for one of his finest socialist stories, "The Strength of the Strong," one which proves that his socialism could sponsor high quality fiction. This story, which Foner calls "among the finest parables in American literature" uses the omniscient but limited narrator, the controlled narrative point of view which had given power to stories like "The Law of Life."[243] In this parable depicting the evolution of capitalism but prophesying its demise, London is attacking Rudyard Kipling for relinquishing his role of prophet to become spokesman for the establishment. Kipling had written a defense of capitalism and an attack upon the socialists' anti-war theory in a parable entitled "Melissa."[244] London's parable was written to attack Kipling's argument that socialism could not prevent war because cooperation necessitates a degenerating laziness that destroys the fabric of society before warfare can be stopped. The motto affixed to "The Strength of the Strong" is "Parables don't lie, but liars will parable—Lip-King (1)." "Lip-King," of course, is a word play upon "Kipling"; and the lying "Bug" who parables in the story is Kipling. The story ends with the socialist hope, uttered by the narrator, that "some day all fools will be dead . . . and all men will be brothers and no man will be idle in the sun and be fed by his fellows (32–33)."

By emulating Kipling's use of parable to attack the Englishman's political ideas, London had found a sub-genre well suited to his purposes and talents. This simplest of all short narrative forms does not require complexity of characterization nor intricacy of thought. Instead, uncomplicated analogy is an ideal vehicle for moral lessons to be taught to a mass audience. London could capitalize upon the "strong truth" and "simple strength of utterance" which he prized and incorporated into his best Alaskan stories. Jesus, of course, taught through parable, and London admired Him for His simple moral understanding and love of humanity, qualities he hoped to portray in "The Strength of the Strong."[245] Moreover, the parable is similar to the form of the best Alaskan tales since simple analogy is similar to archetypal symbolism.

Only one other story is similar in form, technique and theme to "The Strength of the Strong," no matter how suitable parable was for London's socialistic propaganda—"A Curious Fragment." In this story London turns from the pre-historic times of "The Strength of the Strong" to "the twenty-sixth century after Christ, which was the first year of the terrible industrial oligarchy" in America (*WGL*, 257). He restates his attack upon writers who support the establishment and distinguishes them from his ideal artist as propagandist: the first group "was paid by theoligarchy, and the tales they told were legendary, mythical, romantic and harmless," and the other was composed of men like London who were "agitators under the guise of story-tellers" and who "preached revolt to the slave class (258)." A story-teller agitator orates a tale to some "wage-slaves" describing industrial injustice and the consequent brotherhood of the slaves. The oppressed are given courage by hearing about the heroism of one of their number as he faces the tyrannical master in order to present a list of grievances.

It is important that London, in these two socialist stories, has not returned to a completely optimistic theme of mastery. The stories are "dystopian" rather than utopian and concentrate upon the period of oligarchical, capitalistic oppression that, according to the Marxist dialectic, comes before entering the promised land. His metier in these stories, as in his best Alaskan fiction, is catastrophe and suffering.

What differentiates these stories from the Alaskan is that London hopes to prepare his audience for the coming utopia. And even in his self-assumed role of public educator and "agitator" he is more practical than utopian. The assumed audience is the working class, and the story-teller (an extension of London's self concept) is not completely identified with the workers because he has gone further than they through self-education and is prepared to accept responsibility in the new order. At times London, himself, could be contemptuous toward the proletariat. He wrote to Anna Strunsky, for example, "I grow, sometimes, almost to hate the mass, to sneer at the dreams of reform" because they crucify their prophets and remain unfit for leadership themselves.[246] These two stories, however, prove that London hoped to redeem them. In "The Strength of the Strong" he dramatizes the ironic situation of the masses stoning "Split Nose" their collectivist prophet because they have been duped by their corrupt capitalist rulers. Presumably, London's readers would see the folly of this. The final exhortation in "A Curious Fragment" is that "you must prepare . . . by learning to read (275)." By example and exhortation, London provides practical suggestions for redemption and, despite the dystopian action of the stories, assures his audience that "a good time is coming (*WGL*, 275)." Dramatically catastrophic and pessimistic, the stories are coated with optimistic and moralistic propaganda.

As good as "The Strength of the Strong" and "A Curious Fragment" are, as didactic parables, the stories are not as powerful nor as artistically complex as the best Alaskan stories. The shift in emphasis from archetypal symbolism to parable, concomitant with the change from the demonic ambiguities of the Alaskan nightmare to the socialistic certainties, signifies a decline in artistic vitality. Bertrand C. Mayer, writing about Joseph Conrad's fiction, describes a similar phenomenon in terms that could apply to London's. Commenting upon Conrad's change from writing his early impressionistic fiction to propaganda, Meyer observes that Conrad could psychologically "no longer afford those introspective journeys into the self" and the "dream quality" disappears from his fiction.[247] "In the face of danger . . . from storms brewing within the confines of his own mind . . . the artist may yield to the propagandist within himself," Meyer continues, and a "dreamy impressionsim give(s) way to pictorial images conceived in the full light of consciousness."[248] In London's, as well as Conrad's fiction, social and political types replace the archetypal hero and poetry is replaced by slogans.

Perhaps the best known of London's socialist stories, "The Dream of Debs," and the only one dramatizing collectivist triumph, exemplifies the artistic difficulties inherent in his propaganda. The story describes the mechanism and effects of a general strike, as perceived from the first person narrator, Mr. Corf, a member of the upper class. By using an aristocratic, first person point of view, London intends to satirize the naive callousness of upper class reactions to the proletariat. For example, Corf learns so little from his contact with human misery that he concludes the story by observing insensitively that, "The tyranny of organized labor is getting beyond human endurance" and "something must be done (SS, 176)." But this point of view is a clumsy device for London's propaganda. Most of the story shows Corf suffering and emphasizes the violent savagery of the slum dwellers; consequently, the reader identifies too completely with Corf's agony. Moreover, because Corf is politically uninformed, the first person device forces London to draw from his other characters informative speeches, rather than dramatic dialogue. The propaganda motive, in general, inhibits London's artistry. The story is stiffly mechanical not just because of the dialogue, but because London is compelled to attempt brief characterizations of social and political types: the rich, including the dilettantish establishment liberal, the rich thrill-seeking girl, and the monopolist; the General of the militia; the faithful retainer; the kindly working man's wife, etc. As interesting as this story is as socialist argument, it is an artistic failure.

"The Apostate," another favorite of the critics and anthologists, is more successful than "The Dream of Debs" because it isn't ambivalent towards the working class and doesn't attempt to dramatize a complicated body of socialist ideology. In addition, it is a story of disintegration and dehumanization, contexts which characteristically had produced London's better fiction. Johnny, the "apostate," is a "work-beast" produced by a textile mill sweat shop who, as a result of the inhuman working conditions and sub-marginal wages, is ignorant, will-less, and physically misshapen. He has just enough awareness left, after brutalizing days at the machine, to realize that he is nothing more than another moving part in the machine. Without emotion, not even a hatred for the machines or a sense of bitterness, he decides to stop working. He walks out of town, lies in the grass for an afternoon and then hops a freight. Rather than a fictionalization of Marxist ideology, "The Apostate" is more a muck-raking story attacking the inadequacy of child-labor legislation and an irreverent social comment that it is preferable to be a tramp than a work beast.

The last of London's stories using a frankly ideological socialism, "The Mexican," is a companion piece to "The Apostate" since both stories portray the silent anguish of the proletariat facing economic, social and political injustice. However, the mood of "The Mexican" is vengeful rather than pathetically disillusioned, and its youthful protagonist is a victim-rebel instead of mere victim. Artistically it is more successful because it evokes the mythic "Unknown" that suggests both destruction and salvation and identifies its protagonist with that ambiguous, primitive force.

Felipe Rivera, "the Mexican," arrives at the California offices of the Junta attempting to overthrow the Porfirio Diaz dictatorship and asks only that he "work for the Revolution (*NB*, 243)." Despite his silence, the others recognize that

> This slender boy was the Unknown, vested with all the menace of the Unknown. He was unrecognizable, something quite beyond the ken of honest, ordinary revolutionists whose fiercest hatred for Diaz and his tyranny after all was only that of honest and ordinary patriots (244).

The boy is that mysterious, inevitable, telic power that goes beyond intellectual commitment, even beyond patriotic emotion. London identifies him with a primitivistic natural power, an identification which awes the most sensitive and intelligent member of the Junta:

> "To me he is power—he is the primitive, the wild wolf,—the striking rattlesnake, the stinging centipede ... He is the Revolution incarnate ... He is the flame and spirit of it, the insatiable cry for vengeance that makes no cry but that slays noiselessly (251)."

He is a more consciously purposeful Tom Joad from Steinbeck's *Grapes of Wrath* who, like Steinbeck's characters, offers both promise and destruction: He is "a destroying angel," the "hand of God (251, 249)."

Artistically, it is difficult to ask a single character to embody so abstract a concept; but London finds a perfect structural device to permit him to do so. The last twenty-five pages of the story depict a microcosmic prize-fight which pits Rivera against Danny Ward, a boxer from New York. The ring-side crowd is partial to Ward and the boy's silent hatred and determination (equated with determinism in a way that convincingly combines positive will and amoral natural force) battle against bad odds, suspicion and injustice. The fight is portrayed skillfully and dramatically. From a context of brutality, acting brutally and destructively, the Mexican emerges a hated and hating winner: "The Revolution could go on (290)."

The remainder of London's socialist fiction has little merit. In "The Minions of Midas," for example, he employs the dystopian concept that terror will reign before the orderly and humane utopia will be reached that is found in "The Strength of the Strong," "A Curious Fragment" and "The Mexican."[249] But the story is preposterous. The Minions of Midas is a terrorist organization of intellectuals from the working class who refuse to become wage-slaves and who are dedicated to assassinating rich industrialists. The terrorists remain faceless and are known by the reader only through their letters threatening the rich. They are, it is explained, the impersonal principle of destruction that is inherent in the capitalist system:

> *We are part and parcel of your possessions. With your millions we pass down to your heirs and assigns forever.*
>
> We are inevitable. We are the culmination of industrial and social wrong. We turn upon the society that created us. We are the successful failures of the age, the scourges of a degraded civilization. We are the creatures of a perverse social selection. We meet force with force (110).

Unlike the teleological force in "The Mexican," however, this evolutionary principle replaces one inhumane and immoral system with another. The cycle of history is a cycle of injustice; revenge without redemption for the assailants or the victim makes the story a statement of profound pessimism. The story fails not because of its pessimism, however, but because of the repetitious and trite letter device and the problem of an upper-class point of view shared with "The Dream of Debs."

A situation similar to the one in "The Minions of Midas" and the same penchant for trick devices appear in "The Enemy of All the World."[250] Emil Gluck is the product of a brutal childhood environment, injustice before the law and, eventually, a misunderstanding of his economic theories at the university where he works. Therefore, he invents a "secret weapon" and gets his revenge by terrorizing the world. The theme that social injustice will produce a monster, found in "Minions" and "The Apostate," is transmogrified, eventually, into a hack-work piece of science fiction based upon a technological gimmick involving electroplating and wireless telegraphy. London has returned in spirit and substance to the pot-boilers with which he gained entrance into the popular magazines at the beginning of his career (see, for example, the discussion of "A Thousand Deaths" in Chapter I above). The violence and revenge motifs, found in the Northland fiction, have become bizarre rather than a careful comment on human experience.

Stories like "The Enemy of All the World" cannot be described as socialistic; they merely comment upon some aspect of social injustice and are not serious attempts at either dramatizing ideology or writing artistic fiction. Generally, these stories fall into the category of popular fiction that Barrett describes as characteristic of magazine fiction at that time: these stories aim "to present a vivid picture of our own times, whether to criticise some existing evil, or to entertain by telling us something of how 'the other half' of the world lives."[251]

"The Strength of the Strong," "A Curious Fragment" and "The Mexican" hardly constitute a canon of excellent socialistic stories; they are too few. Too many critics have confused the sincerity of London's convictions and the justice of his social indignation with artistic achievement. The truth is that socialistic theory did not provide him a basis for sustained artistic achievement nor produce many stories of quality. By 1910, with the exception of "The Mexican" written in 1911, he had exhausted his interest in socialism as a thematic basis for the short story and discontinued writing such stories. "The PEOPLE" may have sustained him emotionally; artistically they did not.

In April of 1907, having already written all but two of the stories which would be collected in *The Strength of the Strong*, the best of his social emphasis volumes, Jack London and his crew left San Francisco aboard his extravagant yacht, the *Snark*, for a South Pacific tour which lasted until November, 1908. During the cruise he visited Hawaii, the Marquesas, the Society Islands, Tahiti, the Samoan Islands, Figi, the New Hebrides and the Solomons. Finally, suffering from tropical diseases, he was forced to recuperate in Sydney, Australia, before his return by tramp steamer to America, by way of Ecuador and Panama, and to the "Beauty Ranch" in the Sanoma Valley. While on the year and a half long voyage, he wrote numerous articles to finance the trip and, at the same time, wrote *Martin Eden*, his last fiction of major importance. Meanwhile, although troubled by disease, an inept crew, and unexpected and mounting expenses, he composed the short stories that were collected into *South Sea Tales* (New York, 1911), set in Melanesia, and *The House of Pride* (New York, 1912), Hawaiian stories, as well as "The Sea Farmer" and "Samuel," collected in *The Strength of the Strong*.[252] Most of the stories do not warrant individual attention; collectively, however, they reveal London's philosophical pessimism turning into artistic cynicism.

Since these stories were written shortly after the last of London's Alaskan stories gathered in *Lost Face*, one is justified in suspecting that because of the exotic setting inhabited by white adventurers and primitive natives who speak strange languages and practice unique customs, that the events and themes of the stories will be similar to the Northland tales. Indeed, the Melanesian stories in *South Sea Tales* repeat the themes and motifs of the Alaskan stories: the quest for individual and racial identity through the masculine exercising of adventure and the implementation of a "code" or "the law"; the emphasis upon action and comradeship; and an interest in suffering and death as the most universal human experiences. These stories, then, deal with themes with which London was intimately and passionately involved; nevertheless, they are second-rate, perhaps because London had begun to be self-imitative. In these stories, he merely duplicates what he had done so well in the Northland stories when he was intensely involved intellectually, emotionally and artistically in exploring his world view.

South Sea Tales continues but does not really explore Subienkow's summation of life in "Lost Face": "Always it had been savagery—brutal, bestial savagery (*LF*, 7)." The Melanesian spirit of place is a Satanic God of disease who brings out the worst rather than the best in man and whose kingdom is "an inferno."[253] Brutality and suffering are the inhumane qualities of life in London's Melanesia, and if there is a collective hero in these *South Sea Tales*, it is the brutal white man who asserts his racial "inevitability" and matches savagery with savagery by exploiting the natives. Race theory found in the Alaskan stories has turned into racism.

One method London had used previously to define his characters was to emphasize race and occupation (prospector, priest, lawman, gambler, wage-slave). The occupation which defines white men in *South Sea Tales* is "black-birding," forcing Melanesian natives to indenture themselves as field-hands to plantation owners.[254] London's South Seas hero is a slave-trader. Captain Malu in "The Terrible Solomons" is typical:

> Captain Malu was a name for niggers to conjure with, and to scare naughty pickaninnies to righteousness, from New Hanover to the New Hebrides. He had farmed savages and savagery, and from fever and hardship, the crack of Sniders and the lash of overseers, had wrested five millions of money . . . (202–03).

Like the Malemute Kid in "The White Silence" he knows his business; but he is without compassion. Malu is quiet, unassuming, experienced and brutal. In the same story, London employs another old device of his for portraying characterization by contrasting Malu with a "deficient," Bertie Arkwright, who was drawn to Melanesia by a false sense of adventure, is "not inevitable" and has "no constitutional understanding of men and life in the rough (201, 199)."[255]

In a similar paean to the white hero, "The Inevitable White Man," men drinking in Charley Roberts's pub toast the whites who "farm the world" and bring the law. They tell a story of Saxtorph on one of his black-birding raids (238). Saxtorph was "inevitable as death" and was notable for two characteristics: his marksmanship with a Snider and his stupidity (240, 241). His skill with a rifle is the basis for the central dramatic incident of the story, a massacre of natives who resist being recruited: " 'I've seen shooting and slaughter,' " an experienced captain remarks, " 'but I never saw anything like that. . . . Bang, bang, bang, went his rifle, and thud, thud, thud, thud, went the niggers to the deck' (249)." His stupidity explains Saxtorph's racial success: one of the characters remarks, " ' . . . somehow it doesn't seem necessary, after all, to understand the niggers . . . In direct proportion to the white man's stupidity is his success in farming the world' (238)." In both "The Terrible Solomons" and "The Inevitable White Man" the tragedy of racial conflict found in Alaskan stories, particularly those in *The God of His Fathers* and *Children of the Frost*, is absent, replaced by callousness, stupidity and mindlessness.

Rather than probing the tragic implications of South Seas dehumanization, London detaches himself by employing a comic tone. The central incidents of "The Terrible Solomons," for example, are the practical jokes played upon Bertie Arkwright by Captain Malu and other members of the ship's crew. He is tricked into drinking whiskey for tea, into believing that the native cook has poisoned him, into believing that the others lit a stick of dynamite and attached it to one of the natives, and, finally, into believing that the ship is being besieged by savages. Likewise, the tone of "The Inevitable White Man" is inappropriately light for its grotesque subject matter of natives dropping at Saxtorph's rifle shot.

When the comic tone is omitted from a story, a mechanical sadism replaces it as the characters survive by becoming one with the savage environment. In " 'Yah! Yah! Yah!' " a native explains the reason for his passive acceptance of white tyranny by recounting how his village of twenty-five thousand was reduced to three thousand when a mate, who mockingly screamed "Yah! Yah! Yah!" led a dynamiting raid upon the village which was followed by famine and disease. This taught the narrator and other blacks that, "it was very wrong to harm a white man (145)." This is a return to the motif of "the law," now sadistic, as London spends fifteen pages cataloguing the horrors of the genocidal raid. Similarly, "Mauki" portrays sadistic persecution of the native Mauki by Max Brunster, "a degenerate brute," and Mauki's equally sadistic revenge by flaying his antagonist alive, reducing him to a "hideous, skinless thing" (116). Obviously, perverse sensationalism of the stag-magazine variety had replaced London's earlier interest in ordeal and primitivism as elements in a ritual of self-definition. An atavistic conflict between a "primitive savage" and "a degenerate brute" takes men to the nadir of human experience but does not restore them to new values. The tropical zeitgeist is demented.

One story, "The Seed of McCoy," is an exception to the others in the *South Sea Tales* and contradicts their import. If the others repeat the necessity of a tyrannical control over men to advance the white race, "The Seed of McCoy" is an affirmation that good can come of evil, that democracy can grow from an original tyranny and anarchy, and that tenderness, compassion and intelligence can guide men to safety.

McCoy, the grandson of the *Bounty* mutineer and now the democratic governor of Pitcairn Island, offers to guide the *Pyrenees* with her cargo of burning wheat to safety. The ship drifts upon unchartered seas until McCoy directs the ship and crew to the security of a Pacific atoll just as the ship bursts into flames.

London shapes McCoy into a Christ figure who redeems the men aboard the *Pyrenees* whose smoldering fire in the hold is "Hell herself . . . right down there under your feet (268)." The crew is ready to rebel despite the stern, justly administered marine law; but McCoy's spiritual power calms them:

> He spoke to the sailors, and at the first sound of his dovelike, cooing voice they paused to hear. He extended to them his own ineffable serenity and peace . . . McCoy spoke simply; but it was not what he spoke. It was his personality that spoke more eloquently than any word he could utter. It was an alchemy of soul occultly subtle and profoundly deep—a mysterious emanation of the spirit, seductive, sweetly humble, and terribly imperious. It was illumination in the dark crypts of their souls, a compulsion of purity and gentleness vastly greater than that which resided in the shining, death-spitting revolvers of the officers (306–07).

There is a moral, spiritual power beyond force, and the common sailors respond to it, McCoy explains, because " 'Their hearts are good' (308)." This power effects ruler as well as subject: "McCoy's presence was a rebuke to the blasphemies that stirred in his [Captain Davenport's] brain . . . and now he found himself unable to curse in the presence of this old man with the feminine brown eyes and the voice of a dove (313–14)." If he were in another story, Captain Davenport who "was an autocrat of the sea, fearing no man," would have been the hero; but in this, "simplicity" and "gentleness" save (313).

The radical difference in theme between "The Seed of McCoy" and the others in *South Seas Tales* can be accounted for by associating this story with London's socialism. Race theory and racism are absent from "The Seeds of McCoy" and so is the diseased jungle environment. Instead, London is preoccupied with the regeneration of society. According to his dialectical view of history, a corrupt society would consume itself, Phoenix-like, catastrophically, and be reborn purified. McCoy, himself, emerges from an "iniquitous ancestry" since he is "the seed of McCoy," one of the most despicable of the *Bounty* mutineers. His ancestor, with the others, murdered, raped and eventually destroyed the native and white cultures. Finally, after "there was nobody left to kill," the mutineer destroyed himself (310–12). From the first McCoy "who was a power for evil in the early days of blood and lust and violent death" when "God had hidden His face," had sprung the Christ-like McCoy who saves the *Pyrenees* (312–14). Parallel to this sub-plot recounted by McCoy is the situation aboard the *Pyrenees*. The sailors attempt mutiny as the center of their world burns, but a new leader emerges amidst the flames and revitalizes their latent goodness. The men intuitively place their faith in him, just as London places his faith in an ideal social order growing out of evil.

The House of Pride, the other collection of short stories written during the *Snark* voyage, uses civilized Hawaii as its setting and, like "The Seed of McCoy," is more concerned with social issues than with the demonic primitivism of the other stories in *South Sea Tales*. Half the stories ("Koolau the Leper," "Good-by Jack," and "The Sheriff of Kona") comment upon the horrors of leprosy and the other half ("Aloha Oe," "Chun Ah Chun," and "The House of Pride") upon racial and colonial injustice. As *South Sea Tales* pursues the horrors explored in the Klondike stories, *The House of Pride* pursues but does not explore the social insights of stories like those in *The Strength of the Strong* and *When God Laughs*.

Of the stories in *The House of Pride*, only "Koolau the Leper" escapes the liabilities of sentimentality and rises above mere social comment. Although it is a good story, it is so similar to the better Alaskan fiction in both theme and technique, for example, "The League of Old Men," that it proves that London at his best was being self-derivative. Koolau, horribly deformed by leprosy, refuses to be deported to Molokai, the leper colony, preferring a futile rebellion against civilized law enforced by white men. He wages a solitary war as he retreats into the volcanic wilds in order to preserve his freedom: " 'I have lived free, and I shall die free' (86)." But as does Imber in "The League of Old Men," Koolau recognizes the ultimate futility of overcoming the white man:

He was convinced of the hopelessness of his struggle. There was no
gain saying that terrible will of the *haoles* [white men] (84).

He salvages his individual dignity but dies according to "the
law" enforced by whites. London has returned to the ironic
theme of a good man of inferior race destined to submit to the
natural law of white supremacy.

In general, then, *South Sea Tales* and *The House of Pride*
repeat themes and motifs London had explored earlier but, in
comparison, are artistically inferior. Never a consummate crafts-
man, London was careless in his *Snark* volumes. In a letter
puffing his stories, written to an editor in 1908 while London
was aboard the *Snark*, he wrote: "We expect lots of action, and
my strong point as a writer is that I am a writer of action—see
all my short stories, for instance."[256] Not only was London
repeating themes, but the emphasis upon action, realizing that it
was what helped sell other stories, leads him to an unnecessary
multiplication of incident, often repetitious, and an undue
emphasis upon the bizarre. "Chun Ah Chun" in *The House of
Pride*, for example, as did "Mauki" in *South Sea Tales*, repeats
monotonously the protagonist's escapes from brutal masters only
to be caught in similar situations. Too many characters litter the
pages of wordy stories and, sometimes, are unprepared for. In
"Mauki" Max Bunster who is second in importance to Mauki is
introduced half way through the story. Style, too, deteriorates
in these stories. The evocative language of the Indians that
provided stylistic strength to the Alaskan stories is replaced by
the "beche-de-mer" pidgin English of the South Pacific. How
damaging this could be can be seen in the following passage
from " 'Yah! Yah! Yah!' " in which a native tells of his
encounter with a black-birding expedition:

> "One time, me young fella too much, one big fella ship he stop
> outside. Wind he no blow. Plenty fella kanaka we get'm canoe, plenty
> fella canoe, we go catch 'm that fella ship. My word—we catch 'm big
> fella fight. Two, three white men shoot like hell. We no fright. We
> come alongside, we go up side, plenty fella, maybe fifty-ten (five hun-
> dred). One fella white Mary (woman) belong that fella ship (131)."

Only two stories written at this time in London's life have escaped critical oblivion; and they were collected in *The Strength of the Strong* rather than in either *South Sea Tales* or *The House of Pride*: "The Sea Farmer" and "Samuel." London was attached to these stories and insisted that they be published as companion pieces.[257] Written on his trip home, as he recovered from tropical illnesses, they show two ways one can cope with the distress of London's deepening pessimism. In "The Sea Farmer," he makes a positive figures out of Captain MacElrath, the "sea farmer" who "lacked imagination" and never liked the sea (183). The Captain's dream, realized by the end of the story, is to retreat into domestic bliss on a farm, an impulse that *The Little Lady of the Big House* (New York, 1916) proves attracted London himself. Somehow, it is best never to hear the "siren song" of "Romance" nor the shout of "Adventure" (183). "Samuel" dramatizes the other side of the coin. Instead of retreating in a benign way as Captain MacElrath had, Margaret Henan defiantly names child after child "Samuel" even though each one dies horribly. Asked why she insists on naming each son Samuel, she simply responds, "I *like* Samuel," leaving the narrator "puzzling over the why of like" (256–257). Mindless retreat and mindless defiance are at the poles of human responses to mind-numbing existence.

"The Sea Farmer" and "Samuel" have a measure of seriousness to them which is lacking in most of the stories in *South Sea Tales* and *The House of Pride* written on the *Snark* voyage. Most of them show without doubt that Jack London was using his pen merely to fill his coffers and that life without significance was not a philosophical position that could sponsor continually good fiction. In fact, most of the other stories written in this five year period from 1906 to 1911 are potboilers.

From the beginning of his career, London felt no revulsion at publishing work which did not meet his own literary standards. As early as 1899, he wrote to Cloudesley Johns:

Say, I'm having lots of luck with the *Companion*, sending them my

old, almost-ready-to-be-retired stuff. Have you ever tried them? They
pay good and promptly. Though such work won't live it at least
brings the ready cash.[258]

The month before, he wrote to his friend that the *Owl* had paid
$1.50 for "The Handsome Cabin Boy"; the money covered
expenses for stamps and the publication "gave promise of release
from at least one of my early nightmares."[259] "I have succeeded
in disposing of quite a lot of rubbish ... by sending it to the
way down publications," he explained to Johns.[260] From 1899
to 1906, he wrote pot-boilers so that he would have enough
money to meet his expenses and to permit him time to devote
himself to writing better fiction. During the winter of 1902, for
example, while he worked on the fine stories in *Children of the
Frost* and on the *Call of the Wild*, he wrote to Johns, "Lord,
what [a] stack of hack I'm turning out ... I wonder if I'll ever
get clear of debt."[261] From 1906 until 1911, while he wrote
socialist stories and those in the *Snark* volumes, the situation
changed a little. Instead of $1.50 a story, he received $1000
each; instead of merely burying his pot-boilers in "the way
down publications," he resurrected them and collected them
into volumes; and instead of writing for money in order to
permit himself the time to write better fiction, he wrote for the
money alone.

In "Brown Wolf," published in 1906, whose setting is Glen
Ellen, Sonoma Valley, California, on a ranch like the one
London acquired in 1905, the poet Walt Irvine, a protagonist
who is obviously like London himself, says to his wife:

"Mine is no futility of genius that can't sell gems to the magazines
... I am no attic singer, no ball-room warbler. And why? Because I
am practical. Mine is no squalor of song that cannot transmute itself,
with proper exchange value, into a flower-crowned cottage, a sweet
mountain-meadow, a grove of redwoods, an orchard of thirty-seven
trees, one long row of blackberries and two short rows of straw-
berries, to say nothing of a quarter of a mile of gurgling brook. I am
a beauty-merchant, a trader in song, and I pursue utility."[262]

And from 1906 until 1911 London himself was busy changing words into dollars and dollars into "Beauty Ranch," the ill-fated "Wolf House" and the *Snark*. Although he had written pot-boilers before, 1906–1911 were years in which pot-boilers mush-roomed. During these years he published *Moon-Face* (1906) and wrote the stories collected in *When God Laughs* (1911), *The Night Born* (1913) and *The Turtles of Tasman* (1916), four volumes of relatively inconsequential fiction.

The first of these collections, *Moon-Face*, gathers some of the hack work from the "stack" that he had on hand while writing *Children of the Frost* stories and *The Call of the Wild*. Since the subsequent collections of pot-boilers include the same kinds of stories in forms, themes, motifs, techniques and subject matter, an analysis of this volume precludes the necessity of more than a brief mention of the others.

The first two stories, "Moon-Face" and "The Leopard Man's Story," are almost identical in form, theme and technique. Both are first person narratives about patient and elaborate revenge told by perverse protagonists and conclude with surprise endings. In "Moon-Face," the narrator is unexplainedly annoyed by John Claverhouse's (Moon-Face's) laugh and devises a scheme to murder him. He secretly trains Moon-Face's dog to retrieve, knowing that Claverhouse uses dynamite to fish illegally. Then he watches Moon-Face throw a stick of "giant" into a trout pool, the dog retrieve it and the explosion, after which "there was naught to be seen but a big hole in the ground (13)." In "The Leopard Man's Story," a circus leopard trainer tells a tale in which DeVille, a jealous French juggler, kills Wallace, a lion tamer, for looking romantically at his willing wife. DeVille, it is revealed in the last sentence of the story, had sprinkled snuff upon Wallace's back so that when he thrust his head into the lion's mouth during the finale of his performance, the lion sneezed and " 'the jaws came together, *crunch*, just like that' (24)."

In some ways, these two stories are not toally unlike London's better fiction. Violent death, irrationality, revenge and the unusual were at the core of his Alaskan tales. But the

philosophical, symbolic implications have disappeared, leaving
the merely sensational. From a philosophical emphasis upon a
potentially irrational universe, symbolized by the white barrens
of the Alaskan landscape, London shifts his emphasis and portrays irrational man's abnormal psychology. In both these
stories, there is no "spirit of place" to complement human
psychology, not even the diseased South Seas environment. He
moves from the philosophy of "the horror" to the psychology
of the horrible.

London, too, was learning to use the first person narrative in
his better fiction, particularly in his stories which had a tale
within a frame. This would seem to discount the first person
narrator as a distinguishing mark of his pot-boilers. But in the
Alaskan stories, he used it to portray "extraordinary, heroic . . .
action," which Austin Wright discovered as a characteristic
situation in American short stories before the nineteen
twenties.[263] And in the pot-boilers, London uses this narrative
device for different ends, which Wright also found characteristic
of the period—to describe "that kind of private action that
involves a choice extraordinary for the extreme depth of
perversion of values that it reveals."[264]

Frederick Wedmore, writing at the end of the nineteenth
century, adds that the first person narrative device was more
appropriate for "the expression of humour than to the realization of tragedy."[265] Both "Moon-Face" and "The Leopard Man's
Story" affect a light tone while portraying perverse actions.
Grim humor is characteristic of the pot-boilers; and London is
not successful as a comic. Margaret Pope perceived that
London's tragic and ironic stories are more important than his
humorous and mentions that, "he was not a wit and his sense of
humor was the simple one of a child."[266] Slapstick humor,
especially the practical joke, is the comic level of some South
Seas tales ("The Terrible Solomons," for example) and even
some Alaskan stories ("The Passing of Marcus O'Brien" in *Lost
Face*, for example). Often the practical jokes, like the killing one
at the end of "The Leopard Man's Story," are too cruel to be
entertaining. The surprise ending, itself, which London uses as

an agent for his humor is rarely successful in his fiction and characteristic of his pot-boilers.[267]

"The Shadow and the Flash," another story in *Moon-Face*, uses a technological trick as the key to the unusual action. The utilization of technological trickery, like the use of first person narrative to depict the perverse, a comic tone, the surprise ending and the absence of a sense of geographical place, helps to identify this as a London pot-boiler. In "The Shadow and the Flash" Paul Tichlorne and Lloyd Inwood are "as like as two peas" but extremely competitive rivals as children, as college students and as suitors. Brilliant chemists, they each invent a process which makes humans invisible. Each process, however, has a flaw: Paul's makes humans invisible except for a flashing light and Lloyd's except for a shadow. At the climax of the story Lloyd, the shadow, and Paul, the flash, meet on a tennis court, fall into combat and kill one another. Perhaps this is one of London's early stories like "The Rejuvenation of Major Rathbone" and "A Thousand Deaths" that continued on the rounds to publishers until it was finally accepted.[268] Certainly, it capitalizes on the same kind of pseudo-scientific, fantastical device. Sometimes the technological instrument is not as fantastic; nevertheless, it is used to provoke the reading public's interest by reinforcing their interest in the new achievements of applied science. For example, in "The Siege of the 'Lancashire Queen' " (*Tales of the Fish Patrol*) a turbine driven speedboat allows the hero to foil the adversary, and in "Winged-Blackmail" (*The Night-Born*), written in 1910, an airplane is employed to capture a blackmailer by following the carrier pigeon that had brought the threatening letters. In any case, Jack London, who was always fascinated by scientific theory, substitutes technology in his pot-boilers for the more profound scientific-philosophical assumptions behind his important fiction.

In "Planchette," the last story in *Moon-Face*, London moves from technological fantasy to the frankly occult, thereby taking advantage of reader interest in psychic phenomena. The characters, including Chris Dunbar and Lute Story, who are the central characters and can not marry because of some unrevealed guilt experienced by Chris, gather around a medium, Mrs. Grantly, and each in turn experiences automatic writing. Chris's message from Lute's deceased father warns him that the spirit will murder him and has already made two attempts. Twice in the story, horses had thrown Chris and, finally, at the conclusion of the tale, horse and rider plunge down a mountainside to their deaths. This story and similar ones like "The Eternity of Forms" and "The Red One" are the "weird stories" that Barrett noted were highly marketable in turn of the century magazines.[269] In relation to London's other stories, they are a variant of his interest in the material and ideal relationship, the "actual" and the "ideal." In "The Eternity of Forms," for instances, the conflict is between an empiricist and his brother, a philosophical idealist, whom he had murdered.

"Planchette," too, is evidence of London's early, but undigested, interest in psychology. Chris is aware that there are theories of the subconscious but admits little knowledge of them since "psychology is so young a science (258)." Later, London would pursue this interest to greater artistic advantage, but he was not prepared to do so in 1906.[270] More importantly, "Planchette" is like some other London pot-boilers because it is an inconclusive attempt to solve some of his own personal problems or to justify his questionable actions. "Planchette" was written just after London had bought his Glen Ellen Ranch as a home for Charmian, his second wife. The story is set at the ranch, one of Chris's horses, "Washoe-ban," has the same name as one of London's, Lute is athletic as was Charmian, and the medium is short and dark as was London's mother who maintained a life-long interest in spiritualism. Even without explaining the mysterious guilt (which may be London's own) that separates the lovers and brings disaster, it is clear that London used his personal problems as the basis for this story. Similarly, in the anti-Semitic "Bunches of Knuckles" (*The Night-Born*) which was written later, he attempted to whitewash a barroom brawl which had resulted in a law suit against him. In other stories he touched upon other personal problems or pet project: alcoholism in "Created He Them" (*When God Laughs*);

misogamy in "The End of the Story" (*Turtles of Tasman*); environmental determinism as the basis for anti-social behavior in "To Kill a Man" (*The Night-Born*); and prison reform in "The Hobo and the Fairy" (*The Turtles of Tasman*). All of these depend upon pathos to move the audience.

Add these stories to the others mentioned above that had changed from socialism to casual social comment and those which moved from race theory to racism, and one has a sense of the worst London fiction. Perhaps one can best describe his pot-boilers by summarizing the alterations in these stories of his more serious themes, modes and techniques. The best had a strong sense of cosmic and environmental place, the worst, little of this; he shifts from tragedy and irony to comedy and sentimentality; from self-defining ordeal to irrational cruelty; from myth to propaganda; from science to technology; from heroics to histrionics; from universal problems to personal grievances; from an attack on bourgeois morality to a reinforcement of reader prejudices and pseudo-intellectual fads; and from fairly economical and dramatic techniques he returns to the use of multiple incidents and characters, which he had learned to avoid in his apprenticeship.

By 1910 London's artistic impulses and available materials had become so impoverished that he was reduced to buying plot ideas from Sinclair Lewis and culling others from George Sterling.[271] Before retiring for five years (1911–1916) from short story writing, however, London produced two more collections of pot-boilers: *Smoke Bellew* and *A Son of the Sun*, the first serialized in *Cosmopolitan Magazine* and the second in *Saturday Evening Post*. In these London returned to the subject matter and themes that had aroused reader interest in his fiction originally and which had been financially successful for him. They are unabashed self-imitations. Both collections do, however, generate the "spirit of the place" that infused his best fiction, making them better than his other pot-boilers.

In *John Barleycorn* London recalls the time after his return from the *Snark* voyage when he settled on his ranch and wrote *Smoke Bellew*, a series of connected stories about Smoke Bellew's experiences in the Klondike:

...I turned out work that was healthful, and wholesome, and sincere. It was never pessimistic. The way to life I had learned in my long sickness. I knew the illusions were right, and I exalted the illusions. O, I still turn out the same sort of work, stuff that is clean, alive, optimistic, and that makes toward life. And I am always assured by the critics of my super-abundant and abounding vitality, and of how thoroughly I am deluded by these very illusions I exploit (276–77).

In short, Smoke Bellew emerges as a continuation of the rational Malemute Kid characterization which exalted the "life-giving" "secondary truths" and the redemptive quality of masculine adventure. Smoke Bellew is a high spirited, sentimental celebration of the vigorous life in which physical and emotional suffering is minimized and the masculine code of comradeship and emotional well-being is dramatized.

The collection, read as a unit, is remarkably similar to Jack London's first novel, A Daughter of the Snows, in setting, themes, and characters. In each, a young tenderfoot comes to the Klondike from a dilettante's life in San Francisco but (like Stanley Prince in the Malemute Kid series, too) has the potential for "learning the ropes," finds masculine comradeship through adventure and eventually proves himself a worthy husband for one of London's "Mate-women." Even the incidents are almost identical. "The Race for Number Three," for example, depicts a contest to stake a claim and return to record it at the assay office, a contest that occurs in A Daughter of the Snows. Both describe with similar language the jam of dogs, sleds and men at the beginning of the race, the techniques of placing the stakes ("staking the claim"), and the brutal competition and the exhausting race back. In both the rewards of the competition are the same: honor among men, wealth, and the love of the ideal woman.[272]

Other stories in Smoke Bellew prove that London was refurbishing materials he had used before in Alaskan stories. "The Meat," for example, is a continuation of the opening of "In a Far Country." Smoke Bellew and his companion in this and other stories, Shorty, are like Sloper and Bettles who find themselves on the trail with two "incompetents" or "deficients," Stanley Sprague and Adolph Stine who are like Cuthfert and Weatherbee. The Northland code idealizing manly comradeship, sacrifice and "true adventure" is contrasted with self-indulgence, selfishness and false romance—a familiar theme. The difference is that "In a Far Country" confronts "the horror" while "The Meat" extols human triumph. In addition, "A Flutter in Eggs" uses the situation of speculation in egg prices that is the basis for the action in "One Thousand Dozen" (*The Faith of Men*) and "Wonder of Woman" the situation of "Grit of Women" (*The God of His Fathers*). In other stories in *Smoke Bellew* like "The Town-Site of Tra-Lee" and "The Mistake of Creation," Smoke Bellew is a reincarnated Malemute Kid in his roles as master of revels, trickster and righter of wrongs, roles London presented when he was affirming life-giving values.[273]

The last story in this collection, "Wonder of Woman," is a recasting of "Grit of Women," and proves that London even while imitating himself could recapture the power and beauty of his earlier, mythic Alaskan tales. Charmian London records that Jack London "always referred to *Smoke Bellew* as 'hack work,' strictly excluding the last story . . . which he strove to make one of his best.[274] In it Smoke Bellew travels into the unchartered Northland and meets an Indian girl, Labiskwee, who helps him escape from the wasteland. During the ordeal of the escape, both Bellew and Labiskwee approach madness and death as they are caught in an unusual snow storm, called "the white death"; the image of the two figures in the storm is a tableau suggesting at once death and the dazzling light of redemption:

> A pervasive flashing of light from all about them drew Smoke's eyes upward to the many suns. They were shimmering and veiling. The air was filled with microscopic fire-glints (370-71).

They are choked by "dusts of snow wind-driven into sky-scarfs of shimmering silken light (375)." At the climax of their ordeal, Smoke, snow-blinded, finds that Labiskwee, like Pessuk in "Grit of Women," has sacrificed her life for him by hoarding bits of food from her starvation diet so that he might live. By archetypally traveling into the unchartered land and undergoing the ordeals of the trail, Bellew had learned the meaning of love, an illumination that prepares him to return to Dawson and marry the ideal woman.

Other stories in *Smoke Bellew* had repeated the rollicking good humor of the earlier Malemute Kid stories and some in *Smoke Bellew* are not short stories in the usual sense at all since they are inserted merely to establish the background for following stories,[275] but "Wonder of Woman" is characteristic of London's best. The comic tone disappears, the landscape, suggesting with brilliant ambiguity both tragedy and redemption, is evoked mythically as the protagonist descends into the unknown to discover truths that will alter his life. Repetition of past motifs, themes and characterizations did not mean, necessarily, that a story would be inferior.

No story in *A Son of the Sun* equals "Wonder of Women." In essence the volume is another *South Sea Tales* upon which has been superimposed the characterization of David Grief, the "son of the sun." The fundamental situation is absurd: it is as if the Malemute Kid or Smoke Bellew had gone to the diseased tropics and had maintained their masculine bravado.

David Grief is the Blond Hero, the "blue-eyed, golden-tinted, superior man ... questing romance and adventure along the sun-washed path of the tropics" who plays "the game, not for the gold, but for the game's sake (42, 28, 29)." He is the "good guy" who establishes the moral norm, a return to the rational hero who defeats horse opera villainy. Melodrama is the mode. The melodramatic morality and superficiality of characterization can be sensed from the following passage in which one culprit from "A Son of the Sun" describes David Grief to another as the inevitable power of moral right:

> "I tell you only a straight man can buck a straight man like him, and the man's never hit the Solomons that could do it. Men like you and me can't buck him. We're too rotten, too rotten all the way through (10)."

Armed with moral righteousness, Grief becomes, in this series, a private detective who rights wrongs ("A Son of the Sun," "The Devils of Fuatino," "A Little Account with Swithin Hall") or is the moral force who redeems men to their lost sense of the masculine code of honor ("The Proud Goat of Aloysius Pankburn" and "A Goboto Night"). And in "The Jokers of New Gibbon," a story portraying a series of sadistic practical jokes as in "The Terrible Solomons," Grief's role is gratuitious—he is included merely because the series demands that he be.

The composition of the stories in *Smoke Bellew* and *A Son of the Sun* in 1911 marks the end of London's five-year period of decline as a writer of short stories. At this time he was ready to admit a loss of interest in the genre, an interest that he had maintained for the past few years merely because it was profitable. On September 7, 1912, at the time when *Smoke Bellew* and *A Son of the Sun* were in serial publication, he wrote a letter to a staff member of the Century Company revealing his distaste for short story writing and that his only motive for writing stories was money:

> I am trying to avoid writing any more short stories than I can help. ... I am running an expensive ranch ... for months at a time, there are fifty men on the payroll. Then is the time when I rush in and write short stories for $1000 per story for the magazines. Which is the very thing I am trying to get away from. I don't want to write short stories.[276]

Shortly afterwards, his financial problem was solved when he signed a ten-year contract with *Cosmopolitan* to produce a novel a year.[277] A letter written four years later, in 1916, verifies that Jack London had stopped writing short stories after the Smoke Bellew and David Grief series:

> Jumping into the question of short stories: You know that I have written but one short story in the past four years.[278] You know, from our long talk, how I am situated on short stories, and how I hate to tackle any right now ... I don't mean this as an ultimatum; I only mean it to show you how hopelessly prejudiced I am under all circumstances, against tackling short stories at the present time.[279]

Chapter VI

REBIRTH: 1916

Later in that March, 1916, letter to Edgar J. Sisson, despite London's protestations that he did not want to begin writing short stories after his five-year rest from them, he mentions that he had, indeed, been giving thought to writing more:

> I am cudgeling my head now over a possible bunch of short stories, but I must tell you in advance that this one prospect will not consist of related short stories. Each story is a story by itself—if I can see my way to framing up a bunch of these stories. On the matter of short-story writing you and I pull at cross-purposes. This can be better stated as follows: You demand for your purposes that novels should be broken up in the writing into short story units. You demand that short stories be so related that the sum of a collection of short stories constitutes a novel. That is to say, artistically you are playing hell both with the short stories and the novels.[280]

It is clear from the letter that he refused to consider collections of stories like the Smoke Bellew and David Grief series that required an author to violate the demands of the genre, forcing him to provide an inorganic relationship between the stories. By now, anyone familiar with London's writing career should suspect that his resurgent interest in the genre, especially when combined with a desire to make the stories artistic, is a product of an interest in ideas and the hope that they will afford some basis for affirming life. Even though science had unsettled idealistic concepts of man, his temperament insisted that affirmations of the human condition, too, have a scientifically

151

justifiable rationale. Early in his career, with the aid of Kipling's short story forms and techniques, he had used his enthusiastic reading of Darwin, Haeckel, and Spencer to evoke "the stinging things of the spirit" in his famous Alaskan stories. A few years later he readjusted his vision to emphasize a life-giving, "scientific" Marxism to dramatize the "strong truths" about the energy of "the people" in his socialist stories. In both cases he was motivated by a quest for a unifying concept of reality that would have scientific validity. It is not generally recognized, however, that in the last year of his life Jack London wrote a group of stories whose scientific authority derived from his reading of psychology, especially of Carl Jung's *Psychology of the Unconscious* in Beatrice M. Hinkle's 1916 edition.[281]

In 1916 he was once again captivated by theoreticians who proffered him a scientifically defensible rationale for subscribing to humanly sustaining values as he flirted dangerously with nihilism. These last stories are a record of the recurrent philosophical-psychological pattern in his early life and fiction—a movement from an excited sense that revelation is at hand to a bitter and enervating disillusionment.

As early as 1906 in "Planchette" London reveals his interest in psychology. Chris Dunbar, the London surrogate in the story, will not explain unusual events by crediting spiritualism and prefers to explain them psychologically, although the discipline of psychology is too new to do more than promise eventual explanation:

> "We are playing with the subjective forces of our own being, with phenomena which science has not yet explained, that is all. Psychology is so young a science. The subconscious mind has just been discovered, one might say. It is all mystery as yet; the laws of it are yet to be formulated (*MF*, 257–58)."[282]

London, himself, excitedly investigated the new psychological theories that were sparking American interest in the first two decades of the twentieth century. He hoped to learn the "laws" of "the subconscious mind" that were being formulated. From 1914 to 1916, Richard O'Connor writes, London "began delving into the new science—or cause, as it soon became—of exploring the psyche. He devoured the works of Freud, Prince and Jung, fascinated by what he could grasp of their claims for psychoanalysis."[283] While Jack psychoanalyzed Charmian and himself, O'Connor claims, there was a "desperate undercurrent in Jack's probings" as he tried "at the last moment to make the transition from Marxist to Freudian and thereby save himself, like a man sliding down the face of a cliff and grabbing at rocks and bushes to save his fall."[284] Charmian London verifies O'Connor's statements, and she suggests that the summer of 1916 climaxed Jack's intensive reading and discussion when he exclaimed, " 'Mate Woman, I tell you I am standing on the edge of a world so new, so terrible, so wonderful, that I am almost afraid to look over into it.' "[285]

This dramatic statement, recalling the terror that drove him from San Francisco, the wonder that called him to the Klondike and the mixture of despair and joy that infused his Northland stories, was made as London began writing the last of his short stories, published posthumously in *The Red One* (1918) and *On the Makaloa Mat* (1919). "Like Argus of the Ancient Times," in *The Red One*, and six of the seven stories in *On the Makaloa Mat* are without question a product of his interest in psychology.[286]

Although London's biographers mention that he had read the works of Morton Prince, Sigmund Freud and Carl Jung, it is not known what specific books and articles he read, with the exception of Jung's *Psychology of the Unconscious*. Morton Prince's work, even his *The Unconscious* (1913), would have little relevance to London's last stories since this psychologist was concerned primarily with abnormal psychology, an interest that does not appear in London's final stories. Sigmund Freud is of more consequence since London specifically alludes to his ideas in one *On the Makaloa Mat* story, "The Kanaka Surf." Exactly where London encountered Freud's ideas it is impossible to know; however, from 1909 to 1916 they were becoming known to the American public and London would have been aware of them. In 1909 Freud, with other famous psychologists, had participated in a psychological conference sponsored by Clark University that provoked discussion and controversy in American journals and popular magazines. By 1915, Henry F. May writes, "the [Freudian] movement itself was militant and articulate, though small; Freud's major works had been translated and widely reviewed; and the outlines of his theories were discussed in the popular press."[287] Charmian London records, however, that Jack read "most of all, Jung"; and a careful reading of London's stories verifies that *Psychology of the Unconscious*, of all the psychological works available to him, made the most profound impression upon the man and his works.[288] The psychological principles contained in it are uncannily parallel with concerns, even specific ideas, that had preoccupied London's mind and emotions throughout his life and had appeared in his fiction. The stories written in 1916 are so markedly influenced by this volume that it makes his reading of other psychologists irrelevant or only of marginal interest.[289]

Beatrice M. Hinkle's introduction to *Psychology of the Unconscious* compares and contrasts Freud's and Jung's concepts of dreams, sexuality, the libido and the Oedipus complex and emphasizes those ideas which the two psychologists shared. London's stories prove that Jack had not only read this introduction; he read the entire volume with care.

Carl Jung's first chapter, "Concerning Two Kinds of Thinking," contrasts "directed thinking" or logical and scientific thinking with "dream or phantasy thinking":

> The first, working for communication with speech elements, is troublesome and exhausting; the latter, on the contrary, goes on without trouble, working spontaneously ... The first creates innovations, adaptions, imitates reality and seeks to act upon it. The latter, on the contrary, turns away from reality, sets free subjective wishes ... (p. 22).

London had been fascinated by a similar contrast in his most significant fiction. Early in his efforts, the writer had hoped to combine actuality and ideals, realism and romance, rational and subjective responses to life. As he felt the growing fragmentation induced by rationality, he placed more emphasis upon subjective responses and the dream-like in his fiction.[290] Jung, too, was compelled to explain non-rational thought; and the rest of *Psychology of the Unconscious* defines and explores "dream or phantasy thinking" or the "mythic."

While language, the word, represents logical, scientific thought, dream symbols which well up discontinuously from man's unconscious, when properly understood, are actually a unified expression of a man's innermost fears and desires (xix–xx). Furthermore, what a dream is for the individual, myth (including folk and fairy tales) is for groups of people at their most primitive level. This last point did not originate with Jung, however; in fact, London himself was aware of it as early as 1906. As a product of his interest in race, primitives, and atavism, London had learned that dreams were "racial memories" and made that knowledge the premise of *Before Adam*, which was published early in 1907.[291] Considering London's early interest in the subject, he must have been excited as he read the evidence Jung had marshalled for his myth theory, especially when the psychologist exhibited a passage from Nietzsche in support:

> In our sleep and in our dreams we pass through the whole thought of earlier humanity ... In the dream this atavistic relic of humanity manifests its existence within us.[292]

In addition, Jung demonstrated that the major psychologists agreed with Nietzsche's assessment. Freud had written that "it is probable that the myths correspond to the distorted residue of phantasies of whole nations, the secularized dreams of young humanity"; Abraham that "the myth is a fragment of the infantile soul-life of the people"; and Rank and Riklin that myths and fables are "mass dreams."[293] That these myths represent the most elemental, unconscious wishes and fears (an "indestructible optimism" combined with an "accumulation of anxiety")[294] must have appealed to London, also, since joy and terror had always struggled with one another in his work either to complement one another or for final control. Recall, for example, in *John Barleycorn*, the romantic whisper that London heard while drowning in San Francisco Bay or the ambiguous ending of "The White Silence" that combines the Malemute Kid's pride in his ability to participate in adventure with his fear of annihilation. The representation and evocation of strong emotions, intense optimism or pessimism and an enthusiasm for felt life rather than abstracted experience had been the object of and power behind the composition of his best stories.

Just how indebted London was to Jung's study can be seen in the last Alaskan story Jack wrote, "Like Argus of the Ancient Times," which Charmian London incorrectly identifies as a Freudian story.[295] At first, the reader notices little difference between this story and London's early Klondike stories or those in the beginning of *Smoke Bellew*. Old Tarwater, who lives near San Francisco, is called irresistibly to the Klondike gold rush. On the way north, he meets and journeys with four men who appear in other London stories: a carpenter, a miner, a sailor and a businessman who band together for mutual aid. Racing against the time when the winter freeze would stop them, they endure the hardships of Chilcoot Pass, Lake Linderman, White Horse Rapids, and other landmarks which London remembered so vividly from his own experiences. Finally they are forced to make camp for the winter inside the Arctic Circle where Tarwater will face death and restore his spirit. So far, the story, like many of London's others, is largely autobiographical.[296]

But autobiographical materials are merely a backdrop for Jungian fantasy; or, as Franklin Walker has it, London turns from "interpreter of things which are" to "ideas about racial memories he had picked up from Jung's *Psychology of the Unconscious*."[297] According to Jung, a wandering hero, representing "ever-restless desire," undertakes a perilous "night journey" into a mysterious land, representing a subconscious secret, in search of the "treasure difficult to attain" (*P*, pp. 185–233). Late in the journey the sun-hero wanderer faces death, and this confrontation is, ironically, "the highest summit of life" (*P*, p. 320).[298] Finally, the hero returns to water (the womb) and/or emerges in the east reborn. Analogously in "Argus," Tarwater, the seventy-year-old protagonist who is also called "Old Hero" and "Father Christmas," is driven by gold "fever" to search for treasure and becomes lost in a heavy Arctic snowfall during the long night of winter (*R*, 135, 107). As Tarwater comes close to death and drifts between consciousness and unconsciousness, London describes the state of his character's awareness in Jungian terminology:

> more and more time he spent in his torpor, unaware of what was day-dream and what was sleep-dream in the content of his unconsciousness. . . .
>
> Old Tarwater . . . recovered, within himself, the infantile mind of the child-man of the early world . . . and went to myth-making, and sunheroizing, himself hero-maker and the hero in quest of the immemorable treasure difficult of attainment. . . .
>
> Either must he attain the treasure—for so ran the inexorable logic of the shadow-land of the unconscious—or else sink into all-devouring sea, the blackness eater of the light that swallowed to extinction the sun each morning in the east, and that had become to man man's first symbol of immortality through rebirth. . . (*R*, 129–130).

Finally, Tarwater, "turned his back on the perilous west and limped into the sunarising, rebirthing east" where he discovers gold (*R*, 133).

Even though not just this passage but the entire story is cast in Jungian terms and concepts, it might be said that "Like Argus of the Ancient Times" owes little thematically to Carl Jung since, without his aid, London had written many stories in which a hero feels the call of adventure, encounters the hardships of the trail, confronts death and achieves some sense of dignity. But he had stopped writing these stories because the call to adventure had turned out to be an invitation to disillusionment, irrationality and death; and afterwards he turned to writing pot-boilers that avoided "naked truths." Somehow, then, Carl Jung's ideas had restored London's passion for adventure and rekindled those extinguished fires which ended "The Law of Life" and "To Build a Fire" and which symbolized the inability to assert positive values. Apparently, Jung's work helped him find some unique human quality that makes man invulnerable or equal to the crushing forces of nature and capable of overcoming irrationality.

A central concept of *Psychology of the Unconscious* and the most personally significant to London is Jung's concept of the libido. It allowed London, once again attempting serious fiction after four years of pot-boilers, to resurrect his analogous concepts of "true adventure" and "imagination"—those prerequisite capacities for embracing the hardships in nature and wresting spiritual regeneration from a nightmarish encounter with the Arctic wasteland.[299] In his copy of *Psychology of the Unconscious*, London had underscored this definition of "libido" by Dr. Hinkle:

> He, Jung, saw in the term libido a concept of unknown nature, comparable with Bergson's élan vital, a hypothetical energy of life, ... [a] cosmic energy or urge manifested in the human being [and like] the energy of physics (*P*, xxvi).[300]

The restless wanderer, Tarwater, is driven by his often mentioned "fever" which is equivalent to the "unquenchable longing" of libido energy working within the sun-hero, making him continue his perilous journey (*P*, pp. 230–231). His eastward movement and discovery of gold (which has the color of sun and fire and is therefore associated with libido) indicate the measure of Tarwater's success in releasing his libido energy and, simultaneously, revitalizing it (*P*, p. 111). And "if one honors God, the sun or the fire," Jung writes, "then one honors one's own vital force, the libido" (*P*, p. 96). If one reverses this statement, the quality of London's affirmation is captured: if one honors one's vital force by participating in true adventure, he honors life.

Read in this context, a pessimistic story like "To Build a Fire" is the other side of the Jungian coin. The nameless rational man who travels into the Alaskan darkness has no "imagination," no subjective powers, to inform him of the nature of true adventure and the risks involved. He is devoid of psychic energy and, therefore, becomes the victim of the natural forces that crush upon him from without. Consequently, his fatal inability to build a fire, which leaves him to die in darkness, symbolizes his failure or reason's incapacity to affirm and sustain life. Not to honor one's subjective powers brings a denial of life and the symbolic extinction of the fire.

Despite the optimism of "Argus," London must have sensed that the Alaskan materials had been fully exploited, more artistically, years before. The other five Jungian stories, all collected in *On the Makaloa Mat*, use materials from his adopted second home of Hawaii. Because they use Hawaiian settings, they invite comparison with the Hawaiian stories in *The House of Pride* written six years earlier when London was writing stories for frankly commercial reasons.[301] And the Jungian stories are invariably superior to those in *The House of Pride*, testifying to the restorative influence the psychologist's thought had upon the quality of London's fiction. While the earlier stories are repetitive in character and incident, sentimental in tone and superficial in their social comment themes, the Jungian stories in *On the Makaloa Mat* are impressive for their dramatic unity, simplicity, and thematic kinship with London's best fictions. They return to London's most productive themes and subjects: death, the conflict between primitive and modern cultures, and the struggle between optimism and pessimism.

Taking their cue from Charmian London's biography of her husband, several critics have recognized the Jungian basis for "When Alice Told Her Soul." Ironically, it is the only one of these last stories which can be fully understood without knowing Jungian doctrine or symbolism; but the theme of this comic story is derived from a passage in *Psychology of the Unconscious* in which Jung claims that the libido can be released from disturbing subconscious secrets and can find creative outlets if the troubled person confesses his secrets (*P*, p. 233).[302] Alice Akana, the troubled person, runs an exclusive "hula house" where, over the years, she has learned the indiscretions of Honolulu's social elite. Abel Ah Yo, a Bill Sunday style of evangelist, awakens a desire for redemption in her but tells her that she must make a public confession if she is to be redeemed. At this point, the narrator intrudes in order to establish his awareness of the new science of psychology: "Scientifically, though he did not know it and though he continually jeered at science, Abel Ah Yo was right. . . . The result of such a baring would be unity, tranquility, happiness, cleansing, redemption and immortal life" (*M*, 84). Although Alice says, "This rebirth is difficult," "The penitent Phyrne" unburdens her soul of Honolulu's social secrets and sets the rollicking good humor into motion (*M*, 85).

Perhaps this story can be read as London's last effort in the role of social reformer condemning the hypocrisy of the rich and well born. But the humorous characterizations of Alice and Abel Ah Yo, the lighthearted presentations of her confession and his sermons, and the portrayal of the half amused, half scandalized reactions of the public to social hypocrisy, belie a social protest motive. Social comment and comedy combine for one of Jack London's rare successes with humor.

The only other comic story in the volume, "The Tears of Ah Kim," seems to be an eccentric, thematically obscure piece of slapstick. Actually it is almost a programmatic presentation of specific symbols and themes discussed in *Psychology of the Unconscious*. Mrs. Tai Fu has always beaten Ah Kim, her fifty-year-old son, with a bamboo stick, the current reason for the punishment being her disapproval of Li Faa, Ah Kim's fiancée. Although he has always accepted, even relished the beatings, one day the customary lashing causes him to cry for the first time. Shortly afterward, the mother dies and Ah Kim marries Li Faa. The central question, one critic asked recently, is why Ah Kim does not "weep under the beating of his mother's bamboo stick until a certain day."[303]

One suspects that some aspect of the oedipal complex is the intellectual rationale behind the unusual action. In fact, London has dramatized a corollary to the oedipal attachment theory—Jung's concept of "the sacrifice" which is the substance of the last chapter of *Psychology of the Unconscious*. Ah Kim must undergo the pain which derives both from the guilt that springs from his incestuous impulses and his desire to be punished for his rebellious instincts. The bamboo stick, "predominantly a mother symbol," signifies that Mrs. Tai Fu's instrument of authority and punishment is her motherhood, and its phallic connotations reinforce Ah Kim's incestuous guilt (*P*, p. 264). Ah Kim's "submissive and yielding attitude . . . over-compensates for the rebellion and reaction within" (*P*, xxxiv).

To overcome guilt and achieve maturity, Jung writes in his chapter "The Sacrifice," a person must find a "sexual object" to "replace the forbidden mother" (p. 459). This, of course explains the increasing importance of Li Faa in the story as Ah Kim goes through the painful process of sacrificing his infantile wishes in order to transfer his libido energy to another object. In addition, Jung writes, freedom from the mother is symbolized in myths by an allusion to death which is followed by the new, mature relationship which evokes a sense of "eternal germination and renewal" and floral imagery (*P*, pp. 436, 467). It is by Jungian design, then, that at the end of "The Tears of Ah Kim" the mother loses her strength and dies, allowing Ah Kim to marry Li Faa. On his wedding night, Ah Kim explains to his bride why he cried under his mother's last beating: " 'She no longer had strength enough to hurt me' " (*M*, 184). His mother had lost her oedipal power. The bride, in a comic allusion to Jung's "eternal germination and renewal" phrase, is described as shaped like a "watermelon seed"; and, completing the cluster of Jungian symbolism for a mature relationship, Ah Kim calls her "my Flower of Serenity, my Perfect Rest" (*M*, 184).

Despite the solid undergirdings of Jungian thought, the story suffers from appeals to the slap-stick, bizarre, and cruel humor that flawed some of London's less successful stories. Still, "The Tears of Ah Kim," as well as "When Alice Told Her Soul," are curious combinations of Jungian profundities and light comedy that have no real equivalent in any of London's other fiction. Certainly, though, they do not have the stature of the stories for which Jack London is best remembered, particularly the Alaskan tales in which protagonists had gone on the "long trail" into the threatening "unknown" which "lays a man naked to the very roots of his soul." It is the remaining three Jungian stories in *On the Makaloa Mat*—"The Water Baby," "Shin Bones," and "The Bones of Kahelili"—which attest to Jungian thought restoring to his last fiction these important characteristics. Imbued with mythic overtones, they examine the threatening contents of the unconscious and, it is broadly hinted, London's own subconscious in particular.

"The Water Baby," the last story he wrote, is a frame story charged with a simple, lyrical beauty of the kind that had not infused his stories since the Northland tales. And like those first stories, his major theme is the conflict of modern skepticism, born of rationality, with a primitive affirmation whose source is nonrational. Desiring the last, London always was drawn inevitably toward the first. In this story, a modern skeptic named John Lakana (London's own Hawaiian name), fishing with Kohokumu, an aged Hawaiian, lends "a weary ear" to the old man's chants of Hawaiian myths and deities, particularly of Maui, who had slowed the sun, rearranged the heavenly bodies, fished the land up from under the sea and whom Jung associates with oedipal rebirth mythology (*P*, p. 534). Lakana discusses with Kohokumu Christian and Polynesian mythologies, their basis in scientific theories of evolution, the nature of dreams, and, ultimately, the meaning of life and death.

In these discussions, London explicitly links Kohokumu with the most common natural archetype which Jung identifies with the oedipal myths—that of the sun (the hero and libido energy) setting (dying) in the sea (the womb) and rising in the morning (being reborn). The "secret" of his birth, the old man says, is that "the sea is my mother" (*M*, 150). Each time he dives into the sea, he is strengthened, he claims; and in response to this, Lakana thinks, "Shades of Antaeus!" alluding to Jung's commentary upon the story of Antaeus, who could preserve his strength "only through contact with mother earth" (*M*, 150; *P*, 201). The process of returning to the earth for sustenance symbolizes periodic acts of introversion (*P*, 201). Finally, says the old man, he will return to the sea to be reborn:

When I am really old, I shall be reported as drowned in the sea. . . .

This will be an idle thought of men. In truth, I shall have returned into the arms of my mother, there to rest under the heart of her breast until the second birth of me, when I shall emerge into the sun a flashing youth of splendor like Maui himself when he was golden young. (*M*, 150).

During a lull in the fishing, Lakana requests a folk story and Kohokumu obliges him with "The Water Baby," the story within the frame. It is a tale about a young Hawaiian boy who outwits forty sharks in order to catch lobsters for the king and which Charmian London has correctly identified as a "symbolic representation of the Rebirth, the return to the Mother."[304] As he had in "The Tears of Ah Kim," London uses symbols identified by *Psychology of the Unconscious* as connected with libido renewal and growth into emotional maturity. The Water Baby (libido energy, since he speaks the fish language and "the fish is a libido symbol") conquers the sharks (subconscious anxieties, an "incest barrier" which denotes "treasurer guardian" and connotes death) and captures the lobster delicacies (the "treasure difficult of attainment") and thus stays the wrath of the King (avoids destruction and reaffirms life).[305] John Lakana is attentive to the tale, but remains skeptical. The implied tension between civilized skepticism and a natural affirmation of life remains unresolved.

Unlike some earlier stories, frame and story-within are blended together thematically and imagistically: both use folk materials, both invoke the rebirth theme, both employ Jungian symbolism and, literally, both depict fishing. Moreover, unlike in "Argus," the Jungian themes and symbols are used dramatically rather than mechanically and self-consciously. In its simplicity, it is reminiscent of the artistic elegance London achieved in stories like "The Law of Life" and "The Strength of the Strong."

As does "The Water Baby," "Shin Bones," a frame story using the constellation of Oedipal symbolism and the adventurous quest motif, dramatizes the tensions between twentieth-century skepticism and primitive, romantic optimism by invoking Jungian concepts. This time, however, the conflict is within a single character, the modern Hawaiian protagonist, Prince Akuli, who as the last male descendant of the royal family of "Lakanii" (obviously a variant of London's Hawaiian name) is the London surrogate. In "the culminating period of my adolescence" (*M*, 142) or, in Jungian terminology, in the final "budding" stage of libido development (*P*, xxix), Akuli was torn between the competing demands of his father, a cynical businessman in whom there was "no sacredness" (*M*, 133), and his mother, who had reverted to superstitious ancient Hawaiian beliefs by worshiping at the shrine of ancestral bones. The boy himself "could be a skeptic out in the open in the sunshine . . . but . . . was afraid of the dark" (*M*, 121).

Prince Akuli tells a confidant that he was once persuaded by his mother to undertake a dangerous trip to the secret Lakanii burial cave. London knew from his reading of *Psychology of the Unconscious* that any mystery or secret place indicates "a subjectively important secret" which "cuts one off from intercourse with the rest of mankind" and that caves symbolize both the womb and the unconscious (*P*, pp. 233, 375). The Lakanii burial cave, then, is London's own unconscious which he must explore if he is to over-come anxiety and alienation. Akuli's guide is "old Ahuna," who, as an "ancient" like Kohokumu in "The Water Baby," is associated by Jung with revitalizing powers of tapping the unconscious (*P*, pp. 207–208). At first the Prince was reluctant to undertake this particular exploration because, like Jack London facing the exploration of his unconscious it is implied, there were more exciting things to discover—"there were North Poles" (*M*, 119). He goes nevertheless.

No modern reader can misunderstand the detailed anatomical symbolism of London's depiction of this "night journey" to the secret cave since it is common to both Freud and Jung. Prince Akuli has entered the womb, has descended into his own unconscious where he can examine the "great disturbance" which "cuts one off from intercourse with the rest of mankind." Still in keeping with archetypal symbolism, the Prince has an "illumination" in the cave and learns "the great lesson" which he associates with two bones, from a Hawaiian Lancelot and Guinevere, that he takes back (*M*, 137–138). His "imagination" is "fired" by the romance of the Arthurian legend of manly strength, adventure, and passion in which he had once believed but "sobered" and replaced by "things I dare not name" that are associated with his newfound awareness of human mortality—the traditional direction of London's own emotional patterns (*M*, 138, 141). Like a friend from his youth, "on the edge of the grave" Akuli could "sneer at superstition" of any kind, ancient and modern, his mother's superstitious romanticism and his father's callous materialism (*M*, 123). At once, Akuli's experience had been sustaining and sobering. Neither the romantic enthusiasm of Tarwater in "Argus" nor the nihilistic belief that living is madness, which is the import of "In a Far Country" control the story. Instead, a delicate balance is struck between a disturbing awareness of mortality and the calm that comes from the pursuit and acquisition of an understanding that penetrates the illusions of superstition, materialism, and nihilism. By undertaking his quest, Akuli found the meaning of death but also a humble wisdom giving dignity.

But that dignity is tentative and that delicate balance between disturbing awareness and inner peace is weighted towards pessimism. It would seem, then, that London's trip into his own unconscious gave little comfort to the wealthy man who had enjoyed dramatizing himself as a masculine adventurer and heroic lover and who was suffering from physical deterioration and emotional turmoil during the last days of his life. That London's use of Jungian conceptions was turning from a celebration of life's vitality to a final pessimistic preoccupation with death in "Shin Bones" is reinforced by the last Jungian Hawaiian story—"The Bones of Kahelili."

As do "The Water Baby" and "Shin Bones," the stories which reveal the darker side of London's imagination, "The Bones of Kahelili" uses the Jungian concept of an "ancient" revealing a "secret" about the mystery of death to a London surrogate. But if Prince Akuli has made a tenuous peace with life and can await death, Hardman Pool in "The Bones of Kahelili" is more cynical about life and more attracted to death. In this story Hardman Pool, like Jack London at his Glen Ellen ranch, is a wealthy,

benevolent patriarch of a Hawaiian plantation who has become
jaded through the effects of drink and age. To entertain himself,
Pool asks an old retainer, Kumuhana, to reveal the secret of
where Chief Kahelili is buried. In response, the old man tells
him a tale. When he was a young man about to risk mortal
combat for his love, Kumuhana was selected to accompany the
burial canoe of Kahelili as a human sacrifice. When the glass-
covered coffin was thrown overboard, it would not sink,
showing the grotesque face of the corpse, until a horrified priest
broke the glass. The ritual disturbed, Kumuhana escaped his fate
and became the only living person who knows the story.

Without an understanding of London's Jungian interest in
libido theory and its revelation in myths, this story is puzzling.
London, I believe, suggests a hierarchy of "natural obligations"
which culminates in death and implies the impossibility of
spiritual renewal. "The desire for woman must be greater than
the desire for life," Pool extrapolates from the old man's story,
since Kumuhana would risk death to win a bride; and obedience
to authority is stronger than both since he abandons love to
obey the royal command to become a sacrifice (M, 59–61).
What remains implicit is that death is a final obligation stronger
than life, love, or obedience. Reflecting upon the story,
Hardman Pool is most impressed by the mythic significance of
one of the death chants used in the funeral ritual:

> But death is nothing new.
> Death is and has been ever since old Maui died.
> Then Pata-tai laughed loud
> And woke the goblin god,
> Who severed him in two, and shut him in,
> So dusk of eve came on (M, 72).

The riddle of death and rebirth is solved by suggesting the
finality of death, the theme implicit in "Shin Bones." Maui the
sun god of rebirth is dead; or, in other terms, the libido or will
to live is dead. The destructive "goblin god" rules, bringing "the
dusk of eve," a phrase which obsesses Pool and in which he
finds "an intense satisfaction" (M, 76).

It is appropriate that London uses the grotesque at the end of Kumuhana's tale since grotesquery had been synonymous with the overwhelming, malign powers that crushed out life in the Alaskan stories. The protagonists in those stories, like London's autobiographical Hardman Pool, were left without the psychic energy necessary for actively engaging in a contest with death.

While the mature Alaskan stories dramatized the tragedy of youthful, energetic protagonists testing their vitality against the brutal forces of nature only to be drawn catastrophically toward the demonic, the irrational and death-dealing, these last few stories reveal a shift in mood. They dramatize the pathos of aging and disillusioned, even cynical, men awaiting death. While violence and death, the triumph of the demonic, had somehow surprised the earlier protagonists, these last—Jack Lakana, Prince Akuli, and Hardman Pool—are without the capacity for amazement. Carl Jung's system as Jack London found it in *Psychology of the Unconscious*, like the other systems he had found before, had failed on the eve of his own death to give him a sure faith. Hardman Pool voices a sentiment which might be taken as the cast of London's own last thoughts: "We are wise, but the wisdom is bitter" (*M*, 70).

The two remaining stories in *On the Makaloa Mat*, "The Kanaka Surf" and the title story, are not indebted to Jung. "The Kanaka Surf," however, is partially indebted to Freudian psychology. But while Jungian thought had contributed to London's artistry, the Freudian ideas are the occasion for London to return to the bombastic polemics with which he espoused causes and pleaded personal wrongs in his worst fiction.

Lee and Ida Barton are the central characters in "The Kanaka Surf," and as the story opens are about to swim in the treacherous Hawaiian surf. Walking towards the beach, these two magnificent physical specimens are greeted by "gasps . . . indicative of moral shock" from "a score of women" with "soft-fat muscles" and "hot-house complexions" (*M*, 185). London explains their shock with an authorial intrusion which defines Freud's "displacement" principle:

Ida Barton was the cause of their perturbation and disapproval. They disapproved, seriously so, at the first instant's glimpse of her. They thought—such ardent self-deceivers were they—that they were shocked by her swimming suit. But Freud has pointed out how persons, where sex is involved, are prone sincerely to substitute one thing for another thing, and to agonize over the substituted thing as strenuously as if it were the real thing (*M*, 185).

But artists, London claims, are not plagued by self-delusion, and he shifts to a view of this scene as perceived by Stanley Patterson and his wife, two artists (*M*, 187). Stanley Patterson's voice is used, for a lengthy four pages, to praise Ida's boyish muscularity, a masculine beauty that had always figured in London's "Mate Woman" ideal of femininity. This section of the story is climaxed by a long authorial comment which villifies literary critics, among others, who refuse to acknowledge that characters of the heroic proportion of Ida and Lee (and other London characters, it might be added) exist in real life:

> For, be it known in advance, Lee Barton was a superman and Ida Barton a superwoman—or at least they were personalities so designated by the cub book reviewers, flat-floor men and women, and scholastically emasculate critics, who, from across the dreary levels of their living, can descry no glorious humans overtopping their horizons (*M*, 192).

The rest of the story justifies the suspicion that this much has raised: "The Kanaka Surf" is an apology for London's art and life. Ida and Lee Barton are Charmian and Jack London thinly disguised in romantic verbiage. Misunderstood by the world of "dreary folk" who worship the "mediocre and commonplace," their true worth is recognized only by artists and others who have adventured "along the shining ways" (*M*, 192-193). Not only Patterson, the artist, recognizes the Bartons' vitality but so does a "world champion" swimmer, "himself a bronze Hercules . . . the whitest blood man ever burned to mahogany brown by a subtropic sun," who watches them swim skillfully in the dangerous surf (*M*, 197-198). To him, from his shore vantage point, the swimming pair are "Specks . . . they

were of the quick, adventuring among the blind elemental
forces, daring the Titanic buffets of the sea" (M, 201). Having
introduced his old shibboleths of adventure, cosmic power,
physical mastery and white blood, London, through the
champion swimmer, bestows his highest accolade: " 'They aren't
malihinis [tenderfeet]' " (M, 202). In terms of his Northland
fiction, these London characters are not "chechaquos"; and, like
the Malemute Kid, they have been initiated into the romantic
mysteries which set them apart from the rest of human kind.

The final section of the story introduces Sonny Grandison,
who is wealthy, well born, athletic, socially popular,
scientifically informed, politically influential, Harvard educated
and a world adventurer—all, at one time or another, qualities
found in London's idealizations of masculinity (M, 204-205).
The narrator brings him on stage and, then, prepares the reader
for a romantic triangle of Olympian proportion: "Given a
markedly strong and vital man and woman, when a second
equally markedly strong and vital man enters the scene, the peril
of a markedly strong and vital triangle of tragedy becomes
imminent" (M, 206). In the whirl of Hawaiian social life,
Grandison courts a responsive Ida while Lee Barton plays cards
and clouds his suspicions with drink and drugs. Under the
influence of opium, Lee decides to force Ida to a choice
between Grandison and himself by feigning a muscle cramp
when he and Ida are swimming in the "kanaka surf." His ruse
works well, except that he actually begins to drown, and Ida
chooses him. She becomes the "happiest woman in the world"
and he learns the meaning of "the great love" (M, 226).

All this is more London self-dramatizing. Jack, who spent his
last Hawaiian trip being lionized by the social elite, was drinking
to excess, taking drugs to relieve the pain of uremic poisoning
(and eventually to die) and amusing himself with his habitual
card games. Meanwhile he philandered and worried about
Charmian's affairs.[306] Obviously the triangle episode of "The
Kanaka Surf" is a romanticized version of an ugly personal
situation and the sentimental ending a restatement of the myth
of the ideal love between "Mate" and "Mate Woman" that Jack

and Charmian shared in their correspondence and which Charmian tried to maintain in her biographical analysis of her husband's last days.[307] Technically, too, "The Kanaka Surf" is a return to London's earliest practices: it has an essay-exemplum structure which uses an intrusive narrator who postures, moralizes, pastes together shifts in time and place, and mechanically introduces a variety of characters and incidents. Coupled with the unsophisticated form and technique are the personal bitterness and contrived sentimentality of the stories London had written just before retreating from the short story genre in 1912.

"On the Makaloa Mat" is a simple, but wordy, story whose mood is nostalgic and the only story in this volume that is untouched by London's interest in psychology. In it, one character tells a story to another, a favorite device of London's and one which was becoming, by 1916, a stock literary method for others as well. An elderly Hawaiian woman confides to her sister that, fifty years before, she had had a romance with a Hawaiian Prince. The memory of that interlude had sustained her through the ordeal of her arranged and loveless marriage to a white landowner who was the sterotype of the cold New Englander still practicing the Protestant ethic. Although the interlude had been idyllic, she recognizes the claims of modernity and the consequent necessity of having allied herself with the passionless, but financially successful, class who had constructed modern Hawaii. Just as the other stories in this volume had in some way reflected London's earlier stories, "On the Makaloa Mat" reflects the Alaskan Indian tales in which the protagonists remember the glorious past but accept the inevitability of the white man's civilization—loss and acceptance mingle with one another.

Shortly after completing "Like Argus of the Ancient Times" and the stories in *On the Makaloa Mat*, Jack London died at his Beauty Ranch in Glen Ellen, California. Collectively, these stories written in 1916 are a fitting end to his life and writing career because they reflect the wide range of interests, attitudes and abilities that had given birth to the approximately one hundred and eighty short stories that London had written between 1898 and 1912. The 1916 group of stories not only concludes Jack London's career but is representative of it.

Artistically, the differences between "Like Argus of the Ancient Times" and "The Water Baby," "Shin Bones," and "The Bones of Kahekili," are similar to those between London's earliest Alaskan stories and the Northland stories which followed between 1900 and 1908. While "Argus" and early Alaskan stories like "The Wife of a King" are clever in language, light in tone, mechanical in structure, awkwardly didactic and almost overwhelmed with characters and incidents, the three stories from *On the Makaloa Mat* like the second group of Northland stories which include "The League of Old Men," "The Law of Life," and "The Death of Ligoun," are more artistically conceived and executed. Structurally and stylistically, they show the legacy of Rudyard Kipling's short stories and Herbert Spencer's *Philosophy of Style* as well as London's study of magazine short story theory and practice. They are more ironic, symbolic and mythic than his first fiction. Then, too, "The Kanaka Surf" is an unfortunate reminder of the time when London had cynically turned to short stories as a source of ready cash, using techniques he had learned to reject earlier, accounting for many of the pot-boilers which appear in collections like *A Son of the Sun* and *The Night-Born*.

But themes, rather than artistry, were London's passion. And the stories written in 1916 also reflect the thematic concerns of the rest of London's fiction. Through his career, it had been Jack London's scientific reading and personal adventures which accounted for most of the themes and materials of his fiction: at first it was Darwin, Spencer and Haeckel linked with the Klondike and at last Jung with Hawaii. And first and last, London had been preoccupied with a search for salvation amidst hints of certain damnation.

The boyant, enthusiastically optimistic tone of "Argus" recalls London's earliest efforts from 1898 to 1900 to write artistically serious fiction which portrays the triumph of the vulnerable human spirit over a menacing environment. Certain that the godlike in man would triumph, he pitted man's subjective powers against the positivistic facts of life, whether those facts were symbolically present in the Alaskan landscape or in a protagonist's aging body. London suggested in the person of his recurring Alaskan hero, the Malemute Kid, as he did again in old Tarwater, that a scientifically warranted revelation is available to those who exercise "imagination" or release "libido" energy and who take the prerequisite risks. The life-giving, subjective call to "true adventure," properly undertaken could tap the powerful energies of the Haeckelian "soul" or the Jungian subconscious and triumph over the death-dealing wasteland. For Jack London, Jung's *Psychology of the Unconscious* was just the last in a series of romantic calls to completion, to self-identifying and self-sustaining nobility.

Despite the celebration of nobility, like that in "Argus" and "To the Man on Trail," and despite the playful entertainment of positive conceptions such as a dynamic life force which London portrayed in comedies like "When Alice Told Her Soul" and "The Tears of Ah Kim" in *On the Makaloa Mat* and early Alaskan stories like "The Men of Forty-Mile," the romantic call always brought with it eventual reminders of impotence and mortality and, consequently, disillusionment. And the tension between a sought after affirmation and a growing sense of futility characteristically sponsored London's greatest achievement. "The Water Baby," "Shin Bones," and "The Bones of Kahekili" are like the best Northland tales written between 1900 and 1908. His best fiction had revealed a tension between equivalents of old Kohokumu's spiritual vitality and John Lakana's physical-psychological deterioration, as in, for instance, "The Love of Life"; between Prince Akuli's romantic imagination and his modern skepticism, as in "The God of His Fathers" or "The League of Old Men"; and between Kumuhana's knowledge of life and Hardman Pool's jaded awareness of death, both prefigured in the old Indian's consciousness in "The Law of Life." As the Hawaiian stories do, so did the best Alaskan stories dramatize a theme of loss by depicting a noble primitive culture declining in the face of "inevitable" civilization or by portraying protagonists who fail to validate "secondary" truths, having been forced into an awareness of "primary" truths embodied in an external nature to which they either accommodate themselves or succumb.

With the exception of the grotesquery in the burial scene of "The Bones of Kahekili," however, none of these last stories portrays the demonic pessimism of stories like "In a Far Country," "Batard," or "Lost Face" which dramatize an irrational world of pain reflecting "the horror" which is the truth beyond human illusions. But while that sense of the futility of life did prompt London to compose some of his most powerful stories, it also was one of the reasons that led to his intellectual and artistic decline from 1906 until 1912. Partly to detach himself from "the horror," he had written pot-boilers that capitalized upon sentimental celebrations of white supremacy and in general indulged in polemical didacticism to blackmail the reader into accepting his eccentricities, both ideological and personal. "The Kanaka Surf" in *On the Makaloa Mat* is an unhappy sign of that period in his short story career. In it, as he had before, he conjures with his old touchstones: the efficacy of adventure, masculine and feminine heroics, race, social position, wealth and the code which helps one elude death and preserve love and honor.

The pot-boilers contribute to Jack London's notoriety, but it is his best stories that deserve final comment. By standing back from the various, sometimes even contradictory, details of the best short stories in order to perceive general patterns, one is struck by the figure which emerges—a protagonist who is possessed both by demons and a compelling intuition, which he must struggle to verify, that a saving illumination is the reward for agony. Such is the stuff that myths are spun from; and London intuitively, at first, and deliberately, at last, evoked the mythopoeic. Northrup Frye in his *Anatomy of Criticism* has found language that can be used to describe Jack London's most compelling fiction which invokes the demonic and revelatory by myth-making.[308] Frye writes that there are "two forms of metaphorical organization we call the apocalyptic and demonic,

respectively (p. 139)." The "apocalyptic world" presents "the
categories of reality in the forms of human desire" in which an
idealized, abstracted character finds an equivalent to "gold" or
"fire" and is spiritually uplifted (pp. 141–46). The demonic is a
"world of nightmare ... pain and confusion" in which a
"tyrant-leader," "victim" or ironic combination of the two
enters a wasteland "associated with tragic destiny" and
populated by monsters (of which "the wolf" is the most
traditional) and is lost in a maze (pp. 147–50). The applicability
of Frye's remarks to London's best fiction is undeniable.

The fascination of Jack London's short stories is not, as is too
often argued, the product of a robust celebration of turn of the
century popular values. The fascination is born of Jack London's
ability to use his craft to capture the struggle between the most
fundamentally human desire for salvation and the most
fundamentally human fear of damnation.

FOOTNOTES

[1] *Overland Monthly*, N. S., XXXIII, 36–40.

[2] The dates of publication of London's stories are sometimes misleading. During this period from 1899–1902, he also wrote other stories: those collected in *Tales of the Fish Patrol* (1905) were nearly completed before London went to England in the summer of 1902 [see *Letters from Jack London*, ed. King Hendricks and Irving Shepard (New York, 1965), 140]. In this case, since these children's stories exhibit no important technical differences from the more serious stories in the early Alaskan tale volumes, they have been omitted from this discussion. And since the techniques employed in his fourth collection of Alaskan stories, *The Faith of Men* (1904), show no changes from the earlier volumes, *Children of the Frost* is the logical choice as the volume which illustrates the conclusion of London's search for short story form and technique.

[3] *Letters* (to Esther Anderson; Dec. 11, 1914), 437.

[4] Joan London, *Jack London and His Times: An Unconventional Biography* (New York, 1939), p. 195.

[5] *Overland Monthly*, *Black Cat* Magazines, *The Owl*, *Conkey's Magazine*, *Youth's Companion*, *Christmas Wave*, *Atlantic Monthly*, *Harper's Weekly*, *S. F. Sunday Examiner*, *McClure's Magazine*, *Outing Magazine*, *Ainslie's Magazine* and *The News*.

[6] Fred Lewis Pattee, *The Development of the American Short Story* (New York, 1923), p. 337.

[7] *Letters* (to Cloudesley Johns; April 22, 1899), 33.

[8] *Letters*, 437.

[9] "Typhoon" is reprinted in *Dutch Courage and Other Stories* (New York, 1922), pp. 21–31.

[10] IV (Cambridge, Mass., 1957), p. 401.

[11] XCVII (1898).

[12] XXI (June, 1897), 728–40.

[13]Morgan Robertson, LXXXII (Aug., 1898), 206–20; Justine Ingersoll, LXXXII (Aug., 1898), 235.

[14]Herbert Ward, LVI (July–Aug., 1898), 364–77, 517–25.

[15]John R. Spears, XXVIII (April, 1900), 667–68; XXVI (Dec., 1898), 164–72; XXV (June, 1898), 216–19.

[16]For a selective bibliography of Alaskan articles appearing in this periodical, see "Alaskan Articles that have Appeared in The Overland," *Overland Monthly*, N. S., XXX (Oct., 1897), 382.

[17]George B. Waldron, XII (Dec., 1898), 185–88. When convenient the following references to this magazine will be included in the text.

[18]Mortimer O. Wilcox, XII (Dec., 1898), 189–92.

[19]XII, 110–18, 231–40, 353–62, 470–80, 527–34.

[20]*The Responsibilities of the Novelist* (Boar's Head edition; Cambridge, Mass., 1962), p. 238.

[21]*Lost Face* (New York), pp. 63–98. For a discussion of the two versions see Earle Labor and King Hendricks, "Jack London's Twice-Told Tale," *Studies in Short Fiction*, 4 (Summer, 1967), 334–337.

[22]In 1899, at the height of London's apprenticeship, Doubleday and McClure, Co. published *The Works of Rudyard Kipling* which includes: *Plain Tales from the Hills, Soldiers Three, The Story of the Gadsbys, In Black and White, Under the Deodars, The Phantom 'Rickshaw, Wee Willy Winkie and Other Stories, Life's Handicap, Being Stories of Mine Own People, The Light that Failed, Many Inventions, The Jungle Book, The Day's Work, From Sea to Sea.*

[23]*History of American Magazines*, IV, p. 33.

[24]*American Short Story*, p. 263.

[25]For a brief comparison of materials and themes shared by Kipling and London see Abraham Rothberg, "The House that Jack Built: A Study of Jack London" (unpublished dissertation, Columbia University, 1952), pp. 363–65.

[26]V (Nov. 1895), 552–61; VI (March, 1896), 328–37; VII (June, 1896), 23–39; IX (Aug., 1897), 837–59; VIII–IX (Nov., 1896–May, 1897); XII–XIII (Dec., 1898–June, 1899).

[27]XII, 40–44, 176–78, resp.

[28]Richard O'Connor, *Jack London: A Biography* (Boston, 1964), p. 91.

[29]VII (June, 1898), 282.

[30]*Town Topics* (Aug. 31, 1899); *Town Topics* (April 20, 1899); *Town Topics* (May 11, 1899); *Buffalo Express* (June 4, 1899); *Home Magazine* (June, 1899).

[31] O'Connor, p. 110.

[32] *Letters* (Nov. 27, 1898), 4. Jack hoped to marry Mabel, but her indecisive personality and her mother's desire for a better match interferred. She was his first literary confident with whom he shared his early enthusiasms and was the model for Ruth in *Martin Eden* (New York, 1909).

[33] *Dutch Courage*, 28–29.

[34] Joan London, p. 169.

[35] The bulk of the London manuscripts is in the Huntington library. Only a few of these stories found their way into print. Nevertheless, the few published stories are helpful in determining the nature of London's apprenticeship and will be discussed as representative of those stories written before he mined the Klondike vein. Publication dates of the stories are unreliable as guides to dates of composition since London often did not publish stories until years after writing them. My information concerning dating comes primarily from an investigation of the *Letters* which contains a large quantity of business correspondence, as well as personal letters, in which London discussed work in progress.

[36] *Martin Eden* (Rinehart edition; New York, 1956), p. 226.

[37] V (Sept. 1, 1899), 1–3. This story is uncollected and undoubtedly was one of the stories which London wrote early in his apprenticeship, despite the fact that it was published after he had written and published stories of a higher quality.

[38] *Martin Eden*, pp. 225–26.

[39] (May, 1899), 33–42.

[40] See also "The Rejuvenation of Major Rathbone," *Conkey's Home Journal* (Nov. 7, 1899), 5–6, 29, for a similar science fiction story written during this period. It uses the fountain of youth convention.

[41] See Chapter V for an analysis of London's pot-boilers.

[42] *Martin Eden*, pp. 212–13.

[43] *Letters* (to Cloudesley Johns; March 7, 1899), 19–20.

[44] "Prose Fiction: A Bibliography," *Bulletin of Bibliography*, IV–V (July, 1906–Jan., 1908).

[45] "On the Writer's Philosophy of Life" (Nov., 1899); "The Question of a Name" (Dec., 1900); and "Economics in the Klondike" (Jan., 1900), resp.

[46] New York, 1901. This essay originally appeared in the Oct., 1885 issue of *Lippincott's Magazine*.

[47] *Appleton's Journal*, I (May 29), 282.

[48] Matthews, 15–16.

[49]There is no evidence that London studied any specific handbook, although Joan London's statement that Jack "worked laboriously through books on style and structure" might indicate that he was aware of the handbooks in general. The handbooks do, however, summarize the techniques and theoretical arguments London was exposed to in the magazines and are, therefore, more convenient than the magazines as a vehicle for discussion. Barrett's handbook is the most convenient because of its date of publication and representative nature.

[50]For a bibliography of the best handbooks, see Pattee, pp. 337–338. For a satirical treatment of the handbooks, see F. L. Masson, "Simple, Isn't It?" *Bookman*, XLVIII (Feb., 1919), 709–711.

[51]Matthews, p. 16.

[52]London oversimplifies—actually several cabins are involved, and this story does not have unity of place.

[53]London uses the plot from Kipling's "Three—and an Extra" but expanded the characterizations so that there is character development. The story is diffuse in its setting, time and characters.

[54]The situation is the pitting of two white men's wills against an Indian's.

[55]*Letters* (to Anna Strunsky, Oct. 13, 1904), 163–164. He probably objected to the "Scorn of Women" for the same reasons he objected to "The Priestly Prerogative"—the story has too many developing characters, incidents and settings.

[56]Letter to his brother-in-law, 1824, as quoted in *American Short Stories*, ed. Eugene Current-Garcia and Walton R. Patrick (Chicago, 1964), pp. xiii–xiv.

[57]Austin M. Wright, *The American Short Story in the Twenties* (Chicago, 1961), p. 280.

[58]The following are the essay-exemplum stories in the first two volumes: "The Son of the Wolf," *SW*, 21–51; "In a Far Country," *SW*, 69–101; "The Wife of a King," *SW*, 160–189; "The God of His Fathers," *GF*, 1–33; "At the Rainbow's End," *GF*, 230–251.

[59]*Moon-Face and Other Stories* (New York, 1906), 59–85.

[60]Pp. 39–40.

[61]*loc. cit.*

[62]Letter to Mable Applegarth, quoted in Charmian K. London, *The Book of Jack London*, I (New York, 1921), p. 259.

[63]*Letters*, 15.

[64]For a catalogue of the relationships between frame and the story-within, between teller and hearer, see Clara Margolin, *Jack London's Short Stories, Ihre Form and Ihr Gehalt* (Heidelberg, 1926), pp. 19–33.

[65]The following are frame stories which occur in the first three volumes: "An Odyssey of the North," *SW*, 190–251; "Siwash," *GF*, 86–113; "Grit of Women," *GF*, 156–184; "Nam-Bok the Unveracious," *Children of the Frost* (Fitzroy edition; London, 1963), orig. 1902, 39–55; "The Sickness of Lone Chief," *CF*, 92–101; "The Death of Ligoun," *CF*, 113–123; "The League of Old Men," *CF*, 143–160.

[66]See above, p. 11; Alfred Samuel Shivers, "Romanticism in Jack London: (unpublished dissertation, Florida State University, 1962), pp. 39–40, 68–69; Joan London, p. 170.

[67]S. R. Crockett, "On Some Tales of Mr. Kipling's," *The Bookman*, I (Feb., 1895), 24.

[68]Doubleday, rev. ed; New York, 1917. I have used this edition throughout this study for all references to Kipling's stories.

[69]*Plain Tales*, 10.

[70]*Plain Tales*, 171.

[71]*Kipling the Story-Writer* (Berkeley, 1918), p. 32.

[72]*Soldiers Three*, 1–9.

[73]*Soldiers Three*, 1.

[74]*In Black and White*, 1–16.

[75]*Soldiers Three*, 41–82.

[76]Kipling, p. 51.

[77]*Letters*, 106–107.

[78]Actually published in the March, 1901 issue.

[79]*Letters* (Dec., 1900), 115.

[80]*Letters* (To George P. Brett, June 30, 1902), 129.

[81]*Love of Life* (New York, 1906), 203–241.

[82]Barrett, pp. 39–40.

[83]Carl Hovey, *Bookman*, XVII (March, 1903), 84.

[84]*Letters* (To H. A. Hanner, Jan. 29, 1911), 335.

[85]Joan London, p. 287.

[86]For a discussion of the specific recommendations London took from this essay, see Robert Holland, "Jack London: His Thought and Art in Relation to His Times" (unpublished dissertation, University of Wisconsin, 1950), pp. 119–131.

[87]II, p. 50.

[88]Vernon Lee, "On Literary Construction," *Bookman*, II (Sept., 1895), 21.

[89]Spencer, pp. 31–32.

[90]*Ibid.*, p. 28.

[91]Joan London, p. 170.

[92]J. B. P. (Jennette Barbour Perry), "Mr. Kipling as an Artist," *Critic*, XXXIII (Dec., 1898), 473. The story was "Toomai and the Elephants."

[93]For London's theory of primitive language see "The Phenomena of Literary Evolution," *Bookman*, XII (Oct., 1900), 48ff. Some reviewers objected to this element of style—for example, see the *Athenaeum* review of *Children of the Frost* (Jan. 17, 1903), 77.

[94]Kipling's stylistic legacy to London is not all positive, however. "Kiplingesque smartness of diction [is what] Willa Cather later identified as the period mannerism" that infected the stories of many writers [Warner Berthoff, *The Ferment of Realism, American Literature, 1884–1919* (New York, 1965), p. 229]. Many of the "clever" elements of London's style are Kiplingesque.

[95]See below, Chapter V, for a fuller discussion of this decline in interest.

[96]*Letters* (to Esther Anderson; Dec. 11, 1914), 437.

[97]William Dean Howells, *Criticism and Fiction* (Boar's Head edition; Cambridge, Mass., 1962), pp. 19–21.

[98]*Love of Life*, 208.

[99]*Letters* (to Churchill Williams; Oct. 4, 1910), 319.

[100]"Jack London: His Thought and Art," p. 109.

[101]Joan London, p. 169.

[102]*Letters* (To H. A. Hanner; Jan. 29, 1911), 335.

[103]For a discussion of *The Forum*'s intra-mural debate, see Edwin Cady, *Realist at War* (Syracuse, 1958), pp. 29ff. He does not discuss the compromise however.

[104]"Romance and Realism," rev., *Bookman*, I (May, 1895), 257.

[105]"Art for Art's Sake," *Bookman*, I (May, 1895), 241.

[106]*Bookman*, I (Feb., 1895), 12.

[107]See *Martin Eden* pp. 225–226 when Martin rejects the sentimentality and absence of tragedy in popular fiction.

[108]*A Study of Prose Fiction* (New York, 1902), p. 278.

[109]"Rudimentary Suggestions for Beginners in Story Writing," *Cosmopolitan*, XXII (Feb., 1897), 446.

[110]See N. L. Goodrich, "Prose Fiction: A Bibliography," *Bulletin of Bibliography*, IV–V for a full sampling of the articles debating the merits of realism and romance.

[111]Unsigned, *Bookman*, I (Feb., 1895), 48.

[112]Frederick M. Bird, "Magazine Fiction and How Not to Write It," *Lippincott's* (Nov., 1894); Gilbert Parker, "The Art of Fiction," *The Critic*, XXXIII (Dec., 1898), 467.

[113]As quoted by Harry Thurston Peck, rev. of *My Literary Passions, Bookman*, I (July, 1895), 400; *Criticism and Fiction*, 65.

[114]*Criticism and Fiction*, 95, 99.

[115]Cady, *Realist at War*, pp. 35, 251.

[116]*Letters* (To Johns; Aug. 10), 50–51.

[117]P. 76.

[118]"XLV," "Black Riders and Other Lines," *The Collected Poems of Stephen Crane*, ed. Wilson Follett (New York, 1942), 48. It is interesting that London uses "meat" as an equivalent for bold masculine experience in the *Smoke Bellew* stories (New York, 1911).

[119]Quoted by Philip S. Foner, *Jack London, American Rebel* ... (New York, 1947), p. 509; *Letters* (To Johns, Feb. 22, 1899), 15.

[120]*Criticism and Fiction*, pp. 15–16.

[121]Gilbert Parker, "Art of Fiction," 468.

[122]Jack London, " 'Foma Gordyaeff,' " rev., quoted in Foner, p. 512. London praises Gorky for avoiding the conventions of popular romance.

[123]"What Life Means to Me," quoted in Foner, p. 396.

[124]*Letters* (To Johns; March 30, 1899), 26.

[125]*The Beginnings of Critical Realism in America: 1869–1920* (New York, 1930), 323–24.

[126]*Letters* (March 15, 1900), 101.

[127]New York, 1900.

[128]*Letters* (To Ralph Kasper; June 25), 425.

[129]Haeckel, p. 212.

[130]Haeckel, pp. 20-21.

[131] *Letters* (To Johns; March 1, 1900), 96.

[132] *Loc. cit.*

[133]*Letters* (To Johns; April 17, 1899), 29.

[134]*Letters* (To Ralph Kasper; June 25, 1914), 425.

[135]For a good general discussion of London's views about acquired characters in relation to Marx's and Darwin's ideas, written by a biologist, see Conway Zirkle, *Evolution, Marxian Biology, and The Social Scene* (Philadelphia, 1959), pp. 318–337.

[136]" 'A Natural History of American Naturalism,' " *Documents of Modern Literary Realism*, ed. George J. Becker (Princeton, 1963), p. 436.

[137]New York, 1913, p. 112. Sam S. Baskett in "Jack London on the Oakland Waterfront," *American Literature*, XXVII (Nov., 1955), 363–371, cautions that this work is factually inaccurate. But *Barleycorn* is psychologically revealing. What is important here is not the specific conditions of London's youth but, instead, his emotional organization of them. This work is second only to *Martin Eden* in its revelation of London's own emotional and intellectual life.

[138]"In a Far Country," *SW*, 69.

[139]It is important that the earlier "whisper" passage saw life-giving truths beyond appearances; whereas, this passage indicates that the "truth beyond truth" is death-dealing. The early stories ambivalently portray both concepts, but most emphasize life-giving truths. The strongly pessimistic tone of this passage is more typical of London's later mood and was written in 1912.

[140]*White Fang* (New York, 1905), pp. 3–4.

[141]*Rebels and Ancestors: The American Novel, 1890–1915* (New York, 1963), p. 144.

[142]"Jack London's Symbolic Wilderness: Four Versions," *Nineteenth Century Fiction*, XI (1962), 149.

[143]Labor, Earle Gene, "Jack London's Literary Artistry" (unpublished dissertation, University of Wisconsin, 1961), pp. 15, 23–24.

[144]"In a Far Country," *SW*, 72. The trail is at the center of many excellent tales: "White Silence," "Wisdom of the Trail," "An Odyssey of the North" in the first volume. But the technique is often the height of achievement in an otherwise poor story: "Trust" in *Lost Face*, "The Meat" in *Smoke Bellew* and "The One Thousand Dozen" in *The Faith of Man*.

[145]"London's *Heart of Darkness*," *American Quarterly*, X (Spring, 1958), 74. He quotes from Lilian Feder, "Marlow's Descent into Hell," *Nineteenth Century Fiction*, IX (March, 1955), 292.

[146]*Rebels and Ancestors*, p. 152.

[147]"The Unexpected," *Love of Life* (New York, 1906), 126.

[148]"Jack London: His Thought and Artistry," p. 109.

[149]Joan London, p. 209.

[150]*Realism: A Study in Art and Thought*, excerpted as "Conclusions and Applications" in *Documents of Modern Literary Realism*, p. 569.

[151]For a discussion of London's reading and his confused understanding of it see the Holland dissertation and Abraham Rothberg, "The House that Jack Built: A Study of Jack London" (unpublished dissertation, Columbia University, 1952). More systematic studies are: Sam S. Baskett, "Jack London's Fiction: Its Social Milieu" (unpublished dissertation, University of California, 1951) and Roy Werner Carlson, "Jack London's Heroes: A Study of Evolutionary Thought" (unpublished dissertation, University of New Mexico, 1962).

[152]"The Terrible and Tragic in Fiction," *Critic*, XLII (June, 1903), 540–542. See also the opening passage in *Before Adam* (New York, 1907). He shared this idea with Niezsche, although he probably had not read from the philosopher's works at this time, and with Stephen Crane.

[153]See Foner's reprints of London's reviews, pp. 507–524.

[154]*Criticism and Fiction*, p. 65.

[155]"Notes on the Decline of Naturalism," quoted in *Documents of Modern Literary Realism*, p. 579.

[156]*The Development of the American Short Story*, pp. 352–353.

[157]*Letters* (To Johns), 41.

[158]Charles Child Walcutt, *American Literary Naturalism, a Divided Stream* (Minneapolis, 1956), pp. vii–viii.

[159]*Ibid.*, p. 29.

[160]*Realism and Naturalism in Nineteenth-Century American Literature* (Carbondale, 1966), p. 13.

[161]The Kid appears in seven of the nine stories: "Son of Wolf," "White Silence," "To the Man on Trail," "The Priestly Prerogative," "The Man of Forty-Mile," "The Wife of a King" and "An Odyssey of the North."

[162]Letter to Anna Strunsky, Dec. 20, 1902, as quoted in Franklin Walker, *Jack London and the Klondike* (London, 1966), p. 219.

[163]*Letters* (April 7, 1899), 29.

[164]*The Call of the Wild; White Fang*; "Brown Wolf" in *Love of Life*; *Jerry of the Islands*; and *Michael, Brother of Jerry*.

[165]*Jack London and The Klondike*, p. 215.

[166]"Jack London's Literary Artistry," p. 34.

[167]*Lord Jim* (Modern Library edition; New York, 1931), pp. 33–34.

[168]"A Natural History of Naturalism," in Becker, p. 438.

[169]That light and warmth images are associated with life in London's fiction has been noted by several critics including Earle Labor in his dissertation and Ann S. Jennings in "London's Code of the Northland," *Alaskan Review*, I (1964), 43–48.

[170]Joan London, p. 229. Joan London presents this as a quote from her father describing what he desired in the ideal comrade. He never did find this reflection in his self-concept in real life but did create it in the Kid.

[171]The emphasis on love fits in, of course, with London's social brotherhood theme, but love is not extended to all. A capacity for love is found in London's self-extensions: brutes and animals as well as those who live by the code and respond to the spirit of adventure. Code violators are condemned without pity.

[172] P. 229.

[173]*SW*, 120.

[174]"Symbolic Wilderness," 152.

[175]*Lost Face* (New York, 1910), 65.

[176]This character appears in "To the Man on Trail," "The Wife of a King" and "An Odyssey of the North." With some modifications, he becomes the protagonist in London's first novel, *A Daughter of the Snows* (New York, 1902).

[177]"The Priestly Prerogative," *SW*, 143. The priest appears in the same stories as Prince.

[178]London often used "law-giver" in the sense of imposing a Nordic code of race supremacy upon uncivilized or under-civilized cultures (Alaskan, tropical or Mexican). The phrase occurs, for example, in the title of an article extolling the power of Americans in Mexico ("Lawgivers," *Collier's* LIII, June, 1914, 16–17, 28–29). But in these early stories, giving the law is more a recommendation of the code.

[179]Here, implicit, is London's operational belief that it is immoral to gain money without work by "farming" fellow humans. It is one of the minor social themes that recurs throughout his "non-social" fiction. See, for example, "The Passing of Marcus O'Brien," *Lost Face*, 169, for a parallel objection to gambling.

[180]" 'To the Man on Trail': Jack London's Christmas Carol," *Jack London Newsletter*, Vol. 3, no. 3 (Sept.–Dec., 1970), 93.

[181]*Letters* (To Johns, Nov. 11, 1899), 68.

[182]New York, 1905. Despite the publication date, these stories were written during the spring of 1902 (see *Letters*, 140); See also Charmian London, I, p. 348 for London's remark that he deliberately moralized in his stories for boys.

[183]*Fish Patrol*, pp. 71–102.

[184]*The God of His Fathers*, 34–64.

[185]*Smoke Bellew* (New York, 1912); *A Son of the Sun* (New York, 1912). See below, Chapter V, for a discussion of these stories.

[186]*John Barleycorn*, pp. 276–277.

[187]Chicago, 1961.

[188]Wright, pp. 121–123.

[189]Quoted by Wright, p. 123.

[190]Joseph Conrad, *Youth: A Narrative* (New York, 1964), orig. 1902, pp. 5–6. For a comparison of London's and Conrad's treatment of youth and disillusionment, see Sam S. Baskett, "Jack London's *Heart of Darkness*," *American Quarterly*, X (Spring, 1958), 70–76.

[191]For a discussion of confused values, see the Holland and Rothberg dissertations. London relied upon David Starr Jordan's popularizations of Darwin and Spencer, for example.

[192]"Jack London's Quest for Salvation," *American Quarterly*, VII (Spring, 1955), 8.

[193]New York, 1941, p. 35.

[194]P. 41.

[195]P. 330.

[196]Boston, 1955, pp. 75–118.

[197]*The Ferment of Realism*, p. 245.

[198]The dates following the titles are approximate dates of composition. No one has affixed definite dates for the individual stories, but some dates of composition are unsystematically revealed in the *Letters* and provide this rough, but generally accurate estimation.

[199]New York, 1914.

[200]New York, 1911 and 1912, resp. A letter written by London to George Brett in October, 1908 demonstrates that London had prepared these two volumes for publication long before they actually were published: *Letters*, 260–61.

[201]By 1909 London had written not only his best short stories but also *The Call of the Wild* (1903), *The Sea Wolf* (1904), *White Fang* (1906), *The Iron Heel* (1908), and *Martin Eden* (1909), his best novels. After the Snark cruise in 1909 he turned to hack work which produced his seventh Northland collection, *Smoke Bellew* (1912) and a third volume of South Seas tales, *A Son of the Sun* (1912), which are discussed in Chapter V below. Therefore, I have chosen 1909 as the decisive year in London's short story career. Not until the last year of his life did he resume writing serious

stories. It should also be mentioned that during this creative decade London also wrote some volumes of light-weight short fiction: *Tales of the Fish Patrol* (1905), *Moon Face* (1906) and *When God Laughs* (1911).

[202]See *Martin Eden*, pp. 98–107 for Martin's enthusiasm at discovering this work. See also London's letter to Johns saying that "to be well fitted for the tragedy of existence . . . one must have a working philosophy" of life and goes on to mention Spencer's notions of matter and force which are fully presented in *First Principles: Letters* (March, 1900), 101.

[203]*First Principles of a New System of Philosophy* (New York edition, 1876), p. 76.

[204]*First Principles*, p. 29.

[205]"London's *Heart of Darkness*," 75.

[206]"Four Versions," 150–51.

[207]*SW*, 16.

[208]"Jack London's Literary Artistry," p. 12.

[209]*Loc. cit.*

[210]*SW*, 145–159. As I will use the term, "limited" means that the character is the best that he can be but shares limitations inherent in the human condition. "Deficient" will be used as the pejorative term: a deficient character lacks good qualities that, presumably, are available to him.

[211]"Jack London's Literary Artistry," p. 42.

[212]*JB*, p. 12. See above, Chapter III, for a discussion of the other kinds of imagination.

[213]Labor, "Symbolic Wildernesses," 152.

[214]"London's *Heart of Darkness*," 76.

[215]Morris Renek, "Reflections on Violence as a Literary Tool," *Story*, I, no. 1 (May, 1967), 53.

[216]Dallas (second edition, 1957).

[217]*Ibid.*, pp. 8–9.

[218]*Ibid.*, p. 10.

[219]See above, Chapters II–III.

[220]See Zirkle, *Evolution, Marxian Biology and the Social Scene* for a discussion of London's racial views and their relations with his knowledge of biology and socialism, pp. 318–337.

[221] Race, however, is a motif in almost all of the earlier stories. In "The Wisdom of the Trail," for example, Mrs. Eppingwell is capable of mastering the rigors of the trail because of her Anglo-Saxon heritage, and Charlie can practice the code because he has learned the "honor and the law" from whites and is, therefore, superior to his Indian companions.

[222]*South Sea Tales* (New York, 1909), 200–01.

[223]"Introduction," *Documents*, 23.

[224]*South Sea Tales*, 200–01.

[225]Chicago, 1961, pp. 140–44.

[226]*Letters* (To Johns; July 5, 1899), 43.

[227]"Jack London's Literary Artistry," p. 43.

[228]See above, Chapters I–II.

[229]*Letters* (January 30, 1902), 129.

[230] One of the attractions of John Barleycorn was that in bars, London often mentioned, one found men willing to engage in a futile rebellion.

[231]"Batard," *The Faith of Man*, 201–32; "Love of Life," *Love of Life*, 3–42.

[232]*The American Short Story*, p. 245.

[233]*Ibid.*, p. 257.

[234]*Rebels and Ancestors*, p. 187.

[235]"The Theme of Jack London's 'To Build a Fire,' " *American Book Collector*, XVII (Nov., 1966), 17.

[236]*Ibid.*, p. 14.

[237]*Letters* (Sept. 15, 1905), 181.

[238]See p. 181 of *The Sea-Wolf* for a dialogue between Larsen and Maude which dramatizes the conflict between primary and secondary truth.

[239]New York, 1947.

[240]See *The War of the Classes* (1905) and *Revolution* (1910) which are collections of these. Other volumes contain social commentary critical of capitalism: *People of the Abyss* (1903) and *The Road* (1907). *The Iron Heel* is the socialist novel, but *Martin Eden* (1909), *Burning Daylight* (1910) and *Valley of the Moon* (1913) have long sections attacking the injustices and corruption in capitalist America.

[241] Again the publication dates of the volumes are misleading. Magazine dates of publication for the individual stories reveal that all were written from 1906–1911 (and only "The Mexican" after 1909). London himself comments about *The Strength*

of the Strong, not published until 1914, that the "stories were written by me before I started the *Snark* voyage" in April of 1907 (*Letters*, 433): they were written in 1906 as London tried to cure himself of the "long sickness" that had plagued him for three years.

[242]*The Mortal No* (Princeton, 1964), p. 16.

[243]*American Rebel*, p. 108.

[244]*Letters* (To the Editor of *Cosmopolitan Magazine*; August 30, 1909), 287.

[245]See "Chapter XVII," *The Star Rover* (New York, 1915) for evidence of London's interest in Jesus and His simply stated message of unity and love. See also "The Seed of McCoy," *South Sea Tales*, 259–327, discussed later in this chapter.

[246]*Letters* (Dec. 26, 1900), 118.

[247]*Joseph Conrad: a Psychoanalytic Biography* (Princeton, 1967), p. 243.

[248]*Ibid.*, p. 240.

[249]*Moon-Face* (New York, 1906), 87–113; orig. in *Pearson's Magazine* (May, 1901).

[250]*The Strength of the Strong*, 101–133; originally published in *The Red Book* (October, 1908).

[251]*Short Story Writing*, pp. 35–36. See also these London stories: "South of the Slot," *Strength of the Strong*, which portrays the contrast between upper and lower class life by using a protagonist with a split personality; "To Kill a Man and "Under Deck Awnings" in *The Night Born* which portray the insensitivity of rich women to the poor; "Chun Ah Chun," *The House of Pride*, which criticizes colonialism; and "Aloha Oe," *The House of Pride*, which depicts race prejudice in Hawaii. All these stories are sentimental and contrived.

[252]A letter written to Brett on Oct. 25, 1908 from the Solomon Islands proves that London had these stories on hand at this time (*Letters*, 260–61). Although the public thirst for Robert Louis Stevenson's adventurous romances set in the South Seas had been slaked by the turn of the century, London's early interest in his works, especially *Ebb Tide*, shows through in stories like "The House of Mauphi" (*SST*) and "The Pearls of Parlay" (*A Son of the Sun*).

[253]Earle Labor, "Jack London's Symbolic Wilderness," 152.

[254]Black-birding is discussed and serves as a basis for action in four of the eight stories in this collection: "Mauki," " 'Yah! Yah! Yah! Yah!,' " "The Terrible Solomons," and "The Inevitable White Man."

[255]For a discussion of the "deficient," see the analysis of "In a Far Country" above, Chapter IV.

[256]Charmian London, II, p. 148.

[257]*Letters* (To Lute Pease; April 22, 1911), 344.

[258]*Letters* (Sept., 26), 58. See, for example: "The King of the Mazy May," *Youth's Companion* (Nov., 1899), 29–30, and "Pluck and Percinacity," *Youth's Companion* (Jan. 4, 1900), 2–4, for two of London's earliest Klondike adventure stories.

[259]*Letters* (Aug. 10, 1899), 50.

[260]*Loc. cit.*

[261]*Ibid.* (Feb. 23, 1902), 133.

[262]*Love of Life*, 170. Originally, this story appeared in the August, 1906 issue of *Everybody's Magazine*.

[263]*The American Short Story*, pp. 281–83.

[264]*Ibid.*

[265]"The Short Story," *Nineteenth Century* (March, 1898), as quoted in Barrett, p. 123.

[266]"Jack London: A Study in Twentieth Century Values" (unpublished dissertation, University of Wisconsin, 1935), pp. 223–25.

[267]By this time the surprise ending was a cliched technique, although still popular with magazine readers (see Canby, *The Short Story*, p. 307). London used the technique throughout his career but never in a distinguished story. See for example: "The Faith of Men," *The Faith of Men*; "Trust," *Lost Face*; "Just Meat," *When God Laughs*; "Goody-by Jack," *The House of Pride*; and "The Eternity of Forms," *The Turtles of Tasman*.

[268]See above, Chapter I. "The Enemy of All the World," *The Strength of the Strong*, is another of these technological stories which may have been written early in London's career.

[269]"The Eternity of Forms," *The Turtles of Tasman*; "The Red One," *The Red One* (New York, 1918); Barrett, p. 30.

[270]See Chapter VI, below for a discussion of London's use of psychological theories.

[271]See the correspondence with Lewis, dating from Sept. 28, 1910 to Nov. 15, 1911 in *Letters*, 483–89. "Winged Blackmail" (*Night-Born*), "When the World was Young" (*Night-Born*) and "The Prodigal Father" (*Turtles of Tasman*) are the only three stories identified as coming from Lewis. See also Franklin Walker, "Jack London's Use of Sinclair Lewis Plots, Together with a Printing of Three of the Plots," *Huntington Library Quarterly*, XVII (Nov., 1953), 59–74. Joan London claims that Sterling's ideas were the basis for some of the best of London's last stories (p. 327) but does not identify them. "The First Poet" (*Turtles of Tasman*) is one of these—see London's letter to Sterling of Nov. 16, 1910, *Letters*, 321. In this instance, it is possible that London plagiarized, with Sterling's permission, the entire story and not just the plot.

[272]"The Stampede to Squaw Creek" (*SB*) repeats the race incident again. See also,

"A Daughter of the Aurora" (*God of His Fathers*) written while London was writing *A Daughter of the Snows*, which has the same setting and race.

[273]See above, Chapter III, for a discussion of the Kid's roles in "The Men of Forty-Mile" and "The Wife of a King" and their relationship to London's theory of "imagination."

[274]II, p. 202.

[275]"The Taste of the Meat" and "The Meat," the first two stories in the collection, amount to introductory chapters rather than stories.

[276]*Letters*, 363.

[277]*Ibid.* (To George P. Brett; April 22, 1913), 380. In the letter he mentions that he had not written a story for a year and a half and that *Cosmopolitan* was paying him $2200 a month.

[278]A later letter to Edgar Sisson (*Letters*, 414) indicates that this story was "The Princess." Sisson rejected it, and it was published for the first time in *The Red One* (1918).

[279]*Letters* (To Edgar J. Sisson; March 7, 1916), 465.

[280]*Letters*, 465–66. For five years London had devoted himself to writing novels but his efforts were disappointing: *The Valley of the Moon* (1913) and *The Little Lady of the Big House* (1916), like his play *The Acorn Planter* (1915), are sentimental promotions of domestic rural life; *The Mutiny of the Elsinore* (1914) a pot-boiler adventure about rounding the Horn; and *Jerry of the Islands* (1917) and *Michael Brother of Jerry* (1917), sentimental dog stories which combine the elements of social comment and South Seas racism that had flawed his worst short stories.

[281]*Psychology of the Unconscious: A Study of the Transformations and Symbolisms of the Libido—A Contribution to the History of the Evolution of Thought* (New York). Hereafter cited in the text as *P*. Charmian London mentions that Jack owned this volume and underlined various passages in it (II, p. 353).

[282]See above, Chapter V, for a discussion of this story.

[283]*Jack London: A Biography* (Boston, 1964), p. 367.

[284]*Ibid.*, p. 391. It will be demonstrated below that Jack London was more interested in Jungian thought than Freudian.

[285]II, pp. 322–23.

[286]It is surprising that although O'Connor and Charmian London, as well as some others, have mentioned London's late interest in psychoanalysis and that it is reflected in the last stories, no one has pursued the implications of that knowledge. It is doubly surprising since the Hawaiian stories in *On the Makaloa Mat* include some of the best short stories London wrote.

[287]*The End of American Innocence* (New York, 1959), p. 233.

[288]Typically, London's reading was enthusiastically eclectic rather than scholarly, and he seized upon a provocative book rather than thoroughly investigated the field.

[289]At this time, anyway, Jung and Freud were in substantial agreement about fundamental concepts so that it is, when discussing London's fiction, of little importance to distinguish what ideas he took from Freud and which from Jung. Subscribing to both men's views at this time would cause no intellectual contradictions that could lead to thematic or symbolic confusions in a work of fiction.

[290]See above, Chapters I–IV.

[291]New York, p. 9. This work recounts the modern narrator's dreams of prehistory.

[292]Human, All Too Human, II, p. 27, as quoted by Jung, p. 28. See O'Connor for a brief mention of Nietzsche's concept of "eternal recurrence" as it is used by Jack London in The Star Rover (New York, 1915), p. 364.

[293]Quoted by Jung, p. 29.

[294]Jung, xix, p. 30, p. 292.

[295]II, p. 354. She also claims, more accurately, that this story was composed in September, 1916.

[296]See Franklin Walker, Jack London and the Klondike for a comparison of these details to London's own experiences in the Klondike and a list of stories in which similar events transpire: pp. 61, 65, 77, 80, 93, 137, 152, 232–33.

[297]Ibid., pp. 230, 232. For Walker this is a change from "a good yarn, given dramatic cogency through the use of 'actuality' " which "goes to pieces in its latter part, when it departs from London's experiences." He argues that it is improbable that an old man could survive alone in the cold. For that matter, in my opinion, the first part of the story is just as improbable because of Tarwater's age. Moreover, London is sometimes most effective when he "departs from experiences" and becomes mythical and at his worst when cataloging incidents and multiplying characters instead of exercising his "art of omission."

[298]This Jungian pharse, as well as concept, was anticipated in London's fiction years before as a basic irony in many of his stories: the act of killing creates an ecstasy which "marks the summit of life," he wrote in The Call of the Wild, Bantam edition (New York, 1963), p. 49.

[299]See above, Chapters II and III, for a discussion of "true adventure" and "imagination."

[300]Charmian London, p. 358.

[301]See above, Chapter V, for a discussion of this volume.

[302]Charmian London, p. 353.

[303]A. Grove Day, "Introduction," Stories of Hawaii (New York, 1965), p. 17.

[304]Charmian London, p. 354.

[305]*P*, pp. 223, 403, 292.

[306]O'Connor, pp. 368–70, 373–76.

[307]See Charmian London, II, "The Last Summer," pp. 352–396.

[308]Princeton, 1957.

SELECTED BIBLIOGRAPHY

PRIMARY SOURCES

Stories by Jack London

Children of the Frost. Edited by I. O. Evans. London: Arco Publications, Inc,
    1963.
The Complete Stories of Jack London. Edited by Earle Labor, Robert C. Leitz,
    III, and Milo Shepard. 3 vols. Stanford, Calif.: Stanford University
    Press, 1993.
Dutch Courage and Other Stories. New York: Macmillan Co., 1922.
The Faith of Men and Other Stories. New York: Macmillan Co., 1904.
The God of His Fathers and Other Stories. New York: McClure, Philips and
    Co., 1901.
The House of Pride and Other Tales of Hawaii. New York: Macmillan Co.,
    1912.
Lost Face. New York: Macmillan Co., 1910.
Love of Life and Other Stories. New York: Macmillan Co., 1906.
Moon-Face and Other Stories. New York: Macmillan Co., 1906.
The Night-Born. New York: Century Co., 1913.
On the Makaloa Mat. New York: Macmillan Co., 1919.
The Red One. New York: Macmillan Co., 1918.
Smoke Bellew Tales. New York: Century Co., 1912.
A Son of the Sun. New York: Doubleday, Page and Co., 1912.
The Son of the Wolf, Tales of the Far North. New York: Houghton, Mifflin Co.,
1900.
South Sea Tales. New York: Macmillan Co., 1911.
The Strength of the Strong. New York: Macmillan Co., 1914.
Tales of the Fish Patrol. New York: Macmillan Co., 1905.
The Turtles of Tasman. New York: Macmillan Co., 1916.
When God Laughs. New York: Macmillan Co., 1911.

Book-length Fiction by Jack London

The Abysmal Brute. New York: Century Co., 1913.
Adventure. New York: Macmillan Co., 1911.
Before Adam. New York: Macmillan Co., 1962.
Burning Daylight. New York: Macmillan Co., 1910.
The Call of the Wild. New York: Macmillan Co., 1903.
The Cruise of the Dazzler. Edited by I. O. Evans. New York: Archer House,
    Inc., 1963.

A Daughter of the Snows. New York: J. B. Lippincott Co., 1902.
The Game. New York: Macmillan Co., 1905.
The Iron Heel. New York: Sagamore Press Inc., 1957.
Jerry of the Islands. New York: Macmillan Co., 1917.
The Little Lady of the Big House. New York: Macmillan Co., 1916.
Martin Eden. Edited by Sam Baskett. New York: Rinehart and Co., Inc., 1956.
Michael, Brother of Jerry. New York: Macmillan Co., 1917.
The Mutiny of the Elsinore. New York: Macmillan Co., 1914.
Revolution and Other Essays. New York: Macmillan Co., 1910.
The Road. New York: Macmillan Co., 1907.
The Sea Wolf. New York: The New American Library of World Literature, 1964.
The Star Rover. New York: Macmillan Co., 1963.
The Valley of the Moon. New York: Macmillan Co., 1913.
War of the Classes. New York: Macmillan Co., 1905.
White Fang. New York: Macmillan Co., 1906.

Articles by Jack London

"Again the Literary Aspirant." *Critic* 41 (September 1902): 217-20.
"*Foma Gordyeeff*." *Impressions* 2 (November 1901): 85-87.
"*The Jungle*." *New York Evening Journal*, 8 August 1906, 2.
"The Lawgivers." *Collier's* 53 (20 June 1914): 16-17, 28-29.
"*The Octopus*." *Impressions* 2 (June 1901): 45-47.
"Stranger Than Fiction." *Critic* 43 (June 1903): 123-26.
"The Terrible and Tragic in Fiction." *Critic* 42 (June 1903): 539-43.

Miscellaneous Works by Jack London

Jack London Reports. Edited by King Hendricks and Irving Shepard. New York: Doubleday, 1970.
John Barleycorn. New York: Century Co., 1913.
Letters from Jack London. Edited by King Hendricks and Irving Shepard. New York: Odyssey Press, 1965.
The Letters of Jack London. Edited by Earle Labor, Robert C. Leitz III, and I. Milo Shepard. 3 vols. Stanford, Calif.: Stanford University Press, 1988.
No Mentor but Myself: a Collection of Articles, Essays, Reviews, and Letters, by Jack London. on Writing and Writers. Edited by Dale L. Warlker. Port Washington, N.Y.: Kennikat, 1979.

Ancillary Works

Baker, Ray Stannard. "A Story of the Fire Patrol." *McClure's* 12 (November 1898): 19-22.

Bonsal, Stephen. "The Day of Battle: Stories Gathered in the Field." *McClure's* 12 (January 1899): 223-31.

Conrad, Joseph. *Lord Jim*. New York: Modern Library, 1931.

_____. *Youth: A Narrative*. New York: Archer House, Inc, 1964.

Crane, Stephen. "Marines Under Fire at Guantanamo." *McClure's* 12 (February 1899): 332-36.

_____. "The Open Boat." *Scribner's* 21 (June 1897): 728-40.

_____. "The Woof of the Thin Red Threads." *Cosmopolitan* 26 (December 1898): 164-72.

Ewing, Jasper Jr. "Adventures of a Train Dispatcher." *McClure's* 12 (November 1898): 44-48.

Fraser, W. A. "Raja Singh and Other Elephants." *McClure's* 12 (November 1898): 40-44.

_____. "A Tiger in the Tea Gardens." *McClure's* 12 (December 1898): 176-78.

Garland, Hamlin. "Hitting the Trail." *McClure's* 12 (January 1899): 298-304.

_____. "Rising Wolf—Ghost Dancer." *McClure's* (January 1899): 241-48.

_____. "The Trail to the Golden North," *McClure's* 12 (April 1899): 505-7.

Ingersoll, Justine. "The Commodore." *Atlantic Monthly* 82 (August 1898): 235.

Kipling, Rudyard. "In the Rukh." *McClure's* 7 (June 1898): 23-39.

_____. "Quigierern." *McClure's* 5 (November 1895): 552-61.

_____. "The Ship that Found Herself." *McClure's* 6 (March 1896): 328-37.

_____. "Slaves of the Lamp." *McClure's* 9 (August 1897): 837-59.

_____. "The White Man's Burden," *McClure's* 12 (December 1898): 190-93.

_____. *Works*. New York: Doubleday and McClure Co., 1917.

Lewis, Charles B. "The Story of His First Battle." *Cosmopolitan* 25 (June 1898): 216-19.

Mahan, Alfred. "The War on the Seas and Its Lessons." *McClure's* 12 (December 1898-April 1899): 110-18, 231-340, 353-62, 470-80, 527-34.

Robertson, Morgan. "Where Angels Fear to Tread." *Atlantic Monthly* 82 (August 1898): 527-34.

Spears, John R. "The Confessions of a Sea-faring Blackmailer." *Cosmopolitan* 28 (April 1900): 667-68.

Waldron, George B. "500 Years of the Anglo Saxon." *McClure's* 12 (December 1898): 185-88.

Ward, Herbert. "Heroes of the Deep." *Century* 56 (July-August 1898): 364-77, 517-25.

Wilcox, Mortimer O. "The Fore-runners of Empire." *McClure's* 12 (December 1898): 189-92.

SECONDARY SOURCES

Bibliography

"Alaskan Articles that have Appeared in *The Overland,*" *Overland Monthly,* N. S., 30 (October 1897): 382.

Firkins, In Ten Eyck. *Index to Short Stories.* New York: H. W. Wilson Co., 1915.

Goodrich, N. L. "Prose Fiction: A Bibliography of Criticism," *Bulletin of Bibliography* 4 (July 1906-January 1907): 118-21, 133-36, 153-55; 5 (April 1907): 11-13.

Hamilton, David Mike. *"Tools of My Trade"*: *The Annotated Books in Jack London's Library.* Seattle: University of Washington Press, 1986.

Haydock, James. "Jack London: A Bibliography of Criticism," *Bulletin of Bibliography* 23 (May-August 1960): 42-46.

Lachtman, Howard. "Criticism of Jack London: A Selected Checklist," *Modern Fiction Studies* 22 (spring 1976): 107-25.

London, Charmian. "Appendix," *The Book of Jack London,* 2:397-414.

Pattee, Fred Lewis. "Notable Books and Articles on Short-Story History and Technique," *The Development of the American Short Story,* 337-38.

Romm, Charles. "Jack London, a Bibliographical Checklist (1876-1916)," *Publisher's Weekly,* 103 (4 February 1923):1021.

Sherman, Joan. *Jack London: A Reference Guide.* Boston: G. K. Hall, 1977.

Smith, Frank R. "Periodical Articles on the American Short Story: A Selected Annotated Bibliography," *Bulletin of Bibliography* 23 (January 1960-April 1961): 9-13, 46-48, 95-96.

Walker, Dale L., and James E. Sisson, III, eds. *The Fiction of Jack London: A Chronological Bibliography.* El Paso: Texas Western Press, 1972.

Woodbridge, Hensley C., John London, and George H. Tweney, comps. *Jack London: A Bibliography.* Georgetown, Calif.: Talisman Press, 1966. Enlarged edition, Millwood, N.Y.: Kraus, 1973.

_____. "Jack London: A Bibliography, a Supplement," *American Book Collector* 17 (November 1966): 32-35.

B. Short Story Commentary in Books and Articles Appearing in Popular Magazines: 1880-1920

Albright, Evelyn M. *The Short Story: Its Principles and Structure.* New York: Macmillan Co., 1908.

Allen, James Lane. "Two principles in Recent American Fiction." *Atlantic Monthly* 80 (October 1897): 433-41.

Alvord, James Church. "The Typical American Short Story." *Yale Review* 9 (April 1920): 650, 655.

Andrews, E. F. "Rudimentary Suggestions for Beginners in Story-Writing." *Cosmopolitan* 22 (February 1897): 446-49.

"Art of Fiction." *Saturday Review* 78 (17 November 1894): 530-31.

Atherton, Gertrude. "The Novel and the Short Story." *Bookman* 17 (March 1903): 36-37.

Baker Harry Torsey. *The Contemporary Short Story*. New York: D. C. Health and Co., 1916.

Baldwin, Charles Sears. *American Short Stories*. New York: Longmans, Green and Co., 1904.

Barr, Robert, Harold Frederick, Arthur Morrison, and Jan Barlow. "How to Write a Short Story: A Symposium." *Bookman* 5 (March 1897): 42-46.

Barrett, Charles R. *Short Story Writing: A Practical Treatise on the Art of the Short Story*. New York: Baker and Taylor Co., 1898.

Bates, Arlo. "Realism and the Art of Fiction." *Scribner's* 2 (August 1887): 241-52.

Boyensen, Hjalmar Hjorth. "Great Realists and Empty Story-Tellers." *Forum* 18 (February 1895): 724-31.

Briscoe, Margaret Sutton. "Astigmatic Literature." *Literature* 5 (1899): 531-32.

Buckham, James. "Is the Sad Ending Artistic?" *Critic*, N. S. 27 (1897): 291.

Cable, George Washington. "Speculations of a Story-teller." *Atlantic Monthly* 78 (July 1896): 88-96.

Canby, Henry Seidel. *The Short Story in English*. New York: H. Holt and Co., 1909.

_____. *A Study of the Short Story*. New York: H. Holt and Co., 1913.

Crockett, S. R. "On Some Tales of Mr. Kipling's." *Bookman* 1 (February 1895): 24.

Cross, Ethan Allen. *The Short Story: A Technical and Literary Study*. Chicago: A. C. McClurg and Co., 1914.

Dagget, R. M. "Motion and Emotion in Fiction." *Overland Monthly,* N. S. 26 (1895): 614-17.

Darrow, Clarence S. "Realism in Literature and Art." *Arena* 9 (December 1893): 98-113.

Doughty, Francis Albert. "Sound Logic in Fiction." *Critic,* N. S. 26 (1895):

429-31.

Essenwein, J. B. *Writing the Short Story: A Practical Book on the Rise, Structure, Writing and Sale of the Modern Short Story*. New York: Hinds, Hayden and Eldredge, Inc., 1909.

Fuller, Edward. "Art for Art's Sake." *Bookman* 1 (May 1895): 241.

Gosse, Edmund. "Limits of Realism in Fiction." *Forum* 9 (June 1890): 391.

Grabo, Carl H. *The Art of the Short Story*. New York: C. Scribner's Sons, 1913.

Hamilton, Clayton. *A Manual of the Art of Fiction*. Garden City, N.Y.: Doubleday, Page and Co., 1908.

_____. *Materials and Methods of Fiction*. New York: Baker and Taylor Co., 1908.

Harrison, Frederic. "Decadence of Romance." *Forum* 15 (1893): 216-24.

How to Write Fiction. London: Bellaries and Co., n.d.

Lang, Andrew. "The Art of Fiction." *Critic* 4 (24 May 1884): 249-50.

_____. "Realism and Romance." *Contemporary Review* 52 (1887): 683-93.

_____. "Tendencies in Fiction." *North American Review* 161 (August 1895): 153-60.

Lieberman, Elias. *The American Short Story*. Ridgewood, N.J.: Editor Publishing Co., 1912.

MacArthur, James. "Romance and Realism." *Bookman* 1 (May 1895): 257.

Mabie, H. W. "Fiction as a Literary Form." *Scribner's* 5 (May 1889): 620-23.

_____. "Two Eternal Types in Fiction." *Forum* 19 (March 1895): 41-47.

Mallock, W. H. "Relation of Art to Truth." *Forum* 9 (March 1890): 36-46.

Masson, F. L. "Simple, Isn't It? The Literature of the Mechanics of Short Story Writing." *Bookman* 48 (February 1919): 709-11.

Matson, Esther. "The Short Story." *Outlook* 121 (5 March 1919): 406-9.

Matthews, Brander. *The Philosophy of the Short Story*. New York: Longmans, Green and Co., 1901.

_____. "Romance Against Romanticism." *Bookman* 12 (January 1901): 463-67.

Neal, Robert W. *To-Day's Short Stories Analyzed*. New York: Oxford University Press, American Branch, 1918.

Newman, Frances. "The American Short Story in the First, Twenty-five Years of the Twentieth Century." *Bookman* 58 (April 1926): 186-93.

Parker, Gilbert. "The Art of Fiction." *Critic* 33 (December 1898): 466-69.

Pattee, Fred Lewis. *The Development of the American Short Story*. New York: Harper and Brothers, 1923.

Perry, Bliss. *A Study of Prose Fiction*. New York: Houghton Mifflin Co., 1902.

Perry, Jennette Barbour. "Mr. Kipling as an Artist." *Critic* 33 (December 1898): 473.

"The Persistent Mystery of the Modern Short Story." *Current Opinion* 67

(August 1919): 119-20.

"Pessimism in Fiction." *Literature* 3 (1898): 509-10.

Pitkin, W. B. *The Art and the Business of Story Writing*. New York: Harcourt Brace, 1912.

Thayer, W. R. "New Story-tellers and the Doom of Realism." *Forum* 17 (November 1894): 470-80.

Thompson, Maurice. "Critics and the Romancers." *Independent* 52 (4 January 1900): 19-21.

_____. "The Domain of Romance." *Forum* 8 (November 1889): 326-36.

Quirk, Leslie W. *How to Write a Short Story*. New York: Editor Publishing Co., 1904.

Wedmore, Frederick. "The Short Story." *Nineteenth Century* 43 (March 1898): 406-16.

Commentary on London: Books

Baskett, Sam S. "Introduction." *Martin Eden*. New York: Rinehart and Co., 1956.

_____. "Jack London's Fiction: Its Social Milieu." Ph.D. diss., University of California, 1951.

Berthoff, Warner. *The Ferment of Realism, American Literature, 1884-1919*. New York: Free Press, 1965.

Carlson, Ray Warner. "Jack London's Heroes: A Study of Evolutionary Thought." Ph.D. diss., University of New Mexico, 1962.

Cassuto, Leonard, and Jeanne Campbell Reeesman, eds. *Rereading Jack London*. Stanford, Calif.: Stanford University Press, 1996.

Day, A. Grove. "Introduction." *Stories of Hawaii*. New York: Appleton-Century, 1965.

Foner, Philip S. *Jack London, American Rebel*. New York: Citadel Press, 1947.

Geismar, Maxwell. *Rebels and Ancestors: The American Novel, 1890-1915*. New York: Hill and Wang, 1963.

Hendrick, Joan D. *Solitary Comrade: Jack London and His Work*. Chapel Hill: University of North Carolina Press, 1982.

Holland, Robert B. "Jack London: His Thought and Art in Relation to His Time." Ph.D. diss., University of Wisconsin, 1950.

Johnston, Carolyn. *Jack London—An American Radical?* Westport, Conn.: Greenwood, 1984.

Kingman, Russ. *Jack London: A Definitive Chronology*. Middletown, Calif.: Rejl, 1992.

_____. *A Pictorial Life of Jack London*. New York: Crown, 1979.

Labor, Earle. "Introduction." *The Portable Jack London*. New York: Penguin

Books, 1994.

_____. *Jack London*. New York: Twayne Publishers, Inc., 1974.

_____. "Jack London's Literary Artistry: His Symbolism in Relation to His
　　　　Themes." Ph.D. diss., University of Wisconsin, 1961.

Labor, Earle, and Jeanne Campbell Reesman. *Jack London*. Rev. ed. New York:
Twayne Publishers, Inc., 1994.

Labor, Earle, and Robert C. Leitz III. "Introduction." *Short Stories of Jack
　　　　London: Authorized One-Volume Edition*. Edited by Earle Labor,
Robert C. Leitz III, and I. Milo Shepard. New York: MacMillan Publishing
　　　　Co., 1990.

London, Charmian K. *The Book of Jack London*. 2 vols. New York: Century
　　　　Co., 1921.

London, Joan. *Jack London and His Daughters*. Berkeley, Calif.: Heyday
　　　　Books in conjunction with Rick Heide, 1990.

_____. *Jack London and His Times: An Unconventional Biography*. New York:
The Book League of America, 1939.

Lundquist, James. *Jack London: Adventures, Ideas, and Fiction*. New York:
　　　　Ungar, 1987.

Lynn, Kenneth S. *The Dream of Success, A Study of the Modern American
　　　　Imagination*. Boston: Little, Brown and Co., 1955.

O'Conner, Richard. *Jack London: A Biography*. Boston: Little, Brown and Co.,
1964.

Ownbey, Ray Wilson, ed. *Jack London: Essays in Criticism*. Santa Barbara,
　　　　Calif.: Peregrine Smith, 1978.

Parrington, Vernon L. *Main Currents in American Thought*. Vol. 3. New York:
　　　　Harper and Brothers, 1930.

Pattee, Fred Lewis. *The Development of the American Short Story*. New York:
　　　　Harper and Brothers, 1923.

_____. *The New American Literature*. New York: Century Co., 1937.

Pope, Margaret I. "Jack London: A Study in Twentieth Century Values." Ph.D.
　　　　diss., University of Wisconsin, 1935.

Price, Starling. "Jack London's America." Ph.D. diss., University of Minnesota, 1966.

Rideout, Walter B. *The Radical Novel in the United States 1900-1954, Some
　　　　Interrelations of Literature and Society*. Cambridge, Mass.: Harvard
　　　　University Press, 1956.

Rothberg, Abraham. "The House that Jack Built: A Study of Jack London."
　　　　Ph.D. diss., Columbia, University, 1952.

_____. "Introduction." *The Call of the Wild and White Fang*. New York:
　　　　Bantam Books, 1963.

Shivers, Alfred Samuel. "Romanticism in Jack London." Ph.D. diss., Florida

State University, 1962.

Sinclair, Andrew. *Jack: A Biography of Jack London*. New York: Harper and Row, 1977.

Stasz, Clarice. *American Dreamers: Charmian and Jack London*. New York: St. Martin's, 1988.

Stoddard, Martin. *California Writers: Jack London, John Steinbeck, the Tough Guys*. New York: St. Martin's, 1983.

Stone, Irving. *Jack London, Sailor on Horseback*. New York: Houghton Mifflin Co., 1938.

Tavernier-Courbin, Jacqueline, ed. *Critical Essays on Jack London*. Boston: G. K. Hall, 1983.

Walcutt, Charles Child. *American Literary Naturalism, a Divided Stream*. Minneapolis: University of Minnesota Press, 1956.

_____. *Jack London*. ("Pamphlets on American Writers," No. 57) Minneapolis: University of Minnesota Pamphlets, 1966.

Walker, Dale L. *The Alien Worlds of Jack London*. Grand Rapids, Mich.: World House Books, 1973.

Walker, Franklin. *Jack London and the Klondike, the Genesis of an American Writer*. London: Bodley Head Ltd., 1966.

Watson, Charles N., Jr. *The Novels of Jack London: A Reappraisal*. Madison: University of Wisconsin Press, 1983.

West, Ray B., Jr. *The Short Story in America*. Chicago: Gateway Edition, 1952.

Wilcox, Earl J. "Jack London and the Tradition of American Literary Naturalism." Ph.D. diss., Vanderbilt University, 1950.

Williams, Tony. *Jack London—the Movies*. Middletown, Calif.: Rejl, 1992.

Commentary on London: Periodicals

Baskett, Sam S. "Jack London on the Oakland Waterfront," *American Literature* 27 (November 1955): 363-71.

_____. "Jack London's *Heart of Darkness*." *American Quarterly* 10 (September 1958): 66-77.

Berkove, Lawrence I. "A Parallax Connection in London's 'The Unparalleled Invasion,'" *American Literary Realism* 24 (winter 1992): 33-39.

Blackman, Gordon N., Jr. "Jack London: Visionary Realist." *Jack London Newsletter* 13 (September-December 1980): 82-94; Part II, *JLN* 14 (January-April 1981): 1-12.

Bland, Henry Meade. "Jack London." *Overland Monthly*, N.S. 43 (May 1904): 370-75.

_____. "The Work of Jack London." *Overland Monthly*, N.S. 56 (May 1904):

410-16.

Bosworth, L. A. M. "Is Jack London a Plagiarist?" *Independent* 62 (14 February 1907): 247-50.

Brown, Ellen. "A Perfect Sphere: Jack London's 'The Red One.'" *Jack London Newsletter* 11 (May-December 1978): 81-85.

Campbell, Jeanne. "Falling Stars: Myth in 'The Red One.'" *Jack London Newsletter* 11 (May-December 1978): 87-101.

Collins, Billy G. "Jack London's 'The Red One': Journey to a Lost Heart." *Jack London Newsletter* 10 (January-April 1977): 1-6.

Clareson, Thomas D. "Notes on 'The Red One.'" *A Spectrum of Worlds*. New York: Doubleday, 1973.

Courbin, Jacqueline M. "Jack London's Portrayal of the Natives in His First Four Collection of Arctic Tales." *Jack London Newsletter* 10 (September-December 1977): 127-37.

Connell, S. "Jack London Wooed Fame Through the *Overland Monthly*." *Overland Monthly*, N.S. 76 (October 1920): 65-71.

Dickson, D. H. "A Note on Jack London and David Starr Jordan," *Indiana Magazine of History* 38 (December 1942): 407-10.

Dhondt, Steven T. "Jack London's Satires in *When God Laughs*: Overman, Underdog, and Satire." *Jack London Newsletter* 2 (May-August 1969): 51-57.

Eames, Ninetta. "Jack London." *Overland Monthly* 25 (May 1900): 417-25.

Foner, Philip S. "Jack London: An Appreciation." *American Book Collector* 17 (November 1966): 9-10.

Gair, Christopher. "Hegemony, Metaphor, and Structural Difference: The 'Strange Dualism' of 'South of the Slot.'" *Arkansas Quarterly* 40 (spring 1993): 73-97.

Giles, James R. "Some Notes on the Red-Blooded Reading of Kipling by Jack London and Frank Norris." *Jack London Newsletter* 3 (May-August 1970): 56-62.

Graham, Don. "Jack London's Tale Told by a High-Grade Feeb." *Studies in Short Fiction* 15 (fall 1978): 429-33.

Gurian, Jay. "The Romantic Necessity in Literary Naturalism: Jack London." *American Literature* 38 (March 1966): 112-20.

"Jack London, Apostle of the Primitive." *Current Literature* 39 (December 1905): 673-74.

"Jack London Number." *Overland Monthly*, N.S. 90 (May 1932).

"Jack London Special Number." *American Book Collector* 17 (November 1966).

Jennings, Ann S. "London's Code of the Northland." *Alaskan Review* 1, no. 3

(1964): 43-48.

Kirsch, James. "Jack London's Quest: 'The Red One.'" *Psychological Perspectives* 11 (fall 1980): 137-54.

Kratzke, Peter. "Jack London's Optimistic View of the Law: A Reading of *The Son of The Wolf*." *Studies in Short Fiction* 32 (winter 1995): 67-74.

Labor, Earle. "The Archetypal Woman as 'Martyr to Truth': Jack London's 'Samuel.'" *American Literary Realism* 24 (winter 1992): 23-32.

_____. "From 'All Gold Canyon' to *The Acorn-Planter*: Jack London's Agrarian Vision." *Western American Literature* 11 (summer 1976): 83-102.

_____. "Jack London's Symbolic Wilderness: Four Versions." *Nineteenth Century Fiction* 11, no. 7 (1962): 25-27.

_____. "'To the Man on Trail': Jack London's Christmas Carol." *Jack London Newsletter* 3 (September-December 1970): 90-94.

Labor, Earle, and King Hendricks. "Jack London's Twice-Told Tale." *Studies in Short Fiction* 4 (summer 1967): 334-47.

Lay, Wilfred. " 'John Barleycorn' Under Psychoanalysis." *Bookman* 45 (March 1917): 47-54.

London, Joan. "The London Divorce." *American Book Collector* 17 (November 1966): 31.

May, Charles E. "'To Build a Fire': Physical Fiction and Metaphysical Critics." *Studies in Short Fiction* 15 (winter 1978): 19-24.

Mills, Gordon. "Jack London's Quest for Salvation." *American Quarterly* 7 (spring 1955): 3-14.

_____. "The Symbolic Wilderness: James Fenimore Cooper and Jack London." *Nineteenth Century Fiction* 13 (March 1959): 329-40.

Mitchell, Lee Clark. "Keeping His Head: Repetition and Responsibility in London's 'To Build a Fire.'" *Journal of Modern Literature* 13 (March 1986): 76-96.

Moreland, David A. "The Quest That Failed: Jack London's Last Tales of the South Seas." *Pacific Studies* 8 (fall 1984): 48-70.

_____. "Violence in the South Sea Fiction of Jack London." *Jack London Newsletter* 16 (January-April 1983): 1-35.

Murphy, C. G. "Library Collected by Jack London." *Overland Monthly,* N.S., 90 (May 1932): 111-12.

Naso, Anthony J. "Jack London and Herbert Spencer." *Jack London Newsletter* 14 (January-April 1981): 13-34.

Petersen, Per Serritslev. "Science-Fictionalizing the Paradox of Living: Jack London's 'The Red One' and the Ecstasy of Regression." *The Dolphin* (University of Aarhus, Denmark) 11 (April 1985): 35-58.

Peterson, Clell T. "The Jack London Legend." *American Book Collector* 8

(January 1958): 13-17.

_____. "Jack London's Alaskan Tales." *American Book Collector* 9 (April 1959): 15-22.

_____. "Jack London's Sonoma Novels." *American Book Collector* 9 (October 1958): 15-20.

_____. "The Theme of Jack London's 'To Build a Fire,'" *American Book Collector* 17 (November 1966): 15-18.

Pizer, Donald. "Jack London: The Problem of Form." *Studies in the Literary Imagination* 16 (fall 1983): 107-15.

Reesman, Jeanne C. "Jack London—Kama'aina." *Jack London Newsletter* 18 (September-December 1985): 71-76.

_____. "Knowledge and Identity in London's Pacific Fiction." *Jack London Newsletter* 19 (September-December 1986): 91-95.

_____. "The Problem of Knowledge in Jack London's 'The Water Baby.'" *Western American Literature* 23 (fall 1988): 201-15.

Shivers, Alfred S. "The Demoniacs in Jack London." *American Book Collector* 12 (September 1961): 11-14.

_____. "Jack London's Mate-Woman." *American Book Collector* 15 (October 1964): 17-21.

_____. "The Romantic in Jack London: Far Away Frozen Wilderness." *Alaskan Review* 1, no. 1 (1963): 38-47.

Sinclair, Upton. "About Jack London." *New Masses* 9 (November-December 1917): 17-20.

Stasz, Clarice. "The Social Construction of Biography: The Case of Jack London." *Modern Fiction Studies* 22 (spring 1976): 51-71.

Tavernier-Courbin, Jacqueline. "Jack London's Science Fiction." *Jack London Newsletter* 17 (September-December 1984): 71-78.

_____. "'The Wife of a King': A Defense." *Jack London Newsletter* 10 (January-April 1977): 34-38.

Walcutt, Charles Child. "Naturalism and the Superman in the Novels of Jack London." *Papers of the Michigan Academy of Science, Arts and Letters* 24 (1938): 89-107.

Walker, Franklin. "Jack London's Use of Sinclair Lewis Plots, Together with a Printing of Three of the Plots." *Huntington Library Quarterly* 17 (November 1953): 59-74.

Ward, Susan. "Jack London's Women: Civilization vs. The Frontier." *Jack London Newsletter* 9 (May-August 1976): 81-85.

_____. "Jack London and the Blue Pencil: London's Correspondence with Popular Editors." *American Literary Realism, 1870-1910* 14 (spring 1981): 16-25.

Woodward, Robert H. "Jack London's Code of Primitivism." *Folio* 18 (May 1953): 39-44.
Miscellaneous

Becker, George J., ed. *Documents of Modern Literary Realism*. Princeton:
    Princeton University Press, 1963.
Booth, Wayne C. *The Rhetoric of Fiction*. Chicago: University of Chicago
    Press, 1961.
Cady, Edwin. *Realist at War*. Syracuse: Syracuse University Press, 1958.
Frohock, W. M. *The Novel of Violence in America*. Dallas: Southern Methodist
    University Press, 1957.
Frye, Northrup. *The Anatomy of Criticism: Four Essays*. Princeton: Princeton
    University Press, 1957.
Haeckel, Ernst. *The Riddle of the Universe*. New York: Harper and Brothers
    Publishers, 1900.
Hart, Walter Morris. *Kipling the Story-Writer*. Berkeley: University of
    California Press, 1918.
Hoffman, Frederick J. *The Mortal No: Death and the Modern Imagination*.
    Princeton: Princeton University Press, 1964.
Howells, William Dean. *Criticism and Fiction*. Cambridge, Mass.: Walker-de
    Berry, Inc., 1962.
Jung, Carl G. *Psychology of the Unconscious, A Study of the Transformations
    and Symbolisms of the Libido*. Translated by Beatice M. Hinkle. New
    York: Dodd, Mead and Co., 1916.
May, Henry R. *The End of American Innocence*. Chicago: Quadrangle Books
    Inc., 1964.
Meyer, Bernard C., M.D. *Joseph Conrad: A Psychoanalytic Biography*.
    Princeton: Princeton University Press, 1967.
Mott, Frank Luther. *Golder Multitudes: The Story of Best Sellers in the United
    States*. New York: Macmillan Co., 1947.
_____. *A History of American Magazines*. 4 vols. Cambridge, Mass.: Harvard
    University Press, 1938-57.
Norris, Frank. *The Responsibilities of the Novelist*. Cambridge, Mass.: Walker-
    de Berry, Inc., 1962.
Peden, William. *The American Short Story: Front Line in the Defense of
    Literature*. Boston: Houghton Mifflin Co., 1964.
Peterson, Theodore B. *Magazines in the Twentieth Century*. Urbana: University
    of Illinois Press, 1964.
Pizer, Donald. *Realism and Naturalism in Nineteenth-Century American
    Literature*. Carbondale: Southern Illinois University Press, 1966.
Spencer, Herbert. *First Principles of a New System of Philosophy*. New York:

D. Appleton and Co., 1876.

Wright, Austin M. *The American Short Story in the Twenties*. Chicago: University of Chicago Press, 1961.

Zirkle, Conway. *Evolution, Marxian Biology, and the Social Scene.* Philadelphia: University of Pennsylvania Press, 1959.

INDEX

A

Acorn Planter, The (London), 190n. 280

"actuality": and idealism, 144, 154; in London's fiction, xi, 39, 42, 54; in Malemute Kid tales, 58-78; in Northland stories, 50-51. *See also* realism; romance

adventure: stories popularity, 3-7; London's apprenticeship and, 10-33, 54, 75; masculine and London, 12; "true", 158, 172. *See also* magazines; racism

Alaska, as naturalistic symbolism, 49-50, 82. *See also* Klondike

Alaska stories, characterized, 141. *See also Children of the Frost; Faith of Men and Other Stories, The; God of His Fathers, The; Lost Face; Love of Life and Other Stories, The;* Northland tales; *Son of the Wolf, The*

alcohol, 47, 144. *See also John Barleycorn*

Aldrich, Thomas Bailey, 15

allegorical rhetoric, 32

"Aloha Oe", 137, 188n. 251

"Amateur Night" (London), 17

"American Kipling", 7

American Short Story of the Twenties (Wright), 74, 110, 142

Anatomy of Criticism (Frye), 173-74

Andrews, E. F., 38-39

anti-Semitism, 144

"Apostate, The", 123, 128-29, 131

Applegarth, Mabel: and London correspondence, 8; and marriage to London, 177n. 32; as model for *Martin Eden's* Ruth, 177n. 32

"apprenticeship" of London's growth, 8-33, 100

"art of omission" (London's), 191n. 297

artist: as propagandist, 124-25, 126; social role of, 125

Atlantic Monthly (magazine), 4

"At the Rainbow's End" (London), 178n. 58; construction of, 16; flawed, 95

autobiographical form, 36; and Jungian fantasy, 157-59, 165-67; London's, 3, 40, 46, 54, 58-59, 121, 156; and London's psychology interest, 152, 166-169. *See also Martin Eden*

awards and prizes, 3

B

Baker, Ray Stannard, 6

Barrett, Charles R., 13, 19, 25, 29, 131, 144, 178n. 49; on Kipling, 20

Baskett, Sam, 49, 83, 93

"Batard": analogy in, 108; horror in, 110-12, 113, 173

Becker, George, 98

Before Adam (London), 155

Berthoff, Warner, 80

"black-birding", 133, 134, 188n. 254

Black Cat Magazine, 10

"Bones of Kahelili, The" (London), 162, 165-66, 171, 172, 173

Bonsal, Stephen, 5

Bookman, The (magazine), 2, 7, 37

Booth, Wayne C., 99

Brett, George, London's letters to, 100, 185n. 200

"Bunches of Knuckles" (London), 144

Burning Daylight (London), 187n. 240

C

Call of the Wild, The (London), 33, 100, 191n. 298; ritual trip in, 50; writing of, 140

capitalism criticized in London's works, 187n. 240

Century (magazine), 4, 149

character(s): central, 21; "deficient", 134, 186n. 210, 188n. 255; factual control by, 117-18; landscape as, 118-19; London's idealized, 61, 184n. 171; with imagination, 62-65; and narrative functions, 21, 27; occupation, 133; pessimism in, 80-81; psychology, 52; reappearing across stories, 183n. 161, 184nn. 176, 177. *See also* Malemute Kid; narrator; protagonist; themes

Children of the Frost (London), 12, 25; as finest story collection, 96, 100; form changes in, 1; frame stories in, 104-108, 179n. 65; illustrative of London's form quest, 27, 99-101, 175n. 2; nature of the code in, 93; racial conflict in, 134; theme of loss in, 102-103, 109; visual quality of, 29; writing of, 140-41. *See also* "Death of Ligoun, The"; "Keesh, the Son of Keesh";

"Law of Life, The"; "League of Old Men, The"; "Master of Mystery, The"; "Nam-Bok the Unveracious"; "Sickness of Lone Chief, The"; "Sunlanders, The"; themes

"Chun Ah Chun" (London), 137, 138, 188n. 251

code: death of, 93; hero, 86-94; and imagination, 89-93; nature of, 93

colonialism criticized, 188n. 251

color imagery: black oblivion, 113; black philosophy, 122; blond hero, 148; gray subconscious, 113; white death, 147-48; white mysticism, 113, white redemption, 147. *See also* light-dark

compression, 14

Conkey's Home Journal (magazine), 9

Conrad, Joseph, 49, 60, 74, 76-77; similarity to London of, 27

conventions. *See* themes

correspondence: London's genre thought, 100, 149; London's health, 122. *See also* Applegarth, Mabel; Brett, George; Johns, Cloudesly; London, Charmian; Sterling, Carrie; Strunsky, Anna

Cosmopolitan Magazine, 2, 4, 145; novel contract,149, 190n. 277

Cowley, Malcomb, 46, 60

Crane, Stephen: and racism, 5; shared ideas with London, 41, 183n. 152; stories of, 4-5

"Created He Them" (London), 144

Critic, The (magazine), 37

"Curious Fragment, A", 123, 126-27, 130, 131

D

Darwin, Charles: and London, 52, 152, 171; and the soul, 45. *See also* social Darwinism

dating of works. *See* publication dates

"Daughter of the Aurora, A" (London), 190n. 272; as flawed, 95; social comedy in, 95

Daughter of the Snows, A (London): in chronology, 190n. 272; compared to *Smoke Bellew*, 146; as the first novel, 95, 184n. 176; Prince in, 184n. 176; protagonist in, 184n. 176

death: in "In a Far Country", 90-91; in the later stories, xi-xii, 159; in "Law of Life", 26-27; in the Malemute kid tales, 57-78, 84-88; in the Northland, 48; and ritual confrontation in London's stories, xii; 49, 106; in "Sickness of Lone Chief, The", 106-107; understanding of, xii; and values, 57, 60

"Death of Ligoun, The" (London), 100, 171, 179n. 65; form compared to Kipling's, 23; a frame story, 104-105

demonic assertion, 109-10

devices. *See* plot devices

"Devils of Fuatino, The" (London), 149

"Diable-a Dog", 110. *See also* "Batard"

dialogue, 19-21

discursive form, 29

dog stories. *See Jerry of the Islands; Michael Brother of Jerry*

Doubleday and McClure, Co., London's publishers at apprenticeship apex, 176n. 22

dramatic story forms. *See* form

"Dream of Debs, The", 124, 131; and propaganda, 127-128

Dream of Success (Lynn), 80

"dream or phantasy thinking", 154-56

dystopian stories, 126, 127, 130

E

Editor, The (magazine), 2, 13

"End of the Story, The" (London), 145

"Enemy of All the World, The" (London), 131, 189n. 268

environment: and determinism, 145; mastery theme, xi, 114-15, 171-72. *See also* Malamute Kid

epigrams, 18

Escape From Freedom (Fromm), 75-76

essay-exemplum: avoided, 100; compared to Kipling's, 22-24; forms, 8, 16-17, 100; stories, 20-22, 24-25, 29, 32, 170, 178n. 58

"Eternity of Forms, The" (London), 144

"everyman" in London's tales, 92, 119

evolution and literature, 43, 52. *See also* Darwin, Charles

Ewing, Jasper, Jr., 6

F

"facts", 36

Faith of Men and Other Stories, The (London), 81, 110, 175n. 2, 182n. 144; demonic assertion in, 109-10; nature of the code in, 93. *See also* "Batard"; "One Thousand Dozen, The"

Father Roubeau, a reappearing character, 65, 184n. 177

fear, 52

fiction: "Black Cat Story", 10; light-weight short, 186n. 201; naturalism in, 38, 54-55; non-social, 184n. 179; social, 184n. 179; technique, x, 13; theory, 13; Zolaesque "realism" in, x, 38, 41; romantic, 42-43; style, 53. *See also* devices; form; frame stories; "horror"; humor; imagery; literary reviews; magazines; narrator; novels; point of view; protagonist; realism; romance; short stories; socialist stories; technique; themes; theory

"First Poet, The" (London), 189n. 271

First Principles of a New System of Philosophy (Spencer), 43, 82-83, 186n. 202

"Flutter in Eggs, A" (London), 147

Foner, Phillip, 123, 125

force. *See* persistence of force

form(s), x; description versus prescription, 29; development of, 1, 20-21, 32-33; discursive, 29; dramatic, 29; function of, 32; Kipling's imitated, 21-25; simplicity of, 30-31

formula for successful stories, 9, 10

Forum, The (magazine), 37

frame stories: defined, 20, 32, 179n. 65; Kipling's compared to London's, 21-25; narrator in, 142; "Odyssey of the North, An" as, 20-21, 23, 24-25, 29. *See also* "Death of Ligoun, The"; "Odyssey of the North, An"; "Sickness of Lone Chief, The"; "Water Baby, The"

Fraser, W. A., 7

Freud, Sigmund: on dreams/myths, 155; influenced London, 153-56, 158-59, 167-68, 190n. 284, 191n. 289. *See also* Hawaiian stories;

"Kanaka Surf, The"; psychology

Frohock, W. M., 94-95

"From Dawson to the Sea" (London), 8

Fromm, Erich, 75-76

Frye, Northrup, 173-74

Fuller, Edward, 38

futility, London's sense of, xii

G

gambling, 66, 184n. 179

Garland, Hamlin, 6; and London, 37, 50

Geismar, Maxwell, 48, 50, 113

"Goboto Night, A" (London), 149

"God" and "clod" theory, 41-44, 47, 53, 62

"God of His Fathers, The" (London), 14, 172, 178nn. 54, 55; construction of, 16, 96; as one of London's best, 5; symbology in, 96-97, 101

God of His Fathers and Other Stories, The (London), 25; construction of, 15-16; form changes in, 1, 12; motifs in, 95, 100, 102, 134; nature of the code in, 93; quality in, 95. *See also* "At the Rainbow's End"; "Daughter of the Aurora, A"; "God of His Fathers, The"; "Great Interrogation, The"; "Grit of Women, The"; "Siwash"; "Wonder of Woman"

"Good-by Jack" (London), 137

Goodrich, N. L., 13

Gorky, Maxim, praised by London, 42, 52, 181n. 122

"Great Interrogation, The" (London), 20; the Kid in, 71; race in, 71; as sentimentality in, 95

"Grit of Women, The" (London),

179n. 65; death in, 88-89, 106, 147; irony in, 89, 109; as one of London's best, 5; sentiment in, 95; the trail in, 88-89. *See also* "Wonder of Woman"

grotesque. *See* "horror"

H

hack work, 10-11, 33, 131, 185n. 201; *Smoke Bellow Tales* as, 113, 121, 145-149

Haeckel, Ernst, 43, 44-45, 52, 54, 152, 171-72

handbooks on writing, 13-14, 15, 19, 178n. 49. *See also Philosophy of Style*

"Handsome Cabin Boy, The" (London), 140

Harper's Monthly (magazine), 4; Howells in, 37

Harris, Frank, 39

Hart, Walter Morris, 22, 24

Harte, Bret, 39

Hawaiian stories, of London, xi; Freudian and Jungian themes in, xi, 171; symbolism in, xi

Hawthorne, Nathaniel, 13

Hemingway, Ernest, 19

Hinckle, Beatrice M., 152, 154, 159

History of American Magazines, A (Mott), 4

"Hobo and the Fairy, The" (London), 145

Hoffman, Frederick, 124

Holland, Robert, 36, 51

Home Magazine, 2

"honesty", 36

Horatio Alger myth, 80

"horror", the: defined, 110; as horrible, 142; as motif, 100, 105, 115, 121, 147, 167; stories, 10-12, 32, 173

"House of Mauphi, The" (London), 188nn. 252, 254

"House of Pride, The" (London), 137

House of Pride and Other Tales of Hawaii, The (London), 81, 132, 188n. 251; compared to *On the Makaloa Mat*, 159; repeats Northland themes, 138, 159; writing of, 137. *See also* "Aloha Oe"; "Chun Ah Chun"; "Good-by Jack"; "House of Pride, The"; "Koolau the Leper"; "Sheriff of Kona, The"

"House That Jack Built, The" (Rothberg), 79-80

Hovey, Carl, 29

Howells, William Dean, 15; as a magazine reviewer, 37, 40; and Matthews, 35; as a realist, 36-40, 41, 51-52

humor: London's, xi, 9, 172; pot-boiler grim, 142-43, 149; rare success at, 160; slapstick, 142, 148, 160-61

I

"ideal comrade", 61, 66, 124, 184n. 170

idealism (ideals): and actuality, 144, 154; London's, 45, 54; in London's stories, xi, 39-40, 42, 54; and love, 61; in Malemute Kid tales, 58-78; in Northland stories, 50-51; and triumph over actuality, 57; and woman, 168. *See also* actuality; realism

imagery: color, 113, 122, 147-48; floral, 161; light-dark, 108-109, 113, 118, 147; wasteland, 119. *See also* color imagery; light and warmth; light-dark imagination: the code in, 89-93; Jung and rekindled, 158; of the Kid, 63, 68-69; Labor's attention to, 62-63; "thrice cursed", 91-92, 110, 116, 117; as "white logic", 47

"In a Far Country" (London), 178n. 58; compared to Conrad, 49; construction of, 16, 89-94, 118, 146; death motif in, 90-93; explicit mastery of environment theme in, 80; imagination in, 91-92; irony in, 92-93; pessimism in, 173; rationality in, 97; theme of, 105, 165; "white logic" in, 91

"Inevitable White Man, The", 134, 188n. 254

"In the Time of Prince Charley" (London), 9-10, 13, 15

introductory essays, 16

Iron Heel, The (London), 123, 187n. 240

irony: in "In a Far Country", 92-93; in London's work, 85, 87-89, 102, 109, 191n. 298; in socialist tales, 127, 138

irrationality. *See* rationality

Irving, Washington, 15

J

Jack London: American Rebel (Foner), 123

James, Henry, 15

"Jan the Unrepentant" (London), 95-96

Jerry of the Islands (London), 190n. 280

jingoism, 5

John Barleycorn (London): and American values, 46; and London's "long-sickness", 122, 123, 145-46; and morality, 73; opposite emotions in, 156; reveals London's youth, 46-47, 182nn. 137, 139; and secondary truth, 57-58, 76-77; "white logic" in, 47-48, 109

Johns, Cloudesly, and London letters: about apprenticeship, 12, 19-20, 25-27, 139; on the Malemute kid, 59; on philosophy, 43, 44

"Jokers of New Gibbon, The" (London), 149

Jung, Carl G., 190n. 284, 191nn. 289, 298; and Freud, 154; libido concept and London, 159, 166, 172; *Psychology of the Unconscious*, xi, 152, 153-56, 158-64, 167, 172; rekindled London, 153-72. *See also* Hawaiian stories; *On the Makaloa Mat*; symbolism

Junior Munsey (magazine), 2

K

"Kanaka Surf, The" (London), 153, 171; Freudian roots of, 167-70, 173; structure, 170

"Keesh, the Son of Keesh" (London), 27, 100; themes in, 102-104

Kipling, Rudyard: dominated magazine adventure fiction, 6-7, 19, 40; influenced London, x, 1-2, 7, 53, 125, 171, 180n. 94; London praised, 52; plots used by London, 178n. 53; and racism theme, 5; and story structure similarities with London, 20-25. *See also Plain Tales from the Hills; Soldiers Three*

Klondike: London in the, 1, 3, 7, 30; in Garland's work, 6; in London's work, 8, 17, 29, 47, 171. *See also* Northland tales; *Smoke Bellew*

"Koolau the Leper" (London), 137-38

L

Labor, Earle, 48, 60, 83; on death/violence motif, 85; on ideals, 66; on London's quality, 99; on "spirit groping" imagination, 62-63

Lakana, John, London's Hawaiian name, 162

Lang, Andrew, 38

language use: clever, 171; dignified Indian, 100; "force" in, 53; pomposity, 11; quality decline in 138; simplicity of, 27, 30-31, 32; and word play, 125. *See also* imagery; metaphor

law motif, 135

"law giver", 65, 66, 67, 184n. 178

"Law of Life, The" (London), 26-27, 157, 171, 172, 179n. 78; analogy in, 108; "circle of savagery" metaphor in, 111-12; death in, 107-108; London's analysis of, 26-27; as one of London's best, 5, 107; structure of, 29, 100, 107, 112-13, 125; "white logic" in, 109

law-race supremacy, 96-99

"League of the Old Men, The" (London), 99-100, 171, 172, 179n. 65; race theme in, 101-102, 104, 137-38

"Leopard Man's Story, The" (London), 141-42

Letters From Jack London (Hendricks and Shepard), 177n. 35

Lewis, Charles B., 5

Lewis, Sinclair, 145, 189n. 271

libido. *See* Jung, Carl

light and warmth, in London's fiction, 61, 184n. 169

light-dark: and daylight/reason imagery, 118; in black-white-gray imagery, 113; and life-death imagery, 108-109, 147

"Like the Argus of the Ancient Times" (London), 153, 170, 171; as Freudian, 156; as Jungian, 156-59, 163, 165; nobility in, 172

"Lily Maid". *See* Applegarth, Mabel

Lippincott's Magazine, 37, 177n. 46

literary method, scientific, xi

literary naturalism, 37, 38, 43, 44-45, 54-55, 58

literary reviews, 37-42; London's, 41-42

literary theory: "God" and "clod", 41-44, 47, 53, 62; London's development of, x, 29-30, 45

"Little Account with Swithin Hall, The" (London), 149

Little Lady of the Big House, The (London), 139, 190n. 280

London, Bess, 122

London, Charmian: as character model, 168; letters to Jack, 170; on London's psychology interest, 153-54, 156, 159, 163; marriage of, 122, 144, 169-70; recalls London, 33, 66, 147, 190nn. 281, 286; recalls London on Spencer's influence, 30

London, Jack (John Griffith London): adventurous experience of, 3, 46; as "American Kipling", 7; "apprenticeship" of, 8-33, 100; artistic decline of, xi, 121-49; awards and prizes won by, 3; best work of, 25, 81, 148, 159, 171-74, 190n. 286; and Conrad, 27, 49, 60, 74, 76-77; and craftsmanship, 33, 81; and Crane, 41, 183n. 152; critics' rejection of, 85, 143; critiqued his own work, 26-27, 29; and Darwin, 52, 152, 171; death of, 169, 170; decisive year in career of, 185n. 201; didactism of, 16; dual nature of, 40; early writing style of, 8-9; early short stories of, 1, 9, 15, 25, 177n. 35; eclectic reading of, 191n. 288; as editor, 5; emotional life revealed in work of, 182n. 137; in England, 175n. 2; and environment mastery, xi, 114-15, 145, 171-72; experimentation by, 32-33; fame established, 81; first short story publications by, 5; and "force", 43, 51-53; and form, x, 1, 21-25, 30-31; and Freud, xi, 153-56, 158-59, 167-68, 190n. 284, 191n. 289; and futility, xii; and gambling, 66, 184n. 179; and Garland, 37, 50; goals of, 30, 32-33, 52, 57, 107; "God" and "clod" theory of, 41-44, 47, 53, 62; and Gorky, 42, 52, 181n. 122; hack work of, 10-11, 33, 113, 131, 147, 185n. 201; and Haeckel, 43, 44-45, 52, 54, 152; Hawaiian stories of, xi; health of, 169-70; horror stories of, 10-12, 32; and Howells, 36-37, 41, 51-52; idealism of, 45, 54; identification with the Malemute Kid, 59; income of, 32, 132, 139-41, 149, 171, 190n. 277; influenced by Kipling, x, 1-2, 7, 20-25, 31-32, 178n. 53, 180n. 94; as an innovator, 41, 54, 74; inspiration sources, 36, 44, 46-47, 59, 144, 152; and intellect, 83; and Johns letters, 12, 19-20, 25-27, 43, 44, 59; and Jung, xi, 190n. 284, 191nn. 289, 298; and Kipling, 52, 125, 152; in the Klondike, 1, 3, 7, 30; Klondike

influence on London, 8, 17, 29, 47, 171; and Lewis, 145, 189n. 271; life experience and, 1, 3, 122; and literary fads, 10; literary confidants of, 12, 19-20, 25, 43, 126, 177n. 32; "long sickness" of, 122, 123, 188n. 241; magazine publication by, 2; and magazine reviews, 37; and magazine studies, x, 1-4, 7-9, 12-33; 178n. 49; marriage of, 122, 144, 169-70, 177n. 32; and Marx, 52, 152; and *McClure's Magazine*, 4, 5-7, 26, 113; and Nietzsche, 122, 155, 183n. 152, 191n. 292; and Norris, 37, 41-42, 47; pessimism of, 109-101, 112-13, 132, 139, 173; poems of, 9, 11, 32; poetic elements of, 53, 98, 107, 127; posthumous publication of, 153, 170, 190nn. 278, 286; pot-boilers by, xi, 11, 32, 113, 121-22, 131, 139-45, 171; and propoganda, 126-28; psychology and, 38-39, 142-44, 152-74, 190n. 286; quest for quality by, 11-12, 15, 139-41; and the reader, 30-31; as a realist, 35-55; religious interest of, 188n. 245; as reporter, 122; resumed writing, 151-74, 185n. 201; retirement of, 145, 149; as reviewer, 41-42; as a romantic, 36-37, 47; in San Francisco, 7; sentimentality in the work of, 10-11, 95, 137, 159, 170, 188n. 251; serials of, 145, 149; and Sinclair, 52; socialist stories of, 81, 121-49, 150, 160; and the soul, 45; and the *Snark* voyage, 132, 137-39, 145-46, 185n. 201, 188n. 241; and Spencer, 30-31, 43-45, 51-54, 83, 152; and Stevenson, 6, 39, 188n.

252; and strong truth, xi, 51-54, 75, 124, 152; and study of short story forms, 1, 15-16, 178n. 49; style of, x-xi; 15, 17, 21-22, 30-31, 53, 138, 191n. 297; on success as a writer, 2, 3, 9, 29, 35, 52; and suicide,. 122-23; technique development of, x, 10-16, 20, 27-28, 30-31, 45, 178n. 49; theory vs. practice in writing of, 29-30; and violence, 84-86, 94-119, 131, 141; and "white logic", 47, 70-71, 91, 107, 109, 118, 123; and Whitman, 53; youth of, 46. *See also* actuality; adventure; Applegarth, Mabel; autobiographical form; characters; correspondence; Darwin, Charles; death; essay-exemplum; fiction; Freud, Sigmund; Hawaiian stories; idealism; imagery; imagination; irony; language; London, Charmian; London, Joan; magazines; Malemute Kid, the; *Martin Eden*; morality stories; motif; narrator; Northland tales; novels; pessimism; plot devices; short stories; social criticism; socialist stories; Spencer, Herbert; style; realism; ritual; romance; short stories; symbolism; themes; truth; "unknown"; whisper passages; *and names of individual works.*

London, Joan: on Jack's style, 2, 41, 178n. 49, 189n. 271; on Jack's values, 45-46, 62; on Kipling/London, 21-22

"long-sickness", 122, 123, 188n. 241

"Lost Face" (London), 6, 112, 173

Lost Face (London), 121, 124, 132-33, 182n. 144; demonic assertion in, 109-10; nature of the code in, 93; pessimism in, 112-13; pot-boilers in, 113, 142. *See also* "Lost Face"; "Passing of Marcus O'Brien, The"; "Trust"; "Wit of Porportuk, The"

love for all living creatures (idealized character hallmark), 61, 184n. 171

"Love of Life, The" (London), 113-16, 121, 172; flawed epilogue in, 116; theme of, 114, 116

Love of Life and Other Stories, 28, 81; analogy in, 108; dark pessimism in, 112-13; demonic assertion in, 109-10; grotesque climax in, 115; nature of the code in, 93; pot-boilers in, 113. *See also* "Love of Life, The"; "Sun-Dog Trail, The"

Lynn, Kenneth, 80

M

MacArthur, James, 37, 38

magazines: London's reviews in, 41; London's study of, x, 1, 2, 3-4, 8-9, 12-33; *McClures Magazine*, 4, 5-7, 26, 113; popularity of, 2-8; and reviews influencing London, 37-42; and the rise of the short story, 2-7; serials in, 145, 149. *See also* Howells, William Dean; Kipling, Rudyard *and names of individual magazines*

Mahan, Alfred, 5

Malemute Kid, the: appears in seven stories, 57-78, 183n. 161; as an experiment, 73; explicit mastery of environment theme in tales of, xi, 58, 79, 82; failure, 74-75; as an ideal comrade, 61, 124, 184n. 170; imagination and, 63, 68-69, 172; implicit disillusionment theme in,

74-75, 93; implicit human values theme in tales of, xi, 58-78; London's identification with, 59; mastery vs. failure in, 58-59, 73, 117; morality and, 71-73; as most important aspect of London's thought and fiction, 79-80; as narrator, 20-21; and protégé Prince, 64-65, 184n. 176; resurrected later, 73, 146, 147; series combines themes, 57-78; truth in, 57, 58, 60; "unknowable" and, 83-83; whisper in, 58; "white logic" and, 70-71. *See also* Northland tales

Martin Eden (London): and capitalist corruption, 187n. 240; compared to London, 9, 10-12; mirrors London's literary theory, 40-41; reveals London's emotional life, 182n. 137; Ruth-model Applegarth and, 177n. 32; and Spencerian theory, 43, 51; suicide of and London's decline, 121; writing of, 132

martyrdom, 101-102

Marx, Karl: and London, 52, 152; and the soul, 45. *See also* Marxism; psychology

Marxism, 124, 126, 129, 152, 153

"Master of Mystery, The" (London), 29

"Mate Woman" ideal, 168-70

Matthews, Brander, 13, 14; as Howells defender, 35

"Mauki", 135, 138, 188n. 254

May, Henry F., 154

Mayer, Bertrand C., 127

McClures Magazine, 4; and editor London, 5; and Kipling's dominance, 6-7; and London's best stories, 5, 26, 113; racism and individualism in, 5-6

McDowell, Arthur, 52

McTeague (Norris), 45, 47

"Meat, The", 190n. 275; and central "trail" theme, 147, 182n. 144; as imitative, 146

"Men of the Forty-Mile, The" (London): explicit mastery of environment theme in, xi, 58, 67, 79; ideals in, 67-68, 69; imagination in, 68; implicit disillusionment theme in, 74-75, 172; irony in, 87; the Kid in, 66-68, 183n. 161; violence in, 95

metaphor(s): apocalyptic, 173-74; for bold masculine experience, 181n. 118; "circle of savagery", 111-12; demonic, 173-74; Frye's organizational, 173-74; of the human condition, 107, 109; and protagonist use, 188n. 251

"Mexican, The", 124, 129-30, 131-32, 187n. 241

Michael Brother of Jerry (London), 190n. 280

Mills, Gordon, 75

"Minions of Midas, The" (London), 130, 131

miscegenation, 16

misery as mood, 113

misogamy, 145

"Mistake of Creation, The" (London), 147

momentum, 14

"Moon-Face" (London), 141-42

Moon-Face and Other Stories (London), 186n. 201; collection overview, 141-44. *See also* "Leopard Man's Story, The";

"Moon-Face"; "Planchette"; "Shadow and the Flash, The"

morality, 22, 66, 73, 184n. 182; and Howells, 52; and the Kid, 71-73; in "Law of Life", 26, 27; in "A Son of the Sun", 148-49; and Zola, 38

motif. *See* artist; death; "horror"; imagery; irony; law; occult; quest; revenge; ritual; themes; violence

Mott, Frank Luther, 4; on Kipling, 6

Mutiny of the Elsinore, The (London), 190n. 280

mythopoeic prose, xi, 173-74

N

Naass, 14; as narrator, 21, 24, 49

"Nam-Bok the Unveracious" (London), 27, 179n. 65

narrator: and control of story, 15, 125; first-person, 15, 141, 142; functions of, 18-20; Indian, 100-101; intruding, 19, 25, 170; London's, 29; in "Odyssey of the North, An", 20-21, 24; omniscient, 15-17, 20-21, 27, 115-16, 125; and point of view, 15, 17, 19, 27, 115; realism through, 36, 69; stage-manager type, 28, 29, 112; third-person, 27, 29. *See also* essay-exemplum stories; point of view

naturalism. *See* Darwin, Charles; literary naturalism

Nietzsche, Friedrich, 183n. 152; on dreams, 155; "eternal recurrence" concept of, 191n. 292; and London's "long-sickness", 122, 188n. 241

Night-Born, The (London), 124, 171, 188n. 251. *See also* "Bunches of Knuckles"; "Mexican, The"; "To

Kill a Man"; "Under Deck Awnings"; "When the World was Young"; "Winged Blackmail"

nobility, 172

Norris, Frank, 6, 40, 45; and London, 37, 41-42, 47

Northland tale(s), xi, 1, 7, 15, 47-50, 175n. 2; best, 95; and death symbolism, 48, 49-51; dialogue in, 19; first collection of, 1, 12, 17; frame form of, 25; introductory essay in, 17; last collection of, 113; London's approach to, 45; London's fame established by, 81; in *McClures*, 5; narrator in, 15, 17, 19; "Odyssey of the North, An" as, 20-21; seventh after *Snark* cruise, 185n. 201; in six main volumes, 81; ties with socialism stories, 124-25; the "unknown" in, 78-119; white hero in, 98-99. *See also* Alaska stories; *Children of the Frost; Faith of Men and Other Stories, The; God of His Fathers, The; Lost Face; Love of Life and Other Stories, The; Smoke Bellew Tales; Son of the Wolf, The;* themes

Novel of Violence in America (Frohock), 94-95

novels, (London's), 33, 132, 139, 146, 190n. 280; as short story collections, 151; *Cosmopolitan* contract for, 149. *See also* under specific titles

O

occult motifs, 143-44

O'Connor, Richard, 152-53

Octopus, The (Norris), 41-42

"Odyssey of the North, An" (London), 179n. 65; and central "trail" theme,

182n. 144; death core in, 85; death ritual trip in, 49; form compared to Kipling's, 23, 31-32; as a frame story, 20-25, 29; ironic ending in, 87, 102; the Kid in, 71-73, 80, 183n. 161; Prince in, 184n. 176; structure of, 14, 24, 75, 77, 100; "unknowable" in, 83-83

oedipal: myths in London's tales, 162; theory, 160-61

omniscient narrator, 15, 17; in "Law of Life", 27; in "Odyssey of the North, An", 20-21; in "Strength of the Strong", 125. *See also* narrator; point of view

"One Thousand Dozen, The", 147, 182n. 144

"On the Makaloa Mat" (London),170

On the Makaloa Mat (London): as artistic, 171, 172, 173; compared to *The House of Pride*, 159; Freudian stories in, 153; Jungian stories in, 159; posthumous, 153, 170, 190 n. 286. *See also* "Kanaka Surf, The"; "On the Makaloa Mat"; "Shin Bones"; "Tears of Ah Kim, The"; "Water Baby, The"; "When Alice Told Her Soul"

Overland Monthly (magazine), London's first market, 5, 45. *See also* "To the Man on the Trail"

Owl Magazine, The, 140

P

parables in American literature, 125-26, 127

Parrington, Vernon, 43

"Passing of Marcus O'Brien, The" (London), 184n. 179; humor in, 142

pathos, 145

Pattee, Fred Lewis, 7, 53

"Pearls of Parlay" (London), 188n. 152

People of the Abyss (London), 187n. 240

"persistence of force", 43, 51; and style, 53

Perry, Bliss, 38

pessimism: becomes cynicism, 132, 158-59; London's, 109-10, 132; London's darkest, 112-13, 139, 173; of mood, 80-81, 97, 113; most mature story of, 116-18; of South Seas tales, 121, 139

Peterson, Clell, 117

Philosophy of Style (Spencer), xi, 2; influenced London, 30-31, 171

Philosophy of the Short Story (Matthews), 13, 14

Pizer, Donald, 37, 55

plagiarism, 189n. 271

Plain Tales from the Hills (Kipling), 22-23

"Planchette" (London), 143-44, 152

plot devices: and action constructs, 188n. 254; literary, 131, 170; parables, 125-26, 127; plot, 188n. 254, 189n. 267; *Pygmalion* , 69; science, 143; surprise endings as, 189n. 267; technological, 143; voice, 29, 122-23, 168. *See also* analogy; characters; death; imagery; irony; metaphor; narrator; point of view; protagonist; short stories; symbolism; themes

Poe, Edgar Allan, 13

poetic elements: in London's tales, 53, 98, 107; lost in socialist tales, 127

point of view: first person, 15; Indian,

100-101; narrative, 15, 17, 115; omniscient, 115-16, 125; third person, 27, 29

Pope, Margaret, 142

pot-boilers: grim humor in, 142-43; London's, xi, 11, 32, 113, 121-22, 131, 173; narrator in, 142; nature of, 141, 144, 145; for quick income, 139-41, 171; self-imitating, 145

power: moral, spiritual, 136; primitive, 129-30

priest, the: reappears across stories, 65, 184n. 177

"Priestly Prerogative, The" (London), 178n. 55; explicit mastery of environment theme in Malemute Kid tales, xi, 58, 67, 79; imagination in, 62; implicit disillusionment theme in, 74-75; the Kid in, 183n. 161; London's opinion of, 29; structure of, 14, 18, 71-72

Prince, the mining engineer, 20-21, 64-65, 184n. 176

Prince, Morton (psychologist), 153

"Princess, The" (London), 190n. 278

prison reform, 145

"Prodigal Father, The" (London), 189n. 271

propaganda: in London's socialist tales, 126-28; inhibits London's artistry, 128

prose, mythopoeic, xi, 173-74

protagonist: "limited", xi, 86, 97, 101, 111, 117, 186n. 210; as metaphor, 188n. 251; perverse, 141; "spirit groping", xi; as victim of irrationality, 82; violent, 85; and the "unknown", 111; white, 98-99

"Proud Goat of Aloysius Pankburn, The" (London), 149

psychology: Freud/Jung comparison influenced London's, 154; and literature, 38-39; London's last stories and, 152-74; London's shift to, 142-44, 190n. 286. See also Freud, Sigmund; Hinckle, Beatrice M.; Jung, Carl; "Like the Argus of the Ancient Times"; Marx, Karl; Prince, Morton

Psychology of the Unconscious (Jung), xi, 152, 153

publication dates, and story composition dates, 175n. 2, 177n. 35, 185n. 198, 187n. 241

Pygmalion device, 69

Q

quest motif, 91, 119, 163. See also rituals

R

"Race for Number Three, The" (London), 146

race/racism: memory as dreams, 155; in magazines, 5-6. See also themes

Rahv, Philip, 52

"Raid on the Oyster Pirates, A" (London), 68, 77-78

rationality: and code-hero, 86-88; and death/violence motif, 85; and Jung's influence, 158; as London theme, xi, 79-84, 97; loss of faith in, 117; influenced by psychology, 155

realism: defined, 35-36, 41-42; and force, 51-53; and ideals, 39-40; London's writing as, 35-55; in Malemute Kid tales, 58-78; in Northland stories, 51; and psychology, 154-55; unifying, 152; versus romance, 35-41, 44, 58, 118-19. *See also* fiction; romance

"reality", 36; Howells on, 51; London on, 51

"Red One, The"(London), 144

Red One, The (London), posthumous, 153, 190n. 278. *See also* "Like the Argus of the Ancient Times"; "Princess, The"; "Red One, The"

"Rejuvenation of Major Rathborn, The" (London), 15, 143

Remington, Frederic, 4

revenge, 131, 141

Review of Reviews, The (magazine), 2, 13

Rhetoric of Fiction (Booth), 99

Riddle of the Universe (Haeckel), 44

ritual: allied with self-definition and - preservation, 61, 89; death/violence motif, as, 84-87, 89, 104; manhood, 85; motif, 105. *See also* death; trail

Road, The (London), 187n. 240

romance: criticized, 38-39; fiction, x; and idealism, 39-40, 172; and London, 36-37, 40-41, 53, 97; loss of, 109; in Malemute Kid tales, 58-78, 118-19; in Northland stories, 51, 109; popular, 42, 53, 181n. 122; South Seas triangle, 169; versus realism, 35-55, 118-19. *See also* realism

Rothberg, Abraham, 21, 79

S

sacrifice concept (Jung), 160-61

"Samuel" (London), 132, 139

Saturday Evening Post (magazine), 145

science: and realism, 152; as a device, 143; as theme source, 171. *See also* psychology

Scorn of Women, The (London), 178n. 55; social comedy in, 95; structure of, 14

Scribner's (magazine), 4

"Sea Farmer, The" (London), 132, 139

Sea-Wolf, The (London): black pessimism in, 122; romantic flaw in, 123; truth conflict in, 122, 187n. 238; "white logic" and, 123

"Seed of McCoy, The", 135-37, 188n. 245

sentimentality, 10; in London's stories, 11, 95, 137, 159, 170, 188n. 251. *See also* romance

sexual instinct, 16-17

"Shadow and the Flash, The" (London), 143

"Sheriff of Kona, The" (London), 137

"Shin Bones" (London), 162, 163-67, 171, 172

short stories: artistic comparison of early to later, 171; "Black Cat", 10; collected, 170-71; compared to novels, 10, 12-13, 14; death/violence motif, 84-86; dramatic, 19, 20-21, 25, 29; elements, 14-16, 151; formula for successful, 9, 10; and the frame type, 20-21; handbooks, 13-14, 15, 178n. 49; "highest type of", 25; Kipling models, 19, 171; London's analysis of, 14; London's best, 25, 81, 148, 159, 171-74, 190n. 286; in London's decline, 121-49; London's development of, x, 20-33; London's flawed, 29, 66, 70, 81, 145, 190n. 280; and London's writing rebirth, 151-74;

London's theory vs. practice of, 29-30; and the magazine medium, 2-4; moralizing, 22; poetic element in, 53; psychological, 151-73; similarity of Kipling and London's forms, 20-25; theory, 13, 15, 17, 178n. 49. *See also* Barrett, Charles R.; frame stories; hack work; literary theory; magazines; pot-boilers; realism; themes

Short Story Writing: A Practical Treatise on the Art of the Short Story (Barrett), 13-14, 19, 178n. 49

"Sickness of Lone Chief, The" (London), 100, 179n. 65; death in, 106-107; a frame story, 105-108

"Siege of the 'Lancashire Queen', The" (London), 143

Sinclair, Upton, 52

"single effect" intensity, 25

Sisson, Edgar, 151, 190n. 278

situation, 14-15

"Siwash" (London): a frame story, 179n. 65; as sentimentally marred, 95

Smoke Bellow Tales (London): compared to *A Daughter of the Snows*, 146; as hack work, 113, 121, 145-49; metaphor in, 181n. 118; and the resurrected Kid, 73, 146, 147; as self-imitating, 145-47. *See also* "Flutter in Eggs, A"; "Meat, The"; "Mistake of Creation, The"; "Race for Number Three, The"; "Stampede to Squaw Creek, The"; "Taste of the Meat, The"; "Town-Site of Tra-Lee, The"

Snark (ship): 1907-1908 cruise writing, 132, 137, 138, 139; post-cruise writing, 145-46, 185n. 201; pre-cruise writing, 185n. 201, 188n. 241

social comedy, 95

social criticism (themes), xi, 32, 102-104, 124

social Darwinism, 43-44, 54; and the Kid, 73-74

socialist stories (London), 81, 121, 152; compared to Alaskan tales, 127; dystopian, 126, 127; last of the, 160; positive, 123; secondary, 130. *See also House of Pride and Other Tales of Hawaii, The; South Seas Tales; Strength of the Strong, The; When God Laughs*

Soldiers Three (Kipling), 23

"Son of the Sun, A" (London), 148

Son of the Sun, A (London), 121, 145, 148, 171. *See also* "Devils of Fuatino, The"; "Goboto Night, A"; "Jokers of New Gibbon, The"; "Little Account with Swithin Hall, The"; "Pearls of Parlay"; "Proud Goat of Aloysius Pankburn, The"; "Son of the Sun, A"

Son of the Wolf, Tales of the Far North, The (London), 183n. 161; construction of, 15, 17-18, 58-78, 93-94; explicit mastery of environment theme in, xi, 58, 67, 79; first Northland collection, 12, 25, 99; form development in, 1, 12, 14, 58, 95-96, 100; importance of, 94; pessimism in, 80-81. *See also* "In a Far Country"; Malemute Kid; "Men of Forty-Mile, The", "Odyssey of the North, An"; "Son of the Wolf, The"; "White Silence"; "Wife of a King, The"; "Wisdom of the Trail"

"Son of the Wolf, The" (London),

178n. 58; construction of, 16, 17-18, 29; the Kid in, 183n. 161
soul, 45
"South of the Slot" (London), 188n. 251
South Sea romance genre, 188n. 252
South Seas stories (London), 32, 81, 121; repeat Alaskan themes, 132-33; theme variance, 136. *See also Son of the Sun, A*; *South Seas Tales*
South Seas Tales: "blackbirding" in, 133-34, 188n. 254; repeats Northland themes, 138. *See also* "House of Mauphi, The"; "Inevitable White Man, The"; "Mauki"; "Seed of McCoy, The"; "Terrible Solomons, The"; " 'Yah! Yah! Yah! Yah!' "
Spencer, Herbert, xi, 2, 82-83, 186n. 202; "force" of, 43, 51; influenced London, 30-31, 43-45, 51-54, 152, 171; "Unknowable" doctrine of, 82-83
"spirit groping": and ideals, 69; Labor on, 62-63; in Northland stories, 51, 116, 119; protagonists, xi
"Stampede to Squaw Creek, The", 189n. 272
Sterling, Carrie, letter from London, 122
Sterling, George, 145, 189n. 271
Stevenson, Robert Louis, 6, 39, 188n. 252
story-within style. *See* frame stories
"Strength of the Strong, The" (London), 124, 131; construction of, 125-27, 130
Strength of the Strong, The (London), 81, 124, 132, 137, 188n. 251, 189n. 268. *See also* "Dream of the Debs";

"Enemy of All the World, The"; "Samuel"; "Sea Farmer, The"; "South of the Slot"; "Strength of the Strong, The"
"strength of utterance", 30
"strong truth": in London's stories, xi, 51, 54, 124, 152; and style, 53, 75
Strunsky, Anna, London's letters to, 126-27
style: poetic-prose, 53; unites "strong truth" and emotion, 53. *See also* form; language; literary naturalism; realism; short stories; technique; themes
"Sun-Dog Trail, The", 28-29; pessimism in, 112; realism in, 36, 86; ritual in, 86; the "unknown" in, 86-87
"Sunlanders, The" (London), 27
symbolism: of Alaskan landscape, 82, 142; anatomical, 164-65; decline in, 127; dream, 155; Jungian, 163, 164, 165; language, 155; libido, 158, 163, 164; Northland trip ritual, 49-50; oedipal, 160, 162-63; racial, 96-97. *See also* Hawaiian stories; imagery

T

Tales of the Fish Patrol (London), 175n. 2, 186n. 201; morality in, 68. *See also* "Raid on the Oyster Pirates, A"; "Siege of the 'Lancashire Queen', The"
"Taste of the Meat, The", 190n. 275
"Tears of Ah Kim, The" (London), 160-61, 163, 172
technique, x, 13, 178n. 49; London's, 15-16, 30-31
technological stories, 189n. 268

"Terrible Solomons, The", 98-99, 133-34, 188n. 254; humor in, 142, 149

themes, of London: Alaskan repeated in South Seas tales, 132-33, 138; best, 81-82, 97; code versus false romance, 147; confused, 75-76, 95, 96; control, 100; corruption, 187n. 240; disillusionment, 74-75; explicit and implicit, xi, 58, 74, 79; explicit mastery of environment, xi, 58, 67, 79, 97, 114, 116; failure, 119; fountain of youth, 177n. 40; Freudian, xi; humorous, 134-35; Indian, 101; Jungian, xi; as London's passion, 171-74; loss, 102-103, 109, 170, 172-73; minor social, 66, 184n. 179; non-rational/rational, 80-81; optimism/pessimism, 159; race/racial, xi; 20, 71, 96-99, 124, 134, 187n. 221, 188n. 251, 190n. 280; race/racism, 133, 136, 173; rationality, xi, 79-84, 97; rebirth, 163, 166; sadism, 135; social brotherhood, 67, 124, 184n. 170; social criticism, xi, 32, 81, 102-104, 190n. 280; transition, 124; the "Unknown", 82-88; values, 101. See also death; horror; pessimism; rationality; realism; Malemute Kid; values

theory (literary),13; "God" and "clod", 41-44, 47, 53, 62; London's, 29-30; short story, 13, 15, 17, 178n. 49; and the writer-reader relationship, 30-31

"Thousand Deaths, A" (London), 10-11, 15, 131, 143

Three —and an Extra (Kipling), 178n. 53

"Through the Rapids on the Way to the Klondike" (London), 8

time, role of in short stories, 14, 15, 18

"To Build a Fire" (London), 6, 121; imagination in, 62-63, 158; mature pessimism tale, 116-19, 157, 158-59; source story for, 113

"To Kill a Man" (London), 145, 188n. 251

"To the Man on Trail" (London): the first Northland story, 1, 45; ideals vs. actuality in, 64-65, 66, 67, 69; implicit disillusionment theme in, 74-75; the Kid in, 64-65, 183n. 161; nobility in, 172; Prince in, 184n. 176

"Town-Site of Tra-Lee, The" (London), 147

trail, movement on the: as central to London's stories, 18, 49, 182n. 144; ritualistic symbolism of the, 49-50, 88

tricks. See plot devices

"Trust" (London), and central "trail" theme, 182n. 144

truth, in London's stories: death-dealing, 182n. 139; life-giving, 182n. 139; in Malemute Kid tales, 58-78; primary versus secondary, 48, 57, 58, 60, 76-77, 173, 187n. 238, and realism, 36, 47; and romance, 47, 51; and "white logic", 47-48. See also "strong truths"

Turtles of Tasman, The (London), 189n. 271. See also "End of the Story, The"; "Eternity of Forms, The"; "First Poet, The"; "Hobo and the Fairy, The"; "Prodigal Father, The"

Twain, Mark, 7

"Typhoon off the Coast of Japan"

(London), 3, 8, 175n. 9; language pomposity in, 11; structure in, 15

U

"Under Deck Awnings" (London), 188n. 251
unity, 14, 15, 16
"Unknowable, the" (Spencer), 82-83. *See also* "unknown"
"unknown", the: in the Northland tales, 79-119; in the socialist tales, 129; and Spencer, 82-83
utopia stories, 126, 130

V

Valley of the Moon, The (London), 187n. 240, 190n. 280
values: humanly sustaining, xi; death of, 45-46; in London's work, 16, 35, 46-47, 54; Northland negative, 50-51; positive, 121, 158. *See also John Barleycorn*
violence in Northland tales, 84-86, 94-119, 131, 141
visual quality of stories, 29
voice: author's, 29, 168; London's loss of, 122-23

W

Walcutt, Charles, 37, 55
Walker, Franklin, 59, 156
"Water Baby, The" (London), 163, 171, 172; as a frame story, 162
Wave, The, 2
Wedmore, Frederick, 142
"When Alice Told Her Soul" (London): humor in, 172; Jungian basis of, 159-60
When God Laughs (London), 123,

137, 186n. 201. *See also* "Apostate, The"; "Created He Them"; "Curious Fragment, A"
"When the World Was Young" (London), 189n. 271
"Where the Trail Forks" (London), 95
"Which Makes Men Remember" (London), 95
"whisper" passages: and imagination, 62, 156; and "truth" in *Barleycorn*, 57-58, 182n. 139; in Malemute Kid tales, 57, 58, 74, 77
White Fang (London), 48
"white logic": defined, 47, 109; in "In a Far Country", 91; and the Kid, 70-71; in "Law of Life, The", 109; in "Sea-Wolf, The", 123; in "Sickness of Lone Chief, The", 107; in "To build a Fire", 118. *See also John Barleycorn*; truth
"white silence", horror of the, 105, 116
"White Silence, The": and central "trail" theme, 49, 60, 182n. 144; dog analogy in, 108, 113; death in, 48-49, 50-51, 60, 85; imagination in, 63, 68-69; ironic ending of, 87, 156; the Kid in, 60, 63, 80, 82, 133, 183n. 161; structure of, 18, 60, 100; truth in, 77; two-fold theme of, 64-66; "unknowable" in, 83-83
Whitman, Walt, 53
"Wife of a King, The" (London), 178n. 58; compared to Kipling's structure, 22-23, 69; construction of, 16, 70, 171; explicit mastery of environment theme in, xi, 58, 67, 79; ideals in, 65-66, 69-70, 75; implicit disillusionment theme in, 74-75; irony in, 87; the Kid in, 65,

66, 69-70, 183n. 161; London's opinion of, 14, 29; Prince in, 184n. 176; social comedy in, 95

"Winged Blackmail" (London), 143, 189n. 271

"Wisdom of the Trail, The" (London): and central "trail" theme, 182n. 144; death in, 86, 109; explicit mastery of environment theme in 80; idealism in, 65; irony in, 86, 87, 89; race theme in, 187n. 221; rationality in, 86

"Wit of Porportuk, The" (London), 112

"Wolf" as London, 58-59

"Wonder of Woman" (London), 147, 148

"world as world, the" (London), 52

Wright, Austin M., 74, 110, 142

Writer, The (magazine), 2, 13

Y

" 'Yah! Yah! Yah! Yah!' ", 135, 138, 188n. 254

Youth (Conrad), 74, 76-77

Youth's Companion, The (magazine), 4, 6, 68, 113, 139-40; rejections, 8

Z

Zola, Emile, x, 38, 39, 40, 41, 45